D1547506

From Western Deserts
to Carolina Swamps

Lewis F. Roe, 1838–1908. Photo taken at Galesburg, Ill., in 1863.
Courtesy of Lewis T. Roe, Deming, N.Mex.

From Western Deserts
to Carolina Swamps

A CIVIL WAR SOLDIER'S JOURNALS
AND LETTERS HOME

Edited by

JOHN P. WILSON

UNIVERSITY OF NEW MEXICO PRESS
ALBUQUERQUE

© 2012 by the University of New Mexico Press
All rights reserved. Published 2012
Printed in the United States of America
17 16 15 14 13 12   1 2 3 4 5 6

LIBRARY OF CONGRESS CATALOGING-IN-PUBLICATION DATA
Roe, Lewis Franklin, 1838–1908.
From western deserts to Carolina swamps: a Civil War soldier's
journals and letters home / edited by John P. Wilson.
        p. cm.
Includes bibliographical references and index.
ISBN 978-0-8263-5142-5 (cloth: alk. paper)
ISBN 978-0-8263-5144-9 (electronic)

   1. Roe, Lewis Franklin, 1838–1908—Diaries.
   2. Roe, Lewis Franklin, 1838–1908—Correspondence.
   3. United States—History—Civil War, 1861–1865—Personal narratives.
   4. Sherman's March to the Sea—Sources.
   5. Atlanta Campaign, 1864—Sources.
   6. Sherman's March through the Carolinas—Sources
   7. Southwest, New—History—Civil War, 1861–1865—Sources.
   8. United States. Army. Illinois Infantry Regiment, 50th (1861–1865)
   9. United States. Army. Infantry Regiment, 7th.
   I. Wilson, John P. (John Philip), 1935–
   II. Title.

E476.69.R64 2012
973.7'8—dc23
                2011049642

For
Mrs. Amy (Roe) Grant,
*Librarian, Knoxville Public Library, 1947–1958,
and youngest daughter of Lewis F. Roe*

Contents

Figures and Maps

Figures

Maps

Acknowledgments

THROUGH THE TWENTY-FIVE YEARS THAT THIS BOOK WAS A WORK IN PROGRESS, I RECEIVED HELP FROM MANY SOURCES. Two OF LEWIS ROE'S GRANDCHILDREN HAD RETAINED THE original journals, his letters home, and a small number of private papers. Lewis T. Roe of Deming, New Mexico, and Eleanor Verene of Galesburg, Illinois, made all of the surviving journals and nine of the letters available without restrictions. My aunt, Dorothy England of Knoxville, Illinois, ferreted out details of Lewis Roe's life and greatly facilitated my access to the Roe materials in Illinois. Her daughter, Janet Hinck, photographed for me what is probably a Noble Brothers artillery piece now on display in Naperville, Illinois. Edwin Olmstead tutored me on Civil War ordnance and is largely responsible for my present interest, one result of which has been the pulling together of details about the Noble Brothers Foundry's ordnance production for the Confederacy.

Drs. Robert W. Frazer and Harwood P. Hinton read parts of Roe's journals soon after I transcribed them and encouraged their publication. Dr. Donald P. Verene helped bring his great-grandfather's records to publication in a number of ways. The Interlibrary Loan services at the New Mexico State University Library and Doña Ana Community College helped immensely with locating newspaper microfilms and obtaining copies of obscure journal articles and local histories. The online resources of the Internet have been indispensable, particularly in searching for genealogical information, sources of Georgia local history, and Civil War unit histories. Institutions in Georgia, from private groups and county governments up to the state itself, have excellent websites to aid the historical scholar. The computer labs and especially the East Mesa Library of Doña Ana Community College graciously allowed the inputting of text and maps there.

I am also indebted to Holli Pope, a talented designer in Las Cruces, New Mexico, for teaching me the Adobe Illustrator computer program and how to apply this to map-making; to Bob Anglea of Rome, Georgia, for unscrambling the history of land ownership and making a probable identification of the plantation house-cum-hospital at the site of the Battle of Lay's Ferry in northern Georgia; and to Hugh Greeson of Chatsworth, Georgia, present owner of the battlefield area. Also to Mr. and Mrs. Ed Varley of Point of Rocks, Wyoming, for showing me the nearby bluff where many 7th Infantry soldiers, including Lewis Roe, carved their names on June 14, 1860. I would never have found this without the Varleys' guidance; Roe's name unfortunately has not survived there.

Guides to the holdings of libraries and special collections are now widely available on the Internet and can save the researcher immense amounts of time, correspondence, and travel. Even specific documents are sometimes posted as websites. Written inquiries brought copies of useful letters and diaries from the Digital Library of Georgia and the Southern Historical Collection of the University of North Carolina at Chapel Hill. When the Internet did not suffice, inquiries on a variety of topics were posted to the U.S. Army Heritage and Education Center, the Archives and Manuscript Collection of the Seymour Library at Knox College, the State Historical Society of Missouri, the Historical Society of Quincy and Adams County, the Illinois State Historical Library, and the Kansas State Historical Society. Sometimes questions could be resolved and sometimes not, but the respondents were always helpful and I thank them.

Historical illustrations, more than could be included here and some published for the first time, have been provided by the Library of Congress Prints and Photographs Division; the National Archives at College Park, Maryland; the State Historical Society of Iowa; the Peoria (Illinois) Public Library; the Historical Society of Quincy and Adams County; Historic Cheraw; the Hargrett Rare Book and Manuscript Library/ University of Georgia Libraries; and the staff of the Georgia Archives. The latter's website "Vanishing Georgia" is truly a wonder and beyond anything else of its kind. My wife Cheryl deserves special thanks for her patience with me and for the use of her librarian's skills in difficult situations, also for pointing out the recipe "Sherman Strikes Again."

Ms. Dawn Santiago of Las Cruces, New Mexico, prepared the index. To all of the above and to any whom I have neglected, I am most grateful for your assistance during the years of this project.

Introduction

In the early spring of 1858, an Illinois farm boy enlisted in the 7th U.S. Infantry at St. Louis, Missouri. The army was actively seeking recruits at the time, under a threat of war with the Mormons in Utah. Lewis Roe, one of nine brothers, came from a relatively prosperous farming family in Adams County, bordering the Mississippi River. We know little of his early life, but his later writings showed the importance he placed on family ties. He received a good education for the time, including a year in the preparatory class at Knox College in Galesburg, Illinois.

Roe showed no inclination to make military service a career, and he may have joined the army solely for economic reasons. With so many brothers (Lewis was the third oldest), opportunities on the family farm were probably limited. Following enlistment, he spent two years in Utah and participated in "many remarkable incidents and adventures" while stationed at Fort Bridger, but he offered no details about these.[1]

The commander of his Company F, 7th Infantry, had already been promoted to the rank of major and would later be charged as a coward and traitor for surrendering his command in New Mexico at the beginning of the Civil War. Unfortunately, Lewis Roe had nothing to say about Major Isaac Lynde. As for his post commander at Fort Bridger, Maj. E. R. S. Canby, Roe frankly admired Canby and served under him again in New Mexico.

His earliest journal was a small notebook with daily entries, kept during the transfer of the 7th Infantry from Utah to New Mexico in the summer of 1860. The observations were usually brief but covered the entire trip of nearly three months, with only a few pages missing. This march of more than 1,000 miles showed that Roe was not a complainer, and while two officers penned reports at the end of the trek, their accounts evidently have not survived.

At the completion of this transfer, Company F joined the garrison at Fort Craig, New Mexico, and remained there for the next year and a half. Roe's only record from this time is the beginning and final entries of a diary that covered a two-month trip escorting supplies to the military posts in southern Arizona in April and May 1861. Regrettably, the pages are missing for two weeks of the outbound journey, when the party passed through Apache Pass shortly after the notorious Bascom incident there.

In later years Lewis Roe published an article that described affairs in New Mexico on the eve of the Confederate invasion in 1861. Part of the article prefaced his eyewitness account of the Battle of Valverde on February 22, 1862, when Company F formed part of Plympton's Battalion. The article appeared in the *National Tribune* two years after its author's death; whether he wrote it from notes or entirely from memory is not known. Roe wrote out the casualty list for Company F at Valverde, but only a fragment survives among his papers. Captain P. W. L. Plympton's own report on Valverde mentioned Private Lewis Roe as one who behaved bravely throughout the day.[2] Roe's discharge from the army in March 1863 bears an endorsement that he also participated in the skirmish at Peralta. At the beginning of the school notebooks he compiled later in life, our soldier included more details about life with the army in the West. These details and his 1860–1861 journals are unique sources on unreported aspects of pre–Civil War army life— snapshots so to speak—and the Valverde article is a firsthand account by someone who was there.

Lewis Roe's service in the 7th U.S. Infantry from 1858 to 1863 placed him with an old-line regiment that had spent many years doing garrison duty. In the Civil War, this would change; seven of the regiment's ten companies were surrendered without a fight at San Augustin Springs, New Mexico, on July 27, 1861.[3] Roe's Company F was one of the remaining three (C, F, and H), stationed at Fort Craig, New Mexico, and available for duty. These companies continued in New Mexico until the late spring of 1864, then transferred to the East.

After the San Augustin Springs surrender, the local Confederate commander, Lieutenant Colonel John R. Baylor, released the other seven companies on parole. They were sent East in September 1861 and served in noncombat roles, mostly as garrisons at fortifications in upstate New York, until formally exchanged in the summer of 1862. Between December 1862 and July 1863, four of the exchanged companies, seriously reduced in numbers, were brigaded with other understrength regular army infantry units and fought as part of the 5th Army Corps at the battles of Fredericksburg, Chancellorsville, and Gettysburg. By the time of Gettysburg, only 116 officers and men remained in service; of these, 57 were killed or wounded. Such losses rendered the regiment no longer combat-effective, and until the end of the war, the 7th Infantry garrisoned coastal fortifications around New York harbor.[4]

As for Lewis Roe, after mustering out at Fort Union, New Mexico, he walked back to Illinois along the Santa Fe Trail. A few months after arriving home, he married Louisa Smith of Gilson, Illinois, and tried a term of school teaching; where and for how long are not known. Roe evidently had little success at finding employment, and the couple soon had a baby on the way. The federal and state governments offered generous financial inducements to encourage recruiting, so Lewis Roe rejoined the army on February 10, 1864, partly for the money and partly out of patriotism.

His new regiment, the 50th Illinois Volunteer Infantry, had seen hard fighting in 1862 at Shiloh, Tennessee, and Corinth, Mississippi, followed by stretches of garrison duty in consequence of its reduced ranks. This unit and many others whose members reenlisted as veteran volunteers late in 1863 received a one-month furlough in January–February 1864, partly as a reward for veteranizing, as it was termed. The entire regiment returned to Quincy, Illinois, to recuperate and to encourage new recruits. On both counts, this program was a success.

Lewis Roe's journals to March 24, 1865, when he was part of the Army of the Tennessee under Major General W. T. Sherman, plus a final chapter to take him home again, comprise the second part of this book. These journals have been edited as five chapters: the Atlanta Campaign; the March to the Sea; the Carolinas Campaign; his five and one-half months on duty at Rome, Georgia; and the month the army spent at Savannah, Georgia.

Our soldier began keeping a daily journal on April 3, 1864, when his regiment arrived at its camp near Mooresville, Alabama. One month later the troops entrained for Chattanooga, Tennessee, and by the second week of May, Lewis Roe and the rest of the Army of the Tennessee began their invasion of Georgia, called the Atlanta Campaign. The 50th Illinois had a few fights in the first two weeks and advanced rapidly as far as Kingston, Georgia, where Roe's brigade was split off and sent to garrison Rome, Georgia.

The surviving original sections of his journals show that he wrote two-sheet/four-page installments, each with daily entries for about two weeks, and numbered these through mid-January 1865. As he filled each of the double sheets, he penned its number at the top and enclosed it with a letter to Louisa. There were thirty-seven such journal segments, of which Roe destroyed the first twenty-nine after he recopied their contents (with minor editing) into two school notebooks.

From late May to early November 1864, the 50th Illinois helped provide security when Rome became a vast hospital for casualties from the battles around Atlanta. Occasional skirmishing and foraging expeditions broke the routine of garrison life. After the capture of Atlanta in early September, Confederate general John B. Hood marched northward and sent one division to capture Union supplies warehoused at a railroad siding named Allatoona. The 50th Illinois was hastily called in to help defend Allatoona, and Roe provided a dramatic account of that fighting. He received a promotion to corporal and his literacy led him to be assigned as a company clerk.

During the two-month respite that followed the capture of Atlanta, Sherman prepared for his next advance. When the march started, all communications with the North were cut off, but Roe maintained his daily journal and mailed it after the army got to Savannah.

The March to the Sea between November 9 and December 23, 1864, proved to be almost, if not quite, a walk in the park for the Union armies. Sherman's men traveled light and without regular rations, which meant that they turned it into one long foraging expedition. Near the end of the campaign, Roe witnessed the capture of Fort McAllister, but he took no part in the fighting.

The troops spent a month in Savannah engaging in fatigue duties, building breastworks and "doghouses" for shelter, foraging, writing letters, and trying to stay dry. Despite the rain, swamps, and frequent lack of shelter, the soldiers by now were healthy beyond measure. Roe never mentioned becoming ill. He helped to liberate construction materials from a plantation house outside of Savannah; the house survived and continues as an elegant private residence today.

By the end of January 1865 the troops at Savannah had been resupplied and rumors flew as to where they would head next. Roe's brigade moved on January 27, and due to heavy flooding of the Savannah River, his division followed a route separate from the rest of the 15th

Army Corps. They rejoined eventually and pushed rapidly through the swamps of South Carolina. Roe witnessed the burning of Columbia, which in his view happened because the boys got out of hand. The army by now believed that Sherman could do anything and no one anticipated meeting serious opposition. Skirmishers and isolated resistance were simply swept aside. During this march in February and March 1865 there were no opportunities to send mail, and Roe kept a single journal, which also survives.

Roe penned some interesting descriptions during the Carolinas Campaign, such as the burning of the turpentine plantations, which escaped all mention in the *War of the Rebellion, A Compilation of the Official Records of the Union and Confederate Armies*. The explosion of a large ammunition depot at Cheraw, South Carolina, provided another dramatic episode, while he capped his battlefield experiences with an account of the Battle of Bentonville.

By the end of his journals, Lewis Roe had developed into a better than average descriptive writer. His spelling and grammar were always good, but from the first journal in 1860 to the last in 1865, his narrative style improved greatly. One wonders that his language in describing the affair at Bentonville—"'Zip,' 'Zis,' 'thug,' 'Spat' came the bullets, . . ." —didn't give poor Louisa heart failure when she read this! Her husband, of course, came through unscathed.

The journals ended with the arrival of the army at Goldsboro, North Carolina. Roe's participation in Sherman's campaigns was clearly the greatest experience in his life; never again would he or most of his comrades find an involvement with such a cause, or with such leaders. The years after the Civil War were comparatively uneventful. At some point he recopied the original journal segments into two school copybooks, perhaps after publication of the 50th Illinois (Veteran) Volunteer Infantry history in 1894. His editing in the copybooks is minor when compared with the original segments that survive, which suggests that little has been lost by destruction of the first twenty-nine segments. Lewis Roe died at Knoxville, Illinois, in 1908, and apart from his daughter, Amy Grant, I met no one who had actually known him.

Lewis Roe's journals are unique in offering an enlisted man's commentary on the Civil War in both the far West and the Eastern theaters. His experiences in the West have given us a rare firsthand account of the Battle of Valverde and details of such little-known episodes of army life as the long march from Fort Bridger to New Mexico; escorting duty in the Southwest; and a soldier's efforts to understand what was happening around him as the country rushed toward an outbreak of hostilities. Later, he documented the Union occupation of a major city in Georgia and left us a candid account of an enlisted man's experiences with the Army of the Tennessee from Rome, Georgia, to Goldsboro, North Carolina. His relative objectivity, attention to everyday details (the importance of mail; what did a knapsack contain; what did they eat, and how did they get it), and apparent lack of prejudice are unusual qualities for the time.

In the editorial additions to these journals, I sought to identify specific places that Roe mentioned. These include the bluff in Wyoming where many 7th Infantry soldiers carved their names; the site of the Battle of Lay's Ferry in northern Georgia and the probable owner of the plantation house there; and the location and actual name of "Dr. Jones' plantation" outside of Savannah, Georgia. The two maps that show his western travel routes are partly based on field research, including visits to the bluff along Bitter Creek, Sangre de Cristo Pass in the Colorado Rockies, and the sites of Cheyenne Pass and Camp Walbach. On the 1864 map of Rome, Georgia, and vicinity, I relettered many of the names to improve legibility. Names have been added on the Allatoona battlefield drawing to indicate specific locations. Lewis Roe's journals of his army life will, I hope, enlighten, entertain, instruct, and perhaps even amuse the reader.

CHAPTER ONE

The Search for Lewis Roe

I GREW UP IN THE SMALL COMMUNITY OF KNOXVILLE IN WEST-CENTRAL ILLINOIS. AT THE TIME, IN THE 1940S AND EARLY 1950S, I READ A GOOD DEAL AND EVEN HAD A MILD CURIOSITY ABOUT THE early history of our town. An 1854 vintage building known as the Hall of Records housed our city library. The librarian, Mrs. Amy Grant, had local roots herself and was a lady of about seventy years.

The last Civil War veteran in Illinois, Lewis Fablinger of Downers Grove, passed away in 1950 at the age of 103.[1] Although no one from that era lived in Knoxville or even in Knox County, many children of veterans were still active, including Mrs. Grant. She told me that her father served in the Union army and took part in General Sherman's March to the Sea. She also brought one or more of his letters to the library for me to read. Her immediate relationship to a Civil War soldier and the fact that he had kept a journal drew my interest, perhaps because I knew of no Civil War veterans among my own ancestors.

Unfortunately, her older brother out in Kansas had their father's journal and he would not send it back, so unless he came to Knoxville and brought it with him, I wouldn't be able to read it. He did return once with the journal, but I was away in college and he had gone back to Kansas by the time of my next trip home.

Mrs. Grant was the youngest child in her family, born in 1879. She attended Knox College in Galesburg, Illinois, for two terms in 1898–1899 and 1901–1902, and Western Illinois State Teachers' College in Macomb from summer 1905 to June 1907.[2] This educational background no doubt increased her appreciation for the historical value of her father's experiences. So I paid attention when she described the journal. She recalled that he actually compiled it some years after the war, based upon his letters to his wife. The journal was not an actual transcript of these war-time letters, however, and the editorial changes left his later account dif-fering from the contemporary one to some extent.

Mrs. Grant explained that as he finished compiling the journal, her father began to burn his original letters, feeding them into a stove. His wife or an older daughter happened to come into the room at that moment, saw what he was doing, snatched away the unburned letters, and saved them. After her father died in 1908, the journal passed to her oldest brother, who decided that it would eventually go to his own son, named for his grandfather.

I seldom returned to Knoxville after graduating from the University of Illinois and then spending five years in graduate stud-ies. The journal was forgotten when I began a career as an archaeolo-gist in Santa Fe and later in Las Cruces, New Mexico. By the 1980s, I had a business as a consultant and many of my contracts involved historical research. Then in 1984, while rummaging through the ver-tical files at the Fray Angélico Chávez History Library in Santa Fe, I came across an old photocopy of an article printed in the November 3, 1910, issue of the *National Tribune*. This was the national newspaper of the Grand Army of the Republic (GAR), the principal Union vet-erans' organization.

The article, titled "With Canby at Valverde, N.Mex.," had escaped scholars of the Civil War in the Southwest. It appeared to be reliable and written by a participant, but what caught my eye was the signature line at the end—"Lewis F. Roe, Co. F, 7th U.S., Knoxville, Ill." I'd never heard of a Civil War veteran named Lewis Roe in Knoxville, or so I thought. There had been a Roe family when I lived there, and I sent a copy of the article back to my aunt in Knoxville, Dorothy England, with the question—who was Lewis F. Roe?

This was no challenge for her. She wrote back and gently reminded me that Lewis Roe was the father of Amy (Roe) Grant, who had wanted me to see her father's Civil War journal when I was in high school. Those memories came flooding back, and while I now knew who Lewis Roe was, I had no idea he had also served in the Southwest. Although Mrs. Grant had passed away, her daughter, Eleanor Grant Verene, was a customer of my uncle's insurance business in Knoxville. When my aunt gave her a copy of Lewis Roe's article, this delighted her, as the family had no idea that this existed.

The Search for Lewis Roe's Journal

Other materials now began to come out. Mrs. Verene had some family papers, thanks in part to Ella Roe, Mrs. Grant's older sister, who had assumed the role of historian in that family. Mrs. Verene did not have the journal, of course, but she did find a small notebook in which Lewis Roe kept a diary for about four months while serving with the Regular Army before the Civil War, in Company F of the 7th U.S. Infantry. She made a partial transcript of this diary in November 1985 and later allowed my aunt to Xerox the original. From the photocopy I transcribed two largely parallel versions of the march of the 7th Infantry regiment from Fort Bridger, Wyoming, to New Mexico in the summer of 1860, plus another partial diary Roe kept when he, as part of an escort detail, accompanied a train of wagons sent from Fort Craig, New Mexico, to Fort Buchanan in southern Arizona late in the spring of 1861.

The family papers and this notebook now showed that Lewis Roe enlisted in the 7th U.S. Infantry prior to the Civil War, mustered out at the end of his term, and later reenlisted in a volunteer Illinois regiment that formed part of Sherman's Army. My aunt busied herself with the published records of the Illinois Adjutant General's Office and from these we learned the dates of Roe's service with Company C of the 50th Illinois Volunteer Infantry. With her discoveries and some dates in the family papers, we knew enough about his military service by the summer of 1986 for me to request Lewis F. Roe's service and pension records from the National Archives. The pension records especially provided much new information. This incremental approach to the research was unavoidable because the only living person old enough to remember Lewis Roe in that family was a cousin in Florida, who was not available to us. Everyone else had been born after their grandfather died in 1908.

Mrs. Verene also provided copies of nine letters that her grandfather wrote in 1864 and 1865. With respect to the journal, however, we were stymied. Charlie Roe, the older brother who had had it, was now deceased, but his daughter lived in Emporia, Kansas. We tried to communicate with her but were unsuccessful at the time. The whereabouts of Charlie Roe's son, Lewis Roe, was not known. Then in the spring of 1987, Mrs. Verene wrote that this grandson had once worked at the city water department in Emporia.

With this slim lead, I finally called the city of Emporia and learned that Lewis Roe had been employed there from April 1966 until October 1972, not long enough to become eligible for a pension. The city offices had no record of where he might be living. They referred me to Ron Rhodes, supervisor of the city water works, who had known Mr. Roe. From Mr. Rhodes, I learned that Lewis Roe came back to visit now and then (his daughter lived north of Emporia), and he thought that Roe moved to Deming, New Mexico, in 1972 or 1973. This was an incredible coincidence, since Deming lies only sixty miles west of my home in Las Cruces.

The Deming telephone directory showed a Lewis T. Roe living on E. Jote Rd., an address that proved to be a misspelling of Elote Road. The question now was whether I should approach him myself or let his cousin, Eleanor Verene, do so. We decided that I should be the one. Another year passed before I could make a visit.

Finally on December 19, 1988, I drove over to Deming. The Luna County Assessor's Office showed me the location of Lewis T. Roe's house, which appeared to be the only one in an entire Deming Ranchette subdivision situated just southwest of Deming. He was at home when I called. I introduced myself and told him what I was doing and about my interest in his grandfather's journal. This didn't seem to surprise him; he had it right there in the front room and pulled it out for me. I looked through it while we talked, and then I asked about photocopying it. He said that I could take it with me and keep it for a year if I needed to. This was the end of a trail that stretched back almost forty years, and at last I had the opportunity to read Mrs. Grant's father's Civil War journal.

A bit overwhelmed by this good fortune, I returned to Las Cruces and inventoried the documents we had from Lewis F. Roe's own hand. These included:

1. A small notebook with the following:
    a) Pvt. Lewis F. Roe's journal, first version, of the 7th Infantry's march, June 7–July 20, 1860 (incomplete).
    b) Pvt. Lewis F. Roe's journal, second version, of the 7th Infantry's march, June 9–August 30, 1860 (parallel to the first version but lacking entries for June 7 and 8, 1860).
    c) Short diary of Pvt. Lewis F. Roe, April 5–June 2, 1861 (missing entries from April 8 partway through April 23).

2. Surviving installments of Lewis Roe's *original* (daily) Civil
   War journal, 1864–1865:
   > Journal 30th (October 9–15, 1864)
   > Journal 31st (October 16–27, 1864)
   > Journal 32nd (October 28–November 3, 1864)
   > Journal 33rd (November 4–20, 1864)
   > Journal 34th (November 21–December 3, 1864)
   > Journal 35th (December 4–18, 1864)
   > Journal 36th (December 19, 1864–January 4, 1865)
   > Journal 37th (January 6–17, 1865; possibly the last in this
   > numbered series)
   > Unnumbered journal from Camp No. 4 (February 4,
   > 1865) through Camp No. 46 (March 25, 1865)

3. First Notebook, "Record of a Journal Kept by Lewis F. Roe. . . ."
   Includes:
   > Introduction (12 manuscript pages)
   > Transcription of his daily journal (pp. 13–89 with pages
   > missing at the end), April 3–October 21, 1864.
   > Incomplete.

4. Second Notebook
   > Transcription of his daily journal (pp. 1–46 with
   > no pages missing), November 4, 1864, through
   > February 16, 1865. Complete.

5. Personal letters, addressed by Lewis F. Roe to "My Dear Wife"
   or "Dear Louisa":
   > May 24, 1864 (from Rome, Ga.)
   > June 5, 1864 (from Rome, Ga.)
   > June 27, 1864 (from Rome, Ga.)
   > July 24, 1864 (from Rome, Ga.)
   > October 9, 1864 (from Rome, Ga.)
   > January 19, 1865 (from Savannah, Ga.)
   > January 30, 1865 ("30 mi. above Savannah")
   > Date obscured but early to mid-June 1865 (Camp . . . ,
   > probably Louisville, Ky.)
   > June 20, 1865 (from Louisville, Ky.)

6. Article "With Canby at Valverde, N.Mex." in the *National
   Tribune*, November 3, 1910.

Mr. Roe possessed a few other items, such as the draft of an address delivered by his grandfather's older brother Edward D. Roe on Memorial Day 1891 at Silver Lake, Kansas. A square of paper with names on both sides, in Lewis F. Roe's own handwriting, was a fragment from a copy of the Company F, 7th U.S. Infantry casualty list from the Battle of Valverde, New Mexico, on February 21, 1862.[3] These documents suggest that more papers existed at one time. There is nothing to show that Lewis Roe kept other diaries.

When I returned all of Lewis F. Roe's materials to Mr. Roe, he gave me written permission to publish these. Sometime later he found and sent me an original ambrotype of his grandfather in his 7th Infantry uniform, made in Galesburg in 1863. This, too, I copied and returned the original to him. It is used here as the frontispiece. Mr. Roe subsequently sent these records to his cousin, Mrs. Verene, and in June 1990, her son, Donald P. Verene, donated them to Knox College.[4]

At various times between July 1986 and January 1990, I transcribed the two notebooks, the nine journal installments, and the small 1860–1861 notebook; then I checked the typed transcripts carefully against photocopies of the originals. Lewis F. Roe had enclosed installments of his original (daily) Civil War journal with the personal letters to his wife. Eight extant journal segments, numbered 30th through the 37th, each covered one to two weeks. A much longer one, unnumbered, recorded events in February and March 1865. No installments prior to the 30th one have been discovered, and it is now apparent that he fed these, not the personal letters, into the fire as he completed transcribing them into his notebooks. The survival of these original segments is doubly important because the 31st and 32nd ones partly overlap with his first notebook and allow us to fill in the missing pages between October 21 and November 3, 1864, in that notebook. When compared with the second notebook, five of the segments show that his recopying involved only minor editing.

On October 13, 2003, I made a brief visit to the Seymour Library at Knox College to extend the research. The Lewis F. Roe Papers there included a number of items that I had not seen previously, such as his discharge papers from the 7th U.S. Infantry and the 50th Illinois Veteran Volunteer Infantry, and his appointment as a corporal in the latter regiment. An additional thirty-three letters to his wife were also new to me. These letters, three of which lacked one or more pages, were dated between February 17, 1864, and June 1, 1865. The letters at Knox held little new information and have not been used in this book.

Missing from the papers at Knox College were originals or copies of the nine personal letters listed above (No. 5) and the nine Civil War journal installments (No. 2). I have no idea where these have gone. The nine personal letters I had already incorporated into the chapters with the 1864–1865 journals, so their contents have been preserved. Also missing at Knox were the genealogical sections of the Roe family records. These presumably remained with Mrs. Verene and are cited here as Roe family records.

In Roe's journal entry for November 30, 1864 (chapter 8), he said that he again scribbled "in my little book." This suggests that during the Savannah Campaign at least his primary record was a small notebook similar to the one he used in recording his march with the 7th U.S. Infantry in 1860 (chapter 3). If so, then what I have called installments of his original Civil War journal may have been recopied from his "little book" whenever he was about to write home. The close similarity of his handwriting in each installment could mean that the document was written out at a single sitting rather than day by day. Since this "little book" has not survived, there is no way to know what, if anything, he might have added or deleted when writing the installments.

The Search for Background on a Soldier's Life

With the journals transcribed, the next task was to assemble enough background information to write a decent introduction. The introduction that Roe himself wrote at the beginning of his first notebook was invaluable. From his pension file at the National Archives and several pages of Roe and related family genealogical records, we had lists of births and marriages assembled by or with the assistance of his second-oldest daughter, Ella Roe. These and the U.S. Census population schedules from 1860, 1870, and 1880 helped to sort out his own casual references to brothers, an aunt, and cousins in the 1864–1865 journal. We found almost nothing about the first twenty years of his life, prior to joining the 7th Infantry on March 5, 1858. Again, from the time he was discharged from volunteer service on July 13, 1865, until his death

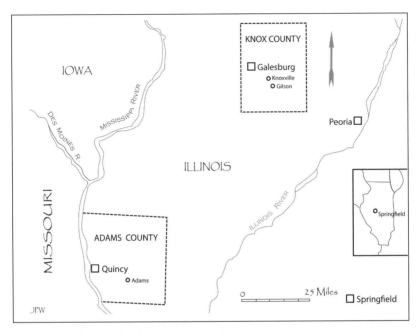

MAP 1. West-Central Illinois. Courtesy of author.

on March 27, 1908, we have few details to cover a period of more than forty years.

Lewis Roe had been born in Adams County, Illinois, and lived almost half of his life there. None of the Adams County histories mentioned individuals or families that could be related to his. Newspapers were another source, and the nine surviving years of the weekly *Knox County Republican* between 1888 and 1910 were examined. These yielded only a confirmation that Roe and his family moved to Knoxville in 1893 and that he participated in activities of the GAR post there.[5]

With little to show thus far, I turned to the two daily newspapers published in Quincy, Illinois, the county seat of Adams County. I read the *Quincy Daily Whig and Republican* from 1858 through 1865 and the *Quincy Herald* from 1859 through 1865. Both papers were virtually complete for these years, but neither published anything about or from Lewis Roe. The *Whig* did an excellent job of news reporting, and it included letters from persons in the 50th Illinois Volunteer Infantry as well as items about that regiment. The *Herald* (which the *Whig* referred to as a Copperhead sheet) had little to say about the regiment following its participation in the battles of Pittsburg Landing (Shiloh), Tennessee, and Corinth, Mississippi, both in 1862.

I borrowed microfilms of the *National Tribune* for the period March 1899 through March 1911. Although Lewis Roe died in 1908, the article published under his name appeared in the November 3, 1910, issue. I hoped that he might have published more, but this was not the case. From a passing reference I discovered the *Western Veteran*, another veterans' newspaper. The Kansas State Historical Society had microfilmed this paper, published from 1884 through 1904. O. H. Coulter, who entered service at age 15 and edited the *Western Veteran* from 1889 through 1904, had served in Company I of Roe's own regiment.[6] Understandably his paper had many articles about this regiment, including rosters of surviving members and regular reports on its reunions. The only reference to Lewis Roe seems to have been his name on the roster for the regimental reunion held in Quincy on September 17–19, 1889.[7]

The *Western Veteran* published the regimental history, *History of the Fiftieth Regiment Illinois Volunteer Infantry in the War of the Union*, with the last regimental adjutant serving as the editor.[8] The paper printed 410 copies of this subscription volume in 1894.[9] It contained one passing reference to Lewis F. Roe, mostly about his previous service in the 7th Infantry.[10]

By itself this well-written regimental history provided ample background for Roe's 1864–1865 Civil War journal. One intriguing feature was the change in literary style about halfway through, at the point where the regiment left its station at Rome, Georgia, on November 10, 1864, to join what became Sherman's March to the Sea. The narrative structure then became a daily journal and the writing style resembled that of Roe's journal. The two appeared to be parallel and independent accounts although their contents were quite different. The probable explanation for their similarities is that the writers shared the same educational backgrounds.

These efforts to fill out Lewis Roe's life proved the folk wisdom of one colleague: that the best subjects for biography are those who died without leaving long, uneventful periods for authors to fill. One senses that for Lewis Roe, the Civil War was the defining experience in his life. He was brave, modest, and also very lucky. Best of all, he left us his account of life in one of Sherman's armies, a role in which he clearly took great pride.

Lewis F. Roe, 1838–1908

Lewis Franklin Roe's parents were Lewis Roe and Caroline (Strong) Roe. He came into the world on August 22, 1838, in the rural community of Adams in Adams County, Illinois. He had two full brothers: Jonas, born in 1834, about whom we know nothing more, and Edward D., born in 1836. His own father died in 1843 and a year later (September 25, 1844) Caroline, a month shy of her thirtieth birthday, married Josiah Read. He was her age or perhaps a year older. Josiah, too, had been married before, to Amy Roe, some nine years his senior and a sister of Lewis Roe. Josiah and Amy had two sons, Franklin and Jonas, born in 1840 and 1842. What became of Amy is not known; perhaps she died in childbirth.

Josiah Read and his new wife Caroline began yet a third family: Warren S., Charles A., Henry W., and William E., born in 1845, 1848, 1849, and 1857 respectively. Lewis Roe thus grew up in a family with nine boys—full brothers, half-brothers, and step-brothers—whom he referred to indiscriminately as brothers. Occasionally in his Civil War journal he called his wife's brothers "brother" as well. The relationships with the cousins, aunt, and uncle he mentioned in his journal are less clear and have not been worked out. Many of Lewis F. Roe's brothers would have been at an age to serve in the Union army, and at least some of them did.

The Roe–Read family, prosperous but not wealthy, farmed in Burton Township in Adams County; Josiah Read reported a personal estate worth $1,000 and real estate valued at $6,000 in the 1860 Census.[11] The boys would have received a basic education at a country school. By 1840 the county seat of Quincy had grown into a city and nearly all of the adult males living outside of towns returned themselves as farmers or laborers. Adams County bordered on the Mississippi River and Quincy had become a river port and a center of manufacturing and commerce.

Lewis received much more than a basic education, as the records of Knox College show him as a member of the preparatory class for one year, 1856–1857. This part of Knox was similar to a high school and the college catalog noted that "Candidates for admission to the Preparatory Class are expected to be familiar with the common English branches." The first-year preparatory course focused on Latin grammar and Latin readings, and Greek grammar and a Greek reader, tempered with algebra.[12] How well he fared with these is not known.

FIGURE 1. At 6th and Maine, downtown Quincy, Ill., ca. 1861–1863. Courtesy of the
Historical Society of Quincy and Adams County.

Lewis Roe noted in his Civil War journal that he spent January 1,
1858, at Gilson, Illinois, a small community a dozen miles from Galesburg and about half that distance from Knoxville. Perhaps it was while
he attended Knox that he first met Louisa Smith, although Knox has
no record of her. Louisa was the eldest of twelve children in the family
of Edmund Smith, a grocer at Gilson.[13] Roe would later marry Louisa
in Knoxville.

We know nothing more about Lewis Roe's early life before he showed
up at the recruiting depot in St. Louis, Missouri, on March 5, 1858, and
enlisted in the Army of the United States for the normal five-year period.
The recruiting officer described him as 5 feet 7 3/4 inches in height with
blue eyes, sandy hair, and a ruddy complexion. Although only nineteen
at the time, he fudged in declaring that he was twenty-two years of age.[14]
He received assignment to the 7th U.S. Infantry.

In 1857 the Mormons in Utah defied the authority of the federal
government, and as a result President James Buchanan sent a small
army to crush this uprising, the so-called Utah War. The plan was for
a summer offensive in 1858, but negotiators reached a compromise
settlement in late June. The army in the meantime had attempted to
recruit additional men for its understrength regular units.[15]

These reinforcements, including the bulk of the 7th Infantry and many recent recruits, were organized as six columns when they marched westward from Fort Leavenworth, Kansas. Roe was sent to join Company F, already on duty at Fort Laramie in present-day Wyoming. He evidently marched with the Fourth Column. A civilian who accompanied this column as a boy of fifteen later wrote a description of their pleasant and largely uneventful trek to Utah.[16]

In his own introduction, Lewis Roe wrote the following about his early army life:

> I served in Co. "F" 7th U.S. Infy. for 5 years, enlisting March 4th
> 1858, at St. Louis Mo. [I] was sent to Jefferson Barracks, 12 miles
> south of St. Louis, where 8 companies of our Regiment was in
> barracks, the other 2 companies (F and H) being at Fort Laramie
> on the Platte river. The 7th Infty. was sent the latter part of May 1858
> to Fort Leavenworth Kan. We went by boat up the Mo [Missouri]
> River. After remaining in camp about a week we started across the
> plains for Salt Lake City, passing through Ft. Laramie. Companies F
> and H joined the column and we proceeded on our way. I was now
> with my Co. "F."
>
> Arriving in Sept. 1858 at Ft. Bridger, Wyoming, our co was
> ordered to remain as garrison for that Post. We had marched about
> 1000 miles. Our route was up the Platte River and the Sweet Water
> river through the South Pass, crossing Green River to Ft. Bridger.
> On the way we passed through several tribes of Indians, the
> Cheyennes, the Sioux, the Crows, the Blackfeet and the Bannocks.
> Saw herds of Buffalos and various wonders of nature.
>
> We remained as garrison of Fort Bridger from Sept. 1858 until
> May 1860, going on frequent Indian expeditions but chiefly as a
> guard to the great Overland Route to California. I might tell of
> many remarkable incidents and adventures while stationed here,
> but as I only write this as preliminary to my journal kept while
> belonging to Co. "C" 50 Ills. [Volunteer] Infty, I will not go into the
> details of my regular army service.[17]

At the time, this country was part of Utah Territory. Fort Bridger lay near the southwestern corner of what is now Wyoming. The post commander there from mid-August 1858 to March 6, 1860, for all but three months of the time Roe spent in Utah, was Brevet Major Edward R. S.

FIGURE 2. Original 1858 officers' quarters at Fort Bridger, Wyo. Author's photo.

Canby, 10th U.S. Infantry.[18] Before two more years had passed, Roe would serve under Canby again, this time at the Civil War Battle of Valverde and the skirmish at Peralta, in New Mexico Territory.

The entire 7th Infantry Regiment transferred from Utah to New Mexico in the summer of 1860 as part of a massive reinforcement that included the 5th Infantry Regiment, three companies of the 10th, and two of the 2nd Dragoons as well.[19] Lewis Roe left Fort Bridger in the second column of his regiment. This march stretched 1,067 miles from Blacks Fork in southwestern Wyoming to Fort Craig on the Rio Grande, and during these three months he kept a daily journal—the earliest such record we have by him. Again, Roe wrote:

> In the spring of 1860 our Regiment (7th Infty.) was ordered to New Mexico and Arizionia. We took up the line of march on the last day of May 1860, taking what was then called the Great Cherokee Trail to N.M. Going east, we crossed the Rockies through Bridger's Pass, on east through Chyenne [Cheyenne] Pass, turning south through Denver City, crossing the hd. waters of the Arkansas River, west through Sangre de Cristo Pass. Thence South through the Mexican cities of Taos, Santa Fe, Albuquerque, down the Rio Grande

through the towns of Los Lunas, Peralto [Peralta], Socorro, to Fort
Craig almost on the southern border of N.M.

Here our company "F" and "H" were ordered to remain as
garrison while the other 8 companies were sent to different forts of
Arizonia. We arrived at Fort Craig on the 3rd of Sept. 1860. We had
accomplish[ed] a march of over 1000 miles through mountains,
passes, over rivers, where it did not seem possible for an army with
a large train to go. Saw but few Indians or Buffalos, but the lofty
mountains, deep cañons were innumerable.

As for his next months at Fort Craig, Roe tells us:

> During the fall and winter of 1860–61 we were chiefly employed as
> guards to the overland mail coaches running from Kansas City to
> San Francisco Cal. Every week the mail coach arriving at Ft. Craig
> would take on an extra coach with 10 or 12 soldiers as guards, cross
> the "*Jornada del Muerto*" (Journey of death) to Ft. Fillmore 110
> miles south. We usually made the trip in 27 hours, coming back
> on the next mail coach.

A partial diary from the spring of 1861 covers a detail that escorted
cattle to Arizona.

Following the Battle of Valverde on February 21, 1862, Colonel Canby
led Company F and other units of his command in pursuit of the Confederates until they eventually left New Mexico Territory in early July.
The summer of 1862 saw Roe and his company assigned to Fort Union,
the principal army supply point in New Mexico. On March 5, 1863, he
mustered out there as a first sergeant. The frontispiece is an ambrotype,
taken in Galesburg, Illinois, in 1863, that shows him wearing the sword
belt plate authorized for sergeants and officers in the infantry.[20] By his
own account, Lewis Roe walked from Fort Union back to St. Joseph,
Missouri, on the Santa Fe Trail in company with Michael Fitzgerald,
also discharged from Company F:

> My time expired on the 4th of March 1863. I started for home,
> passed through Raton Mts. by Raton pass, striking the headwaters
> of the Arkansas river, followed down the river to the great bend,
> thence northeast to Kansas City. Up the mo [Missouri] river to St.
> Joe thence by rail to Quincy, arriving home April 8th, 1863. Was
> married in Aug. 1863. The war of the rebellion was still going on.

He evidently kept up a correspondence with Louisa Smith while in Utah and New Mexico, because on August 13, 1863, Thomas Vaill, minister of the Presbyterian Church at Knoxville, married Lewis and Louisa.[21] Just fifteen days later, the school commissioner of Adams County signed a second grade teaching certificate, making Lewis Roe eligible to receive a contract to teach elementary students in the one-room schoolhouses that were the principal public schools of the time.[22] When or how long he taught is not known; a second grade certificate had to be renewed annually but school terms might be for as little as two months.

An Adams County infantry regiment had been mustered into service on September 11, 1861, as the 50th Illinois Volunteer Infantry. Now, two years later, the Civil War was at its height, and the government began offering generous financial incentives for men already in service to accept discharges and reenlist as veteran volunteers for three years. The draft that was supposed to begin in Illinois on January 5, 1864, offered an additional inducement. Lewis Roe would have been aware of all this, and in his introduction he said, "It did not seem right for me a trained soldier to remain at home and the Gov offering 402 dollars bounty I enlisted."

So, partly from a sense of patriotism and partly because of the government bounty, with a private's pay of $13 a month, Lewis Roe went back into uniform. His prior service made him eligible for enrollment as a veteran volunteer. This was probably the best-paying employment that he could have found. The *National Tribune* for August 8, 1907, gave a thorough explanation of the bounty system that evolved during the Civil War and confirmed that Roe would have received a bounty and premium of $402, paid in installments. With their first daughter (Carrie May) due in May, he had his new family's welfare to consider.

Lewis Roe went off to join his regiment near Mooresville, Alabama, and from there to participating in the first weeks of Sherman's Atlanta Campaign, followed by garrison duty at Rome, Georgia, and a major battle at Allatoona. He and his comrades accompanied the month-long March to the Sea and continued up through the Carolinas to Bentonville and finally to Goldsboro, North Carolina. For Roe, this was the end of the war. The journal doesn't mention that he received a promotion to corporal on October 1, 1864.[23] Although his daily entries end at Goldsboro on March 24, 1865, the regimental history continues day-by-day through the return to Quincy and final discharge of the soldiers on July 13, 1865.

Within a year after his return home, the Roe family moved to Missouri for reasons unknown. Their second daughter, Sarah Ella, was born at Cream Ridge, Missouri, in June 1866, and the next child, Minnie, at Cream Ridge one and a half years later.[24] Cream Ridge was a small nineteenth-century village in north-central Livingston County, Missouri. The family may have moved their place of residence because Medicine Township in the northeastern corner of Livingston County saw three sons—Charles, Herbert, and Frederick—arrive in 1870, 1871, and 1874, respectively. Charles was born just six days after the census-taker visited the Roes.[25]

The 1870 Census population schedule listed the family as having a personal estate valued at $200 and real estate worth $800. This suggests a small farm of perhaps eighty acres, probably all that one person could work unaided. The schedule included no neighbors with familiar names, such as relatives or service comrades. Perhaps the family moved a second time because a 1907 declaration in Roe's pension file claimed that he had resided at Wheeling, Missouri, up until 1876. Wheeling is a small town at the east-central edge of Livingston County.[26]

With a young family, a small farm, and only his wife to help with the work, Lewis Roe probably had trouble making ends meet during the decade they lived in Missouri. At this time, Missouri was instituting Normal Schools to better prepare its teachers for the common schools. The only two Normal Schools, at Warrensburg and Kirksville, had two six-week terms of instruction. Whether Roe attended either is not known, but on October 1, 1872, he did receive a second grade teaching certificate from the County Superintendent of Public Schools in Livingston County.[27] The county that year had ninety-nine primary schools and issued 122 certificates to teachers, so Lewis Roe should have had little trouble in finding a position. Annual school terms ran from four to eight months, the length probably depending upon the money available in individual school districts. He farmed as well and saw his certificate renewed in 1874 and 1875.[28]

Once again for reasons not known, the Roe family returned to Burton Township, Adams County, Illinois, in 1876. They settled on a farm adjoining those of his mother and stepfather (now retired), his half-brothers Warren, Charles, and William, and his aunt, Ruth Roe.[29] He took the examination offered by the Adams County Superintendent

Figure 3. Lewis and Louisa Roe in later life. Photo courtesy of
Mrs. Eleanor Verene, Galesburg, Ill.

of Public Schools and received teaching certificates in 1880 and 1882.[30]
County directories returned him as a farmer there in 1886 and 1892.[31]

On the first day after passage of a new federal law, the Act of June 27,
1890, Lewis Roe filed a declaration for an Invalid Pension. He claimed
among other things that he was gradually going blind. These claims
were decided on a case by case basis, and initially he received a relatively generous pension of $12 per month, reduced to $8 per month in
April 1895. Periodically he made applications to have this increased,
but evidently without success.[32] In the meantime, the Roes and most of
their children moved to Knoxville in February 1893.[33] Perhaps they did
so to be nearer his wife's family, who presumably still lived in Gilson.
A year after their arrival, Lewis and Louisa, with two of their daughters
and youngest son, joined the Knoxville Presbyterian Church.[34]

By the 1890s, the old soldier wasn't really able to work, though the
Roes had a garden, and he drove a cart and horse around town selling
his vegetables. He may have helped other people with their gardens
as well.[35] He participated in veterans' affairs, being elected chaplain of
the G. W. Trafton Post No. 239 of the GAR at Knoxville in December
1893 and again in January 1895. His regiment held a reunion each fall
at Quincy, Illinois, but he is shown attending only the one in 1889.[36]

Unfortunately, the only Knoxville newspapers that survive from the end of August 1895 to the time of Roe's death in 1908 are for part of 1900 and 1901. This run carried no mention of him. No one still living in the 1990s recalled Lewis Roe, although older Knoxville residents knew his children.

Louisa died in 1906, and an obituary for Lewis Roe from an undated number of the *Knox County Republican* said that he passed away suddenly at his home in Knoxville on Friday evening, March 27, 1908. The GAR and WRC [Women's Relief Corps] members attended the funeral as a body; pall bearers were GAR comrades with the post commander in charge of graveside services. The post adjutant sent a letter of condolence to the youngest daughter, Amy Roe, noting that "He was a faithful and consistent member, ever working for the best interest of our order."[37] He rests in the Knoxville cemetery.

FIGURE 4. Lewis Roe's grave, Knoxville, Ill. Photo courtesy of Mrs. Eleanor Verene, Galesburg, Ill.

CHAPTER TWO

Retracing the March of the 7th Infantry, June–August 1860

LEWIS ROE'S FIRST JOURNAL IS ACTUALLY THREE INDIVIDUAL JOURNALS, WRITTEN IN SEQUENCE IN A SMALL, HANDMADE NOTEBOOK WITH PAGES THAT MEASURE 2.93 BY 4.56 INCHES. Sixty-six pages survive, all with writing, the leaves stitched together along the binding margin with heavy thread. There are no covers, and sheets are missing both front and back. Approximately four pages have been lost near the center. The contents of the small notebook were listed earlier; here we are considering only the two versions of his 1860 journal. All of the entries were made in ink, in the handwriting of Lewis F. Roe. None of the pages are numbered, and there are no sketches or maps.

The Two Versions of the 1860 Journal

After puzzling over this little notebook for more than a decade, I am inclined to accept the opinions of my aunt and Eleanor Verene that Lewis Roe simply wrote his journal of the 1860 march from Fort Bridger to Fort Craig twice. His first version began on June 7, 1860, at Fort Bridger when the first subcolumn departed (Roe was in the second subcolumn). It ended with the entry for July 20. The second version began June 9, and it continued through the end of the march on August 30, 1860. It is separated from the first one by a shorter diary of escort duty in April–June 1861. Either he left blank pages after the abrupt end of the first diary on July 20, or there are pages now missing at that point. My conclusion is that we have simply lost some pages.

Whether this has meant significant gaps in the record of the 1860 march, I very much doubt. Comparisons of entries for the same days show that the two versions were sometimes identical; in other places similar contents had different phrasings; and occasionally one entry included observations not found in the other. Where they differed in length, the second version was usually longer. I have chosen it as the primary narrative here.

Why he bothered to rewrite his journal is not evident, as the information added (or deleted) usually has no particular significance. There are no contradictions between one account and the other. Publishing the two versions side by side was considered and put aside because the contents largely duplicate one another.

The first version is drawn upon for the June 7 and 8 entries, and elsewhere when it has something unique. Lewis Roe wrote both in any case and the two versions are probably contemporary with one another within the same year.

Confirming a Route

The daily journal of an extended march by a regimental-size or larger unit is quite rare outside of wartime contexts such as the Mexican War journals of Lt. Col. W. H. Emory and Capt. A. R. Johnston.[1] Perhaps the best example is *The March of the Mounted Riflemen from Fort Leavenworth to Fort Vancouver, May to October 1849,*[2] although this retracement of the Oregon Trail had quite different objectives. It was also almost twice the length of the 7th Infantry's trek. Such narratives show that the frontier army was quite capable of unsupported marches across vast stretches of roadless country. Roe's 1860 journal documents substantial changes in the two years since he and others had passed that way before.

In the absence of any well-established roads, the 7th Infantry in 1860 followed a series of trails and trail segments, some named and others not. I worked out their actual route from a combination of modern topographic maps, distances and directions in the journal, other overland accounts and itineraries, place names, and the findings by overland trail researchers. In Wyoming, the most important sources were the U.S. Geological Survey's (USGS) 1:100,000 scale topographic maps from the Evanston quadrangle on the west to the Laramie quadrangle on the east; and the Topozone.com version of the USGS Point of Rocks, Bitter Creek NW, Black Buttes, Bridger Pass, and Islay 7.5' quadrangles. In Colorado, I had two 1:100,000 scale USGS sheets for

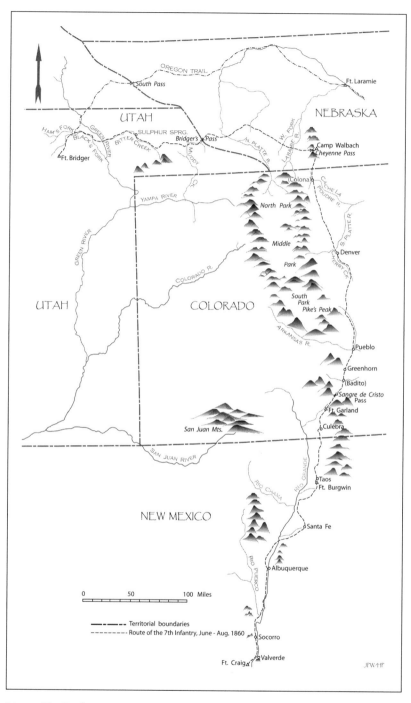

Map 2. The Rocky Mountain West in 1860. Courtesy of author and Holli Pope.

the country northeast of Denver, the Blanca Peak sheet for south-central Colorado, the La Veta Pass 7.5' topo map, and the Internet websites for the Cherokee Trail.[3] There was also the map and other remarks in Janet Lecompte's *Pueblo, Hardscrabble, Greenhorn,*[4] and the U.S. Forest Service 1:126,720 scale map of San Isabel National Forest. For Wyoming and Colorado, the reprinted diaries, maps, and retracements in Lee Whiteley's trail guide and volume 3 of Jack E. and Patricia K. A. Fletcher's *Cherokee Trail Diaries* proved most helpful.[5] South of the Colorado line, any number of maps from 1846 to the present aided in plotting the route across northern New Mexico.

The map work left a few locations needing confirmation, so on May 3–8 and again on October 19–24, 2003, I visited several of the places that Roe had known or passed in southern Wyoming and Colorado. These included Fort Bridger State Historic Site, the sandstone bluff with upward of 100 soldiers' names carved on it (Roe's Camp 9), Bridger Pass (Camp 15), Cheyenne Pass (Camp 24), and Sangre de Cristo Pass (Camp 44). My questions were whether Lewis Roe's and the modern locations for these place-names coincided, and to confirm the place where he carved his name, if the rock still existed. Roe's descriptions proved to be accurate, and my comments about all of them are given below.

The Cherokee Trail

The third day out from Fort Bridger, Lewis Roe claimed that "Turning to our right we took what is called the Great Cherokee Trail" (Camp 4). The Cherokee Trail, first traveled in 1849 and 1850, led from the Cherokee Nation in eastern Oklahoma to Fort Bridger, and from there by several routes to California or Oregon. Across southern Wyoming it followed at least three routings. The branch taken by the 7th Infantry had actually been pioneered by Capt. Howard Stansbury in 1850.[6] An engineer party under Lieutenant Francis Bryan surveyed a route that led through Bridger Pass in 1857, and the army then improved Bryan's trail by grading hills, filling ravines, and other construction in 1858.[7]

Sometime after this, emigrant trains began to travel this way. Ben Holladay's Overland Stage Line followed this road in 1862, and parts of it became known as the Cherokee Trail where the improved road superseded earlier trails that had borne this name.[8] Capt. Randolph B.

Marcy wrote in the itinerary for his 1858 march from Fort Union, New Mexico, to Fort Bridger, Wyoming, that "The *Cherokee Trail*, noted, extends from the Cherokee nation [in modern Oklahoma] to California and has been traveled for several years by emigrants."[9] By 1860 this had become the principal route used by emigrants and other travelers, including the 7th Infantry, across southern Wyoming. Completion of the first transcontinental railroad in 1869 made all of these earlier trails obsolete.

The March of the 7th Infantry

The army required orders and reports to cover every significant movement, and the march of the 7th Infantry from Utah to New Mexico was no exception. Lt. Col. Pitcairn Morrison, commanding the regiment, led the first subcolumn the entire distance. He left Fort Bridger on June 7 and arrived at Fort Buchanan, Arizona, on October 3. Maj. Isaac Lynde had charge of the second subcolumn, which departed June 8 and marched into Santa Fe, New Mexico, on August 17. William D. Kirk, a civilian wagon master whom we will meet again later, led the ox train that hauled the regiment's gear.[10]

In a letter reporting his arrival in the Department of New Mexico, Lieutenant Colonel Morrison said that he was enclosing the journal of the entire distance, "embracing in marginal notes, and topographic sketches; such descriptions of a General Nature, as may be useful in correcting former Maps, and in giving information to the Emigrants, or to Commanders of bodies of troops, traversing the Country." He referred also to a detailed report of the march of the remainder of the first general column by Maj. Isaac Lynde, commander of the second subcolumn. Lewis Roe's company was part of Lynde's command.[11]

Much of Morrison's October 18 letter was given over to complaints. He obviously had had no maps or guides, "not even a pocket compass." The ox train sent to haul supplies was more than useless, in his opinion, for long marches with troops. He considered the march had been delayed about twenty-five days by the ox-drawn wagons and bad roads, especially on the section along Bitter Creek. While en route he had sent a brief letter from Fort Garland, Colorado, and Major Lynde reported after he arrived in southwestern New Mexico and established a new post there.[12]

I queried the National Archives as to the whereabouts of Lieutenant Colonel Morrison's journal and Major Lynde's detailed report. Neither had been published, and an extensive search of military records failed to yield either document. The Register of Letters Received that noted Morrison's October 18 letter did not indicate any enclosures, or that anything had been forwarded to another office.[13] As a result, the primary record of this long march appears to be the small notebook kept by Pvt. Lewis F. Roe, Company F, 7th Infantry.

Unlike his regimental commander, Private Roe was not one to complain, other than about bad water or a poor camp. He made entries consistently and often in good detail, noting place names and keeping track of the distances marched, occasionally giving the compass directions as well. Most of the place-names are identifiable, though Roe had obviously never studied French. The following sections are a travelogue that will allow the reader to follow this march with reference to modern place-names, and provide explanations where needed. Other annotations are offered in chapter 3 in endnotes to the daily entries.

From Fort Bridger to Cheyenne Pass

After leaving Fort Bridger, the second subcolumn followed the Overland Trail eastward down Blacks Fork [of the Green River] to Church Butte, then marched northeast to Hams Fork and crossed it on a bridge near its juncture with Blacks Fork. The column continued easterly on the same road, which for a while paralleled Blacks Fork. When they came to Green River, they camped, then ferried across to the site of the modern town with this name. The troops followed the Cherokee Trail upstream along Bitter Creek and on June 13 rested at the location of present-day Rock Springs, Wyoming.

Two days later and still along Bitter Creek, Roe's subcolumn reached Sulphur Spring, their Camp 9 and the point where the stream here bends from south to west. The Union Pacific Railroad now parallels Bitter Creek east as far as Point of Rocks, Wyoming, then follows south along this creek for another twenty miles.

At Point of Rocks, the Cherokee Trail continued east while the Overland Trail bore south. Apart from the railroad, some modern graded roads, and the Black Buttes Coal Co. facilities, the country south of Point of Rocks is still largely undisturbed. Initially I searched for anything resembling the features Roe described in his diary entry for June 15, 1860, as I especially wanted to see if his name and native place carved in soft sandstone had survived. To me, nothing corresponded with the diary description, so I sought help and was directed to Mr. and Mrs. Ed Varley at Point of Rocks, Wyoming. This roadside community on Interstate 80 lies about one-half mile north of the old Point of Rocks Stage Station and Bitter Creek.

From Roe's description of a sulphurous spring that flowed from a crevice in a very high rock and soldiers' names cut into the soft sandstone, the Varleys immediately recognized that this site, well-known locally, lies about 1.2 miles southeast of the Point of Rocks turnoff on Interstate 80 and east of Bitter Creek. They took me to it, and the situation was just as Lewis Roe described. There is no doubt that this is the right location.

There are some natural panels on the cliff face just above the spring and other panels extend around the west-facing bluff here for one hundred feet or more toward the southeast, with soldiers' names and dates on every exposure. There are dozens, perhaps more than one hundred of these, many partly eroded due to weathering. Access above the spring is now precarious because of a steep talus slope and loose soil (and an evil-smelling marsh below). Dates include 1860, 1863, and 1865, and three of the more complete inscriptions read:

C W HUTTE	WILFORD PALMER	G. LOESCH
June 14	June 1860	C° C 7 Inf.
1860		

The Varleys and I looked at these panels carefully but saw nothing that resembled Lewis Roe or Adams Co., Illinois. Perhaps what he carved has weathered away.

From their campsite, on June 15 the subcolumn marched south, past the later sites of the Laclede Stage Station and Fort Laclede. Roe's Soda Springs perhaps marks the location of Fort Laclede. They continued to the later site of Dug Springs and arrived on the 19th at Muddy Creek ("Little Muddy Fork of the Platte River"), where they made a good camp about 2.5 miles below what would soon be known as Washakie Stage Station. Despite a poor road, they made good time with their ox train (not mentioned by Roe) through a narrow defile to another camp (14) at the eastern end, then split away on June 22 toward the northeast. Four miles farther along, they crossed the Continental Divide at Bridger Pass.

Although it has a prominent name, Bridger Pass was not explored until 1850 and was not opened for wagons until after 1858. From then until 1862 this route became the newest "cutoff" on the Cherokee Trail. In 1862 the Overland Stage Line located along it and built stations ten to fifteen miles apart. This then served as the principal corridor to the west until 1869, when the Union Pacific and Central Pacific railroads met at Promontory Point, Utah. Completion of the railroad caused the stage line to cease operation, and other traffic dwindled away as well.[14]

The deep chasm that Roe and the others passed through on June 21 is a narrow defile, now blocked from access at a bridge across Muddy Creek near its east entrance. Bridger Pass is actually a broad, open valley with rolling hills and ridges, between the much higher Atlantic Rim to the north and Miller Ridge—the Sierra Madre to the south. BLM Road 3301 approximates the old Overland Trail closely for more than seventeen miles here, and a sign marks the Continental Divide.

From Bridger Pass, the Overland Trail continued east to the North Platte River, then swung northeastward. The troops crossed Pass Creek on June 27. Since Lieutenant Bryan had mentioned Rattlesnake Creek in 1857, the route now evidently led eastward around the north side of Elk Mountain and on across the Medicine Bow River about at the community of Elk Mountain, then southeastward roughly parallel to modern Interstate 80 for twenty-one miles to the crossing of Cooper Creek. Approximately eight miles beyond, the modern interstate and the old Overland Trail diverge, and the two subcolumns continued southeastward to the Laramie River or just beyond. They next bore east along Lieutenant Bryan's tracks, south of modern Laramie, Wyoming. After crossing what Roe called the Black Hills, now part of the Sherman Mountains, everyone arrived at Cheyenne Pass on July 4.

Cheyenne Pass to Fort Garland

Cheyenne Pass, a short twenty miles by road north of Cheyenne, Wyoming, still bears this name. As used by Lewis Roe and others at the time, Cheyenne Pass was a prominent gap in a north-side ridge line at a very well-watered location, immediately west of the present-day Lorenz

FIGURE 5. Looking west at Cheyenne Pass, Wyo. Author's photo.

Ranch. It is now accessible only from the east, by a road into this ranch from Wyoming Route 211. The ranch buildings are spread across the area, separated by South Lodgepole Creek.

However, the U.S. Geological Survey's Islay, Wyoming, 7.5' topo map now shows Cheyenne Pass as a gap, traversed by Bean Creek, in a much higher ridge line 1.5 miles farther west. Since the same map locates the site of Camp Walbach one-quarter of a mile north of the Lorenz Ranch, there is little question but what Cheyenne Pass in the 1858–1860 period was the more eastern location, by the modern ranch. Sprague's[15] location of Cheyenne Pass is also this one. Since no one was home there, I did not search for the remains of Camp Walbach, which as Roe said had been built in the winter of 1858–1859.

The regiment rested one day at Cheyenne Pass before turning to the right and continuing very nearly due south. They marched along the eastern base of what he called the North Park Mountains, now part of the Front Range. Their road here did not coincide with any named trail. The route Horace Greeley, editor of the New York Tribune, took from Denver to Cheyenne Pass in 1859 appears to have lain to the east, a continuation of the Trappers or Taos Trail. Capt. Randolph B. Marcy's and Col. W. W. Loring's itineraries of their 1858 march from New Mexico to Fort Bridger indicate that their course lay more toward the west after they passed beyond the Cache la Poudre River in northern Colorado.[16]

FIGURE 6. Denver, Colo., ca. 1860. Courtesy, Colorado Historical Society,
negative F10540.

On July 9, Roe's subcolumn passed through what was evidently the
earliest settlement of La Porte, Colorado, soon after it had been organized by a town company and settled in 1860 as the town of Colona.
Two days south of there they came to St. Vrain. This was the St. Vrain
stage station, where M. A. Allen built a log cabin in 1860 and his wife
or widow later added a hotel. Old Fort St. Vrain, a fur-trade post built
in 1837 and abandoned about 1851, would have been a nameless ruin by
1860, lying on the banks of the South Platte some twenty miles closer
to Greeley, Colorado.[17] Denver now lay just ahead.

This bustling town, already a small city, was not yet two years old.
The soldiers camped on Cherry Creek, rested for a day, and looked
over Denver. The subcolumn had rejoined the Cherokee Trail at the
Cache la Poudre crossing. Now, on the move once more, the marchers followed the trail south up Cherry Creek, then down Fontaine qui
Bouille Creek past a series of well-recognized camping places until
they reached the Arkansas River at what is now Pueblo, Colorado.
Their route as far south as present-day Colorado Springs lay to the
east of modern Interstate 25, but from that point to Pueblo it followed
very close to present-day I-25. Pueblo was named for an adobe trad-
ing fort established in 1842 and abandoned around 1850.[18] Permanent

settlers returned there in 1859 as a result of the Colorado gold rush that year, but Roe apparently found the place deserted.[19] Here they left the Cherokee Trail for the last time.

From the Arkansas River crossing at Pueblo, the troops turned toward the southwest along the Trappers or Taos Trail that connected the upper Arkansas with the settlements at Taos, New Mexico.[20] The men's spirits improved as they neared New Mexico and passed the Greenhorn settlement, probably their Camp 42, where a few people continued to live. They forded the Huerfano River near modern Badito and then ascended to the Sangre de Cristo Pass. From what Roe says, this clearly was not a wagon road, but it had been a well-marked route of commerce for trappers and traders out of New Mexico for forty years or more. In 1819, soldiers from the Spanish presidio at Santa Fe had built a short-lived fort at the eastern base of Sangre de Cristo Pass to keep Americans out of New Mexico.[21] Lewis Roe did not mention this site, though its ruins were visible as recently as the 1930s.

The place name Sangre de Cristo Pass is shown on both the USGS La Veta Pass, Colorado, 7.5' topo map and the U.S. Forest Service's San Isabel National Forest map. This pass lies on the crest of the Sangre de Cristo Mountains south of the Huerfano River Valley in south-central Colorado and is no longer used in its higher reaches. Nineteenth-century maps show this route clearly.[22]

From the caldera called McDowell Park at the top of the moun-tains the marching columns followed an easy grade down the west-ern slope along Sangre de Cristo Creek until finally on July 27 they tumbled into Fort Garland, near the eastern side of the San Luis Valley. Fort Garland, now in southern Colorado, lay in New Mexico Territory at that time.

Fort Garland to Fort Craig: Trail's End

At Fort Garland the subcolumns lay over for eight days, principally to allow the oxen to recuperate. The march then resumed, again head-ing south. The men passed the small Mexican village of Culebra, later renamed San Luis, then continued through Costilla ("Casteo") and other unnamed villages, probably including Questa (Roe's Red River), San Cristobal, and Arroyo Hondo—all but the last only a few years old at the time. Their route closely paralleled Colorado Route 159 and

FIGURE 7. Fort Garland, N.Mex., Christmas 1859. Sketch by Dr. C. H. Alden.
Courtesy, Colorado Historical Society, negative F1609.

New Mexico Route 522. Lewis Roe's entry for August 8 is confusing because U.S. Hill actually lies south of Talpa, New Mexico, between there and the Rio Pueblo east of Picuris Pueblo. This is an instance of a mislocated place because Roe sometimes made his diary entries after the date indicated. In any event, the regiment came into Taos, New Mexico, on August 9 and the nearby military post of Cantonment Burgwin one day later.

Leaving Burgwin on August 11, they took what is now known as the old road to Taos, New Mexico, Route 518, south from the post and down U.S. Hill, so named because the road was built as an army construction project in 1854.[23] Later travelers would echo Roe's description of "very bad roads." Once at the Rio Pueblo, they followed downstream as it became the Rio Embudo. Roe tells us it was dry at the time, which would have been most unusual (especially in August) but not impossible. The troops reached the Rio Grande at the village of Embudo, then bore left and followed roads that approximate New Mexico Route 68 and U.S. Route 84 south to Santa Fe, the capital of New Mexico Territory. For many years, Santa Fe also served as the headquarters of the Military Department and later District of New Mexico.

Santa Fe fell far short of Roe's expectations, but he had to spend only one day there. At this point the regiment divided or "disorganized," as Lieutenant Colonel Morrison put it, and Roe noted the assignments of all ten companies in the regiment. His own route followed the Santa Fe River and dropped down La Bajada Hill to the Rio Grande again. The companies marched down the east side of the river to Albuquerque, New Mexico, then crossed over and continued south along the west bank to Socorro. The roads at that time hugged the river more closely than do the present highways.

Roe's mileage from Albuquerque to Socorro is excessive (96 miles); the distance today is not more than 75 miles. The only Pueblo Indian village he could have passed is Isleta, which is north, not south, of Los Lunas. These little discrepancies also show that not all of his journal entries were made on the indicated dates. As far as we can see, none of these lapses bear importantly on the journal's reliability.

From Socorro, one day's march put them about at the abandoned site of Fort Conrad, which for some unknown reason, Roe called Whiskey Point. In more recent times, the railroad siding here has been called Tiffany. Finally, on August 30, the end of their 1,067-mile march came in sight at Fort Craig, New Mexico.[24] Here Lewis Roe and Company F would remain for the next eighteen months.

One might expect the sight of hundreds of soldiers—the entire 7th U.S. Infantry and two companies of the 2nd Dragoons—to have excited some comment. They met a few Indians and several emigrants every day, but very little was said. Philander Powell, diarist with an Arkansas company en route to California ("Californey") did note on July 9, 1860, that they "camped on a stream where there are 600 soldiers camped."[25] The stream was the Cache la Poudre.

Both Denver and Santa Fe had newspapers at the time; the Denver paper commented on July 12 that the first division of the eastern column of the Utah Army passed through the city. It consisted of two companies and an immense baggage and sutler's train. "The troops and equipage presented rather a sorry appearance," which the paper attributed to recent severe rain storms.[26] The *Santa Fe Gazette* gave a more complete report:

> The second column of the Troops, consisting of 5 companies of the
> 7th Infantry, ordered from Utah to this Territory arrived in this city
> on the 17th inst. [August 17]; having left camp Floyd on the 16th of

May under the command of Maj. Lynde. The companies were offi-
cered as follows: Brevet Maj. Gatlin Company "F," Brevet Maj. Paul
Company "I," Capt. McLaws Company "D," Capt. Jones Company
"A," and Capt. Stevenson Company "B."

The column continued its march on the 19. inst., to be
distributed as follows: One company to be stationed temporarily at Albuquerque: Two companies to be stationed temporarily at
Los Lunas: Three companies at Fort Craig: Two companies at the
Miembres in order to take post in that vicinity, and two companies
under Col. Morrison at Fort Buchanan.[27]

In New Mexico, the men of the 7th Infantry would soon be introduced
to war; two of the companies inside of two months, on a campaign
against the Navajo Indians, and the rest when the Civil War came to
New Mexico the following year.

Denver in 1860

Lewis Roe and the 7th Infantry had passed through three cities—
Denver, Santa Fe, and Albuquerque—on their march to New Mexico.
Roe expressed his disappointment with Santa Fe and Albuquerque,
but he liked Denver, where the 1860 Census recorded a population of
4,749, the great majority of whom were Midwesterners like Roe him-
self. The *Rocky Mountain News*, published weekly since 1859, described
Denver as Roe and his comrades must have seen it, in the issues for
June 6 and June 20, 1860 (both p. 2):

> We doubt if a better field for the study of various characters and
> phazes [phases] of human nature, and its multifarious occupations
> can be found than in a stroll thro' the streets of our city.

In the spring of 1859, Denver consisted of three hundred log huts, "covered with mud." But now,

> Lofty buildings are rising on the business streets; solid and
> substantial brick edifices. . . . Gorgeous saloons, with mirrors and
> paintings, lighted from glittering chandeliers, meet the eye of the
> passerby on every corner. . . . The brass muzzles of Ambrotypists'
> cameras peer out from upper story windows, seeking to
> Daguerreotype the crowd as it passes.

As for the people,

> Flashing silks and the widest expanded [hooped] crinolines sweep
> past the corners. . . . Ladies promenade its streets, . . . arrayed in the
> newest, costliest silks . . . made up in strict conformity with the latest
> Paris fashions. . . . But the greatest diversity is in the rougher sex.
> Hardy, brown faced, weather-beaten men . . . from the plains, the
> mountains and the mines, with a profusion of buckskin patches, red
> shirts and hairy faces, crowd every corner [and] fill up the stores.

Enterprising small merchants had set up shop along the principal
streets; some in tents, others from the rear end of a wagon, and still
others from a box on the sidewalk. These small dealers offering "an
endless variety of all kinds of traps," seemed to thrive. "Traps" was syn-
onymous with "all kinds of merchandise." To supply everyone,

> Great trains of huge Prairie freighters [i.e., wagons] arrive and
> depart almost daily, and more than a thousand emigrant wagons
> arrive every week.

Many of these wagon trains simply discharged their cargoes or passed
on to the mountains with their mining machinery. The reporter concluded that

> We are daily expecting the arrival of an organ [grinder] and mon-
> key, . . . and sundry other necessary evils that inhabit the streets of
> a large city.

CHAPTER THREE

Fort Bridger to Fort Craig; Lewis Roe's 1860 Diary

June 7 [1860]

Ft. Bridger. Camp No. 1. The first column struck camp and took up the line of march for Arizona. Our column will follow tomorrow.

June 8th

Black's Fork. Camp No. 2. Our column started today, one company at a time goes on guard. The guard has to remain in camp until the command and all trains are out. Our company (F) being on guard it was late before we started. Got into camp after dark. Well, I am once again upon the march. I am not sorrow [sorry]. But I know not what may befall me. Day's march 18 miles.

June 9th

Ham's Fork. Camp No. 3. Followed down Black Fork. From thence due east about 10 miles down Ham's Fork. We crossed this stream on a bridge. Encamped 2 miles below. Day's march 16 miles.

June 10th

Ham's Fork. Camp No. 4. Turning to our right we took what is called the Great Cherokee Trail. This road is not traveled much. We have passed several mountaineers' ranches. Forded Ham's Fork twice. Direction southeast. Day's march 12 miles.

June 11th

Green River. Camp No. 5. Leaving Ham's Fork on our right, our road ran over high table lands which we ascended by steps, getting up one hill only to find another still higher before us. At last after having ascended a long hill, the most beautiful sight that I have ever seen was presented to our view. Below us we could see Green River now winding its way through small but beautiful bottoms, then again dashing madly through chasms and over rocks while on the other side is to be seen high mountains. Then away in the distance like some ancient castle is seen what is called Church Peak, on account of its having some resemblance to a church.[1]

We now commenced to descend by steep pitches, sometimes having to lock both wheels of our wagons. Finally we found ourselves in a long narrow chasm or canyon called Rabbit Hollow. Emerging from this we came upon a fine level bottom on which we encamped. Found the first column encamped here. Direction southeast. Day's march 18 miles. Distance from Ft. Bridger to Green River 64 miles.

June 12th

Green River. Camp No. 6. Crossed the river today on a ferry. Swam the mules. This river is very swift and deep; hard swimming the mules. We worked hard all day. Encamped immediately after crossing.

June 13th

Bitter Creek. Camp No. 7. The road leaving Green River runs eastward along Bitter Creek. Encamped at a small spring at the foot of a snow topped range of mountains.[2] Direction east. Day's march 16 miles.

June 14th

Bitter Creek. Camp No. 8. A hard, hard day's march. Dry, hot and very sandy. Our road ran along this creek all day. Water was always near but it was impossible to drink it. So much alkali in the water that it is entirely unfit for use. Several boys fell out, too much worn out with the thirst and sand to travel any farther. Encamped at the mouth of Bitter Creek Canyon. Direction east. No water, no wood, no nothing. Day's march 22 miles.

June 15

Sulphur Springs. Camp No. 9. Through Bitter Creek Canyon all day. Dry, hot and sandy. Sick ambulances crowded. I took a few spoonsfull of vinegar which seemed to refresh me so that I was able to get along very well. Encamped immediately after getting out of the

FIGURE 8. Soldiers' names from 1860 (and later) on bluff above Sulphur Spring,
    near Bitter Creek, Wyo. Author's photo.

Cañon at Sulphur Spring, which flows out of a crevice in a very high
rock. Sulphur Springs is about 3 rods from Bitter Creek. The water
tastes very much of sulphur. Here we found the names of several of the
boys of the first column cut in the soft sandstone. I left mine here also,
together with the name of my native place.[3] Direction east. Day's march
10 miles.

June 16

    Bitter Creek. Camp No. 10. Still along this creek. I think we must
be getting near the head of this stream as it is smaller and the water
does not taste so much of alkali. A very poor camp. Direction south. I
wish we were out of these mountains so we could get some air. Day's
march 16 miles.

June 17

    Soda Springs. Camp No. 11. These springs are near Bitter Creek.[4]
They are the best on the route so far. We appear to be getting out of
the mountains or at least I can see through them. Away in the distance
I can just distinguish a snowy range of mountains. Direction south. I
think tomorrow's march will be over a level plain. Day's march 18 miles.

June 18

Camp No. 12. Our route today lay over a flat, level plain or a kind of park. Directly ahead of us is a snowy range of Mts. Plenty of game here; you can see the antelopes scudding away in every direction. The Dragoons [have] seen several bears; killed one. Direction east. Encamped at a small spring, name not known.[5] Day's march 22 miles.

June 19

Little Muddy Fork of Platte River. Camp 13. Heavy, sandy road all day. The road after leaving the flat plain ran through small knolls and bluffs. We are getting nearer to a range of snow-topped mountains. Direction east. Encamped on a small stream, name not known.[6] Found the 1st column encamped here. Day's march 16 miles.

June 20

Little Muddy Fork of Platte River. Camp 13. No movement today. Waiting for the first column to get ahead. We have been marching too fast for the first.

June 21

Little Muddy Fork of Platte River. Camp 14. Through Little Muddy Canyon. A very bad road, now climbing the side of a mountain and now in a deep chasm. The command got far in advance of the train. Direction northeast. Encamped at the base of Bridgers Pass. Distance 18 miles.

June 22

Bridger's Pass. Camp 15. Passed over the main chain of the Rocky Mts. today. There is something strange and pleasant in the feeling or knowledge that you stand on the dividing ridge between the Atlantic and Pacific Oceans. We commenced ascending the slope of Bridger's Pass about 8 o'clock in the morning. We ascended one hill after another. It is about 4 miles from the base to the summit. There is a flat about half a mile. Then commenced the descent, which is similar to the ascent. Direction east. While on the summit I could see a snow-topped range [of] mountains, which they tell me is the other side of the Platte River. Day's march 18 miles.

June 23

North Platte River. Camp 16. Our route today lay over a fine rolling prairie. First view of the Medicine Bow Mountains. Encamped on [North] Platte River.[7] Found the first column here. Day's march 20 miles. Distance from Green River 171 miles. Distance from Fort Bridger 235 miles.

June 24

North Platte. Camp 16. No movement today. The river is rising rapidly.

June 25th

North Platte River. Camp 16. No movement yet. Waiting for the first column to cross. A young man named Lynch belonging to our Co. (F) while attempting to go down the river on a raft was drowned. He started from Bridger with high hopes. Alas, how soon were they dashed down. Perhaps I may be the next; God only knows. The 1st column crossed today; we tomorrow.

June 26th

North Platte. Camp 17. Crossed the river today in the same manner as we did Green River, that is, swimming the mules. The men ferried across. Encamped immediately after.

June 27th

Pass Creek. Camp 18. After leaving the Platte River our road ran over a fine level prairie. Seen several antelopes. Encamped on Pass Creek at the base of the Medicine Bow Mountains. Day's march 12 miles.

June 28

Medicine Bow Creek. Camp 19. Through mountains all day, a very bad road. Met a large train of emigrants going to California. Medicine Bow Mountains are covered with pines. Came up with the first column. Day's march 18 miles.

June 29

Medicine Bow Creek. Camp 19. Lay over today to let the first column get ahead. Several of the boys went hunting; had quite a feast of venison.

June 30

Cooper's Creek.[8] Camp 20. Our road which had been running nearly east now turned due south along the base of the Medicine Bow Mountains. We appear to have a level road for some distance ahead. Away in the distance like a black cloud is seen a low range of mountains. The troops were mustered today. Distance 21 miles.

July 1st

West Fork of Laramie River. Camp 21. A fine road all day but very dusty. I was just beginning to think that we had a long, long day's march. I could not see any prospect of wood or water ahead when all at once I came on the edge of a high bluff. Beneath was the most beautiful green bottom I have ever seen. The grass knee high. The bottom is about half a mile wide here is no wood. I believe a wagon is going about 3 miles up the stream for wood. Distance 16 miles.

July 2nd

Laramie River. Camp 22. This is quite a large stream. We could just ford the river although some of our knapsacks got wet in crossing.[9] This bottom is something [somewhat?] similar to the one on which we encamped last night. We found no wood here. Wagons were sent some six or seven miles for wood. Found a grave here. Day's march 14 miles.

July 3rd

Gold Ridge. Camp 23. After traveling 3 or 4 miles in the morning our road struck the Black Hills. We ascended a hill near a mile long, the top of which was covered with pines. Encamped on Gold Ridge, so called on account of fine particles resembling gold. Several picked it up, thinking it was the pure gold. Distance 16 miles.

July 4th

Chyenne Pass. Camp 24. Chyenne [Cheyenne] Pass divides the Black Hills from the North Park Mts. Came up with the 1st Column here. In the evening we had a temperance lecture out on the green. Day's march 12 miles.

July 5th

Chyenne Pass. Camp 24. No movement today. I visited the
remains of a fort, Fort Walbash [Walbach], about a mile from here. It
was built in the fall of 1858 by 2 or 3 companies of the 4th Artillery.[10]
Major Lynde left here for Fort Laramie for his wife and family. 80 miles
from here to Laramie. ~~Day's march~~

July 6th

Crow Creek. Camp 25. We are marching south along the eastern
slope of the North Park Mountains. There is on our left as far as the eye
can reach a perfectly level plain. I am once more out of the mts. for the
first time in 3 years. Day's march 10 miles.

July 7th

Camp 26. Marched southward along the base of the North Park
Mountains. In the same direction today as yesterday, over a rolling prairie. Encamped at a small spring, name not known. Several Indians came
into camp. They were Arrapohoes [Arapahos]. Day's march 16 miles.

July 8th

Camp 27. A very poor camp. We had to dig wells for water. We
meet every day several Emigrants from Pikes Peak going to California;
some to the Park Mts. to hunt for Gold. Day's march 16 miles.

July 9th

Cache La Poudre river. Camp 28. Here is quite a settlement or
town but it is now deserted, all the inhabitants having gone to the
[gold] mines. This is a large stream for this *country*. Distance 12 miles.

July 10

Camp 29. Still along the base of the North Park Mts. Encamp on a
small stream, name not known. Distance 16 [miles].

July 11

St. Vrains. Camp 30. Since leaving Chyenne Pass we have been
marching due south. Distance today 16 miles.

July 12

Camp 31. Encamped on a dry creek; poor camp. First view of the
famous Pike's Peak, which is in the Middle Park Mts. Distance 15 miles.

July 13

Camp 32. Marched 14 miles.

July 14

Denver City. Camp 33. Marched through Denver City or the (gem of the Mts.). Encamped 3 miles from the city on Cherry Creek. Some very fine Brick buildings for so young a city. Distance 8 miles.

July 15

Denver City. No movement today. A great many of the boys are in the city on pass. Denver has a population of about 3,000 inhabitants although thousands are passing through here every day.[11]

July 16th

Cherry Creek. Camp 34. We are marching up this stream, getting closer under the Park Mts. Cherry Creek is different from any that I have ever seen. This is a porous stream, sometimes the water will entirely disappear. It will sink in the sands, then some 8 or 10 rods farther on it will rise again. Pike's Peak still in sight. Day's march 10 miles.

July 17th

Cherry Creek. Camp 35. Still along this stream. The days are getting very hot. We had a long day's march. Several [men] gave out; were picked up by the guard. Day's march 22 miles.

July 18th

Camp 36. Left Cherry Creek to our right. Passed through several groves of pines. While crossing a small rivulet today some of the boys picked up a small quantity of quicksilver placed there by the miners to collect the gold. Encamped on a small spring, name not known. Distance 21 miles.

July 19

Jimmy's Camp.[12] Camp 37. First view of Greenhorns Peaks. These are 2 peaks alone by themselves. Encamped about 6 miles from Pike's Peak and opposite to it, which [sic] has been in sight for several days. Distance 20 [miles].

July 20

Fountaine qui *Boullie*. Camp 38. Col. Morrison of the first column seems to be hurrying things some. We are ordered to keep one day's march in [the] rear of the first column. In order not to lose ground we are compelled to make long marches. Encamped on a tributary of the Arkansas. Distance 21 miles.

July 21

Camp 39. We are following this stream [Fountain Creek] down, which is a tributary of the Arkansas. There are a few log cabins scattered here and there but most of them are now deserted. Distance 18 [miles].

July 22

Arkansas River. Camp 40. Crossed the Arkansas River and encamped for the first time in New Mexico. Thus far it has been the opinion that we were going to Arizonia. Now the boys begin to think that we are going to some part of New Mexico. Others say that we are to be stationed somewhere on this river. At the place of crossing is a new bridge, as it is on the main road to Cal[ifornia].[13] Distance 4 [miles].

July 23

Camp 41. We are traveling along the base of the South Park Mts. Since leaving the Chenne [Cheyenne] Pass we have had a good road over a fine rolling prairie. Greenhorns peaks still seen in the distance. Day's march 20 miles.

July 24

Greenhorns Ranch. Camp 42. Greenhorn peaks seem to be some distance to our left. There are Mexicans living in this Ranch, the first I have seen. Day's march 8 miles.

July 25

Camp 43. The men of the first column must have broken down or something else must be the matter as we are making very short marches. The men in our column seem to be in excellent spirits. 11 miles.

FIGURE 9. Sangre de Cristo Pass, Colo., looking NE from camp of August 11, 1853. From *Pacific Railroad Surveys*, tinted lithograph by John Mix Stanley.

July 26

Sangre de Christos [Cristos] Pass. Camp 44. This pass which divides the Ratoon [Raton] Mts. from the South Park Mts. we commenced ascending early in the morning. The road ran over high and stony hills. At last we came to a long and very steep hill. The command divided itself into small parties, so many to each wagon, and by a good deal of pulling, pushing, shouting, yelling &c. we succeeded in reaching the top. Then commenced the descent. By tying on ropes and using caution we got safely down. We found ourselves in a beautiful valley about 1/2 mile square.[14] The mountains around were covered with groves of pine. Distance 15 [miles].

July 27

Ft. Garland. Camp 45. Came through a long, narrow Cañon through which runs a stream of water. Crossed this stream about 50 times. After leaving this Cañon the road ran over table lands. Arrived at Ft. Garland in the midst of a heavy rain. Found the first column here. Encamped about 2 miles from Fort Garland near old Ft. Massachusetts, now in ruins.[15] Ft. Garland is garrisoned by 2 Co. of 10th [Infantry]. Day's march 17 miles.

[*No entries for the period July 28 through August 4.*]

Aug. 5

Calebbro [Culebra]. Camp 46. Due south along the western slope of the Ratoon mountain. Calebbro is a small Mexican village. Here is some cultivated land, the first I have seen since leaving Leavenworth in 1858. Day's march 15 miles.

Aug. 6

Casteo [Costilla]. Camp 47. The Ratoon Mts. on our left, Spanish Peaks on our right. Casteo is a large place. The Mexicans seem to be quite a gay race of people. Several fandaga [fandangos] tonight. Distance 14 [miles].

Aug. 7th

Red River. Camp 48. Passed through several Mexican villages today. Encamped on Red River, which is only about ankle deep. All of [the] Red River bottom is under cultivation. The farms are all watered by irrigation. Distance 16 miles.

Aug. 8th

Camp 49. Through the mountains today; very bad road. The road after leaving Red River runs in the shape of U.S. From this it is called the US hill. Day's march 14 miles.

Aug. 9th

Taos. Camp 50. Passed through a fine country today, most part of which is under cultivation, all watered by irrigation. They appear to make the water run in ditches where to me it seems impossible to make it run. Distance 15 miles. Distance from Ft. Bridger 755.

Aug. 10th

Camp Burgwin. Camp 51. Entered the Taos Cañon. Encamped in the center of it. Here is a detachment of Mtd. Rifles.[16] Came up with the first column. Distance 10 miles.

Aug. 11

Camp Burgwin. Camp 51. No movement today. The mountains on each side are covered with pines.

Aug. 12

Camp 52. Over the Taos mountains. Very bad roads; high and heavy hills. D[istance] 15 [miles].

Aug. 13

Camp 53. Passed through several villages today. All the bottoms which it is possible to irrigate are under cultivation. Distance 12 miles.

Aug. 14th

Rio Grande. Camp 54. Followed down the dry bed of a creek until we reached the Rio Grande. The valley of the Rio Grande is all under cultivation. Distance 18 miles.

Aug. 15th

Rio Grande. Camp 55. Followed down the Rio Grande today; passed through several villages. Distance 18 miles.

Aug. 16th

Camp 56. Left the Rio Grande. Encamped at the junction of the Leavenworth road.[17] Day's march 19 miles.

Aug. 17th

Santa Fe. Camp 57. Arrived at Santa Fe, the Capital of New Mexico, today. Found the first column here. Distance 9 [miles]. Distance from Ft. Bridger 857 [miles].

Aug. 18th

Santa Fe. Camp 57. Our Regiment was divided today. H and C companies with headquarters to Ft. Buchanan, Arizonia. B and G to build a new fort on the Rio Membres [Mimbres], Arizonia. A & E to Albuquerque. I to Los Lunes [Los Lunas]. K, D & F to Ft. Craig. Santa Fe is not near as good looking a place as I expected to find it. On the contrary, it is a dirty, filthy place. Streets very crooked. The plaza looks more like a cow yard than anything else.

[*No entries for August 19 and 20.*]

Aug. 21st

Camp 58. Our 3 companies commanded by Major Gatlin started for Ft. Craig today. Our road ran over a rolling prairie in a southwest direction. Little or no cultivation. Distance 16 miles.

Aug. 22nd

Rio Grande. Camp 59. Came on the Rio Grande again today. Here as before the bottom is under cultivation. Distance 28 miles.

Aug. 23

Rio Grande. Camp 60. Followed down the Rio Grande. The farms or patches under cultivation are mostly walled in with adobes. Distance 25 miles.

Aug. 24

Albuquerque. Camp 61. Arrived at Albuquerque. E Co. stationed here. This place is even worse than Santa Fe. Such a dirty place I have never seen. Distance 10 miles.

Aug. 25th

Los Lunes [Los Lunas]. Camp 62. Crossed the Rio Grande at Albuquerque and still continued down the river. Encamped at Los Lunes. Day's march 22 [miles].

Aug. 26th

Rio Grande. Camp 63. Still down the river. Passed through several villages, one of them an Indian village settled by the Pueblos. Distance 25 miles.

Aug. 27th

Rio Grande. Camp 64. We have been making rather long marches but I suppose we will be soon at our journey['s] End. Distance 24 miles.

Aug. 28

Socorro. Camp 65. This is quite a large town. The farther down the river we get, the more sandy it gets the bottom. Days march 25 miles.

Aug. 29

Whiskey Point. Camp 66. We have been making very long and hard marches. Some of our animals have given out. Distance 25 miles.

Aug. 30

Ft. Craig.[18] Camp 67. We have at last arrived at our journeys end. D[istance] 10 [miles]. Total distance from Ft. Bridger 1067 miles.

CHAPTER FOUR

Escort Duty in the Southwest and the Battle of Valverde

L EWIS ROE WAS EXCEEDINGLY LUCKY DURING HIS ARMY CAREER. HIS INCOMPLETE DIARY OF ESCORT DUTY FROM FORT CRAIG, NEW MEXICO, TO SOUTHERN ARIZONA AND RETURN IN THE spring of 1861 shows that he missed, sometimes by only a day, most of the ambushes, raids, and other violence that swirled around him at that period. Later, between 1862 and 1865, he fought in four major battles at Valverde, Rome Crossroads, Allatoona, and Bentonville, from which he came away with a slight wound in the left shoulder at Allatoona and a minor one in the leg at Valverde.

A series of events that started on February 4, 1861, touched off an eleven-year war with the southern Apaches in New Mexico and Arizona. At Apache Pass, a gap between the Dos Cabesas and Chiricahua Mountains in southeastern Arizona, the Chiricahua Apache chief Cochise cut his way out of a tent during a parley being held at a Butterfield Overland Mail station and then besieged the 7th Infantry company that had been sent there to find a kidnaped boy. On February 6, the Apaches ambushed a New Mexican wagon train just west of the station. Eight teamsters perished, including at least two who died lashed to the wheels of the burning wagons. Attacks climaxed on February 19 when the army hanged six captured Apaches. This Bascom Affair, named after the lieutenant in charge of these troops, is one of the best-known events in early Arizona history.[1]

No sooner had this episode quieted than a wagon master leading a public train of wagons toward Fort Buchanan took the train, loaded with army supplies, into Mexico and sold its contents there.[2] Then on April 28, Apaches attacked a stagecoach at Doubtful Canyon and killed the five men aboard. Two of them were tortured to death.[3]

In the midst of these and other incidents, Lewis Roe departed Fort Craig, New Mexico, on April 5 as part of a twelve-man escort with a provision train and a herd of commissary cattle for forts Buchanan and Breckinridge in Arizona. From April 8, when the train and escort were still following the Rio Grande downstream, until they arrived at Fort Buchanan on the 24th, the original diary unfortunately is now missing. The party left the Rio Grande at some point and headed west, perhaps joining the Overland Mail route at Cooke's Spring in southwestern New Mexico. We know that the wagons passed through Apache Pass from Roe's "Declaration for an Original Invalid Pension" in 1890, where he claimed that he contracted scurvy there in May 1861.[4]

In any event, the normal course of travel would have been to continue past Dragoon Springs to the Overland Mail station on the San Pedro River, then south up the San Pedro until the road again bore west around the southern point of the Whetstone Mountains and eventually reached Fort Buchanan. The loss of the diary pages for April 8–23 probably happened after 1950, because Lewis T. Roe of Deming, New Mexico, volunteered that he remembered reading what his grandfather said about passing the burned wagon train where the teamsters had been tied to the wheels.

When the account resumed on April 23, the escort had been alert for attacks. Then at midnight on April 24, according to Roe, Indians tried to run off the beef herd at Fort Buchanan and awakened the garrison. Perhaps this incident is what a Los Angeles paper meant when it said that Indians had lately charged through the fort stealing the picket ropes.[5]

With tensions running high, Lt. Gurden Chapin, commanding at Fort Buchanan, detached twenty men from his garrison to increase the size of the returning escort. On the return trip, Roe tells us that the day after they passed the San Pedro station, the Indians helped themselves to forty-four mules there. He ceased to keep a daily diary after he arrived at Fort Breckinridge on the lower San Pedro on May 3. During the march back, the need for constant watchfulness probably took most of his time and energy, and we learn nothing more about the raids on other trains and mail stations at this time. Later, in the introduction to his 1864–1865 journal, Roe added:

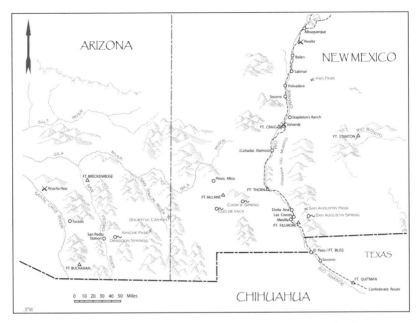

MAP 3. Southern New Mexico and Arizona in 1861–1862. Courtesy of author.

In March 1861 I was ordered on detail as guard to a Quartermaster's [wagon] train to Fts. Buchanan & Breckinridge in the western part of Arizonia, 300 miles distant. There were 12 of us. We were attacked by the Apache Indians but reached Ft. Craig again with the loss of about half of our mules.[6]

April 5, 1861 [Fort Craig, N.Mex.]

Detailed this morning on escort with a provision train for Forts Buchanan & Breckinridge in Arizonia. There are 12 wagons. 6 of them for Breckinridge and 6 for Buchanan. Our Escort consists of 12 men. We got started about 9 o'clock in the morning. Encamped at the 15 mile Flat.[7] D[ist.] 15 [miles].

Adobie Wall. Apr. 6th. Camp No. 2. Down the Rio Grande all day. Encamped at the adobie [adobe] wall, so called from 2 clay banks which looks like an adobie wall in the distance.[8] 13 miles.

Cañon La Moose [Cañada Alamosa]. Apr. 7. Camp No. 3. This is quite a large Mexican settlement. A good deal of land around it under cultivation.[9] Dist. 16 [miles].

Willow Band [Bend] of the Rio Grande [April 8]. Camp No. 4. Still down this stream. The grass is getting better. There is plenty of cottonwood trees all along this river. Dist. 15 miles.

[*Pages missing; journal resumes part-way through entry for April 23.*]

. . . herd but we keep a good look out—scarcely sleep at all at night. The boys are very much fatigued. I do not think the Indians will get our herd except they do it by *hard fighting*. D[ist.] 13 [miles.]

Fort Buchanan. Apr. 24th. Camp 20. We are here at last. H & C companies [7th Infantry] are stationed here. We had a great shaking of hands with the boys, a great many questions to ask and asked great many. As soon as we could get away from the boys we spread our blankets, pulled off our shoes (what we had not done before leaving Fort Craig) intending to have one good night's sleep at least. But about 12 o'clock we were awakened by the "*alarm*" being sounded in the Fort. We seized our muskets, stood ready. We found out in about half an hour that the Indians had followed us into the Fort but finding us on our guard they undertook to get the *Beef herd* of the Post. The "*alarm*" was given too quick. They had to "skedaddle." Day's march 18 [miles].

Whetstone Springs.[10] Apr. 25th. Camp 21. Homeward Bound over the same road we traveled in coming here. 20 more of an Escort joined us as our force was not deemed sufficient. Day's march 18 miles.

Rio San Pedro. Apr. 26th. Camp 22. Day's march 13 miles.

Dragoon Springs. Apr. 27. Camp 23. Found Escort & Train all safe, the boys glad to see us together again.[11] Divided the loads among all the wagons. Our teams which had been 8 mule teams were now reduced to 4. Dist. 13 miles.

Rio San Pedro. Apr. 28th. Camp 24. Kept on the overland mail road today. Mail station here. Distance 18 miles.

Rio San Pedro. Apr. 29th. Camp 25. Down this river. Very good bottom road. Day's march 15 miles.

Rio San Pedro. Apr. 30th. Camp 26. The Indians appear to be following us again. They run off 44 mules from the mail station yesterday where we first struck the river. Distance 18 miles.

Rio San Pedro. May 1st. Camp 27. We have been traveling due north. Dist. 20 miles.

Rio San Pedro. May 2nd. Camp 28. Dist. 20 miles.

Fort Breckinridge.[12] May 3rd. Camp 29. Arrived at the Fort and unloaded. We are to remain here some time to rest our animals. This place is garrisoned by D & G companies of the 1st Dragoons. Dist. 12 [miles]. Total distance traveled from Fort Craig 496 miles.

Started from Fort Breckinridge for Fort Craig on the 8th of May. Arrived at Fort Craig on the 1st of June. Found the company [F] had left for Albuquerque. Distance from Fort Breckinridge to Craig about 400 miles.

Stapleton's Ranch.[13] June 2nd. Camp [No. 1]. Started for Albuquerque this morning. Crossed the Rio Grande. Proceeded up the river. Day's march 13 miles.

Although nothing indicates that this diary continued past June 2, 1861, Roe referred back almost forty years later to an incident that he said took place on July 4, 1861, but which other evidence shows must have happened about June 4. This was in his only published article, which is reprinted later in this chapter.

In the introduction to his first notebook, Roe continued with what happened upon returning from the trip to Arizona:

> Rumors of the great conflict of the secession of some of the southern states began to reach us. Still no one dreamed of war. We only thought it a wrangle in Congress. On our arrival at Fort Craig we found our Co [F] had gone to Albuquerque. Thither we followed them. About this time, our officers began to go home on furlough.

They afterward resigned and became Brigadier and Major Generals in the Rebel Service. Fully two thirds of them thus resigned. They were natives of the south.

After remaining in Albuquerque about a month we heard of the capture of Ft. Sumter, of Bull Run, in a kind of listless way. We could not realize that war had actually commenced. We were so far away no thought that we would be engaged in it ever entered our heads. Meanwhile, the Companies of our regiment that was in Arizona were ordered to Ft. Fillmore. The garrison of Ft. Craig now consisted of Companies "H," "C," and "F."[14]

Roe apparently kept no diary while at Fort Craig, but he may have had other records now lost to us.

In early July, Confederate Lt. Col. John R. Baylor brought the Civil War to the Southwest when he led a battalion of his 2nd Regiment, Texas Mounted Rifles, into El Paso, Texas, and the deserted post of Fort Bliss. Three weeks later, Baylor took his 258 men forty miles up the Rio Grande; occupied Mesilla, New Mexico; skirmished with some ineptly led federal troops from nearby Fort Fillmore; and then captured nearly seven hundred of them at San Augustin Springs when they sought to retreat.[15]

Roe's account of this period in his introduction is not always reliable, but he was all too correct about the high desertion rate of army officers and in stressing that the rank and file did not know what was going on. In his words,

It was rumored that a Texan army of rebels were preparing to invade N.M. Col. Canby, then commanding the Dept. of N. Mexico, raised about 3,000 Mexican volunteers to resist the invasion. The Rebels arriving at Ft. Fillmore demanded the surrender of the 7 companies of our regt. stationed there, which was cowardly done by Major [Isaac] Lynde without a shot being fired.

He failed to mention that at least several dozen enlisted men deserted, including Pvt. Morris Phillips from his own company, who deserted at Fort Craig on February 15, 1862.[16]

By late September, Baylor's strength had increased to some 830 men.[17] This was too few to do more than harass the federal garrison at Fort Craig, which included Roe and three companies (C, F, and H) of the 7th Infantry.

Then in December, Confederate Brigadier General Henry Hopkins Sibley arrived from San Antonio, Texas, leading his Sibley Brigade of some 2,700 men. With these and part of Baylor's forces, he began his advance up the Rio Grande in February 1862. The two sides skirmished south of Fort Craig on February 16 and along a ridge line a mile east of the Rio Grande on the 20th. The main battle came the following day when the Confederates, now badly in need of water, tried to reach the river again at the tiny village and fort known as Valverde, just north of Fort Craig.[18]

At Valverde, Roe's Company F fought as part of Plympton's Battalion, a five-company unit whose main role was in support of Capt. Alexander McRae's six-gun battery. In later years, Roe published an article on the Battle of Valverde and the events that preceded it, which is reprinted below. Lewis Roe's account parallels those of Captain Plympton and General Canby.[19] Captain Plympton mentioned him by name as one of those who behaved bravely throughout the day, particularly in the effort to retake McRae's battery.[20] Private Roe received a promotion to first sergeant after the battle, as the replacement for First Sergeant James Rockwell, killed during the fighting.[21]

Back in July 1861, sixteen 7th Infantry men from the Fort Fillmore garrison had refused to accept parole at the San Augustin Springs surrender and were held as prisoners of war.[22] Roe now tells us that they managed to stay together for the next six months and eventually escape, avoiding the Texans as they made their way to Fort Craig. Perhaps Sergeant William James and Pvt. James O'Brien, both of Company G, 7th Infantry, and attached to Company F at Valverde, were two of the escapees. They died there on the battlefield.[23]

Company F of the 7th Infantry suffered the heaviest casualties of any federal unit at Valverde. Officially, fifteen were killed (including the two attached from Company G) and twenty-seven wounded, with two missing.[24] This would put the casualty rate for that company at 73 percent. The fragmentary casualty list for Roe's company may include more than battlefield casualties, as he listed Corporal John P. Rumble and a Pvt. Joseph Fulgion [Falgan?] as killed, while both the official list and the February post return for Fort Craig included Corporal Rumble as wounded while a report signed by Col. Benjamin Roberts on February 22 listed Fulgion as missing.[25] Company F clearly fought until the survivors were finally forced to give way and recross the river to escape annihilation.

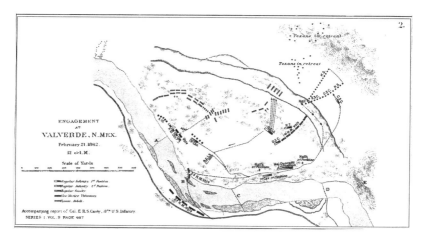

FIGURE 10. Engagement at Valverde, N.Mex., February 21, 1862. From *Atlas to Accompany the Official Records of the Union and Confederate Armies* (2003) [1891–1895], plate 12 no. 2.

While Roe's article ended abruptly, his introduction included a parallel account of Valverde and the events that followed it:

> The rebels marched up the Rio Grande arriving at Ft. Craig. Col. Canby depending on his Mexican volunteers attacked the rebels, but before our skirmish line was driven in, our Mexican vols. turned and ran every man for himself, leaving 250 of us facing 3,500 rebels. The result was we were badly cut up, our Co. "F" suffering the worst. We went into battle that morning (Feb. 21, 1862) Sixty men strong. We came out only 14 able to march. 21 were shot dead, the remainder wounded, but one man in our Co. escaped without a bullet mark. I rec [received] a slight wound in my leg. My coat was shot through the breast; it was a close call.
>
> The rebels demanded the surrender of the fort but Col. Canby refused, leaving us in Ft. Craig. They proceeded up the Rio Grande, capturing towns and cities and finally entering Santa Fe. Meanwhile 2 regiments of Colorado volunteers entered N.M. from the north. We followed the rebs from the south. A battle was fought near what was called Pidgeon's [Pigeon's] Ranch. The Texans were routed and we joining with the Colorado Vols. pursued them down the Rio Grande, capturing great numbers. Arriving again at Ft. Craig we remained there a short time, then left for Ft. Union in the northeastern part of N.M.[26]

Lewis Roe and his company also fought in the Peralta affair on April 15.[27] By June, his Company F was at Fort Union, the principal military supply depot in New Mexico, where it remained for the next year.[28]

With Canby at Valverde, N.M., February 21, 1862

Editor, *National Tribune*: Concerning the campaign in New Mexico in 1862, I wish to give an account as I remember it, especially the part taken in it by Col. [Edward R. S.] Canby's forces. I must first say a word about the condition of the Regular Army just previous to the war. The early Spring of 1861 found the 7th U.S. [Infantry] (to which I belonged) distributed as follows: Co's. F, C and H in Fort Craig, on the Rio Grande, 100 miles south of Albuquerque; of the remaining seven companies, four were at Fort Buchanan and three at Fort Breckinridge, in western Arizona.[29] We were in almost total ignorance of what was going on in the States, having no mail communications at that time, Butterfield's overland mail having stopped; but we had rumors innumerable.

One thing was apparent, however; we were being deserted by our officers. Col. [Thomas T.] Fauntleroy, commanding the Department of New Mexico, on leave of absence, went south into Texas. He was succeeded by Col. W. W. Loring, of the Mounted Rifles, who only remained a short time, when he, too, left on leave of absence, taking the Texas route. Col. [Daniel] Ruggles, 5th U.S. [Infantry], followed in the same way.[30] Col. E. R. S. Canby finally became Department Commander, and he stuck.

While our Department Commanders were thus deserting us, the same thing was going on among the line officers. The 7th U.S. [Infantry] lost Capt. Lafayette McLaws (Co. D), Capt. and Brevet Maj. Richard Gatlin (Co. F), Lieutenant [Robert R.] Garland (Co. C), Lieut. [John S.] Marmaduke (Co. B), and Lieut. [Joseph] Wheeler, of the Dragoons [RMR].[31] All these left at Fort Craig. Officers left from other companies of the 7th in the same proportion, so we were practically an army without officers.

The rank and file did not know what was going on. One day, as I was wandering about Fort Craig, I picked up a fragment of a letter written by the Post Surgeon of one of the forts in Arizona to the Post

Surgeon of our fort, in which, after some account of the news from the States, were these words: "D——n old Abe Lincoln and his friends. H——ls too good for them. For my part, if the worst comes, I'm with the South." This fragment opened my eyes, and I knew why our officers were leaving us.[32] On July 4, 1861, while our company was on the march to Albuquerque, we met Col. [Henry Hopkins] Sibley and escort on their way south. We halted for an hour's rest, and as we were parting Col. Sibley stuck his head out of his ambulance, saying: "Boys, if you only knew it, I am the worst enemy you have."[33]

The mystery was solved when a few months later he came back into New Mexico at the head of a force of Texan rebels.

Col. Canby in Command.

Upon Col. Canby assuming command, the forts in Arizona were ordered abandoned, their garrisons concentrating at Fort Fillmore, N.M., on the Rio Grande, 10 miles north of the Texas line and 120 miles south of Fort Craig.[34]

Early in 1862 rumors were afloat that there was a force of Texans variously estimated at from 3,000 to 4,000, marching to invade New Mexico; also that there was a regiment of volunteers from Colorado coming to our assistance. A regiment of New Mexican volunteers, made up of peons and greasers, was also raised. Meanwhile the Texans came on, and encamped opposite Fort Fillmore, N.M. They were encamped there for some time, and a demand was made for the surrender of the fort.[35]

What follows was told me by one of the comrades of the 7th who was there. Col. Lynde, commanding the fort, refused, but agreed to evacuate. Two companies were sent out in advance, one hour afterward two more, one hour after them the remaining one went out. The Texans overtook them, and they were taken without firing a shot.[36] The prisoners were drawn up in line, and this offer was made to them:

"To all who take service with us in the C.S.A. will be given $26 per month, a horse, saddle and bridle, and all each can make besides." To the honor of the Regular Army be it said not one soldier accepted the offer. They were then paroled. Eighteen of them refused to be paroled, saying they had sworn to uphold the honor of Old Glory, and they would take no other oath. This when they fully expected to be shot for their stubbornness. They were kept as prisoners, but finally made their escape and joined us at Fort Craig, just in time to take part in the bloody battle of Valverde. The 18 were commended in General Orders by Col. Canby.[37]

Of course, all was excitement at Fort Craig. The Texans were on the march up the Rio Grande, and we had only about 300 white troops to meet them. We had a regiment of Mexicans, but they did not amount to a "row of pins." The garrison of Fort Craig consisted of two companies, 2nd Dragoons; one company, 2nd Art.[Artillery]; one company of 2nd Colo.[Colorado] (who had just arrived), three companies (F, C and H) of 7th U.S. under Capt. Plympton, two companies of 5th U.S. under Capt. Wingate.

The Texans Open the Fight.

On Feb. 19, 1862, the Texans appeared before Fort Craig, making a show of force, but withdrew on the 20th. They appeared on the opposite side of the river. A portion of our troops were sent across the river on picket. The rebels opened with a few cannon shots, doing no damage. On the morning of the 21st they moved up the river, still on the opposite or eastern side. Leaving a few troops in the fort, Col. Canby put our forces in motion also up the river on the western side. At a wide bottom called "Valverde" we crossed over. The Mexicans did not cross, but remained on the west bank. We formed line of battle, threw out skirmishers and advanced. The Texans were found posted behind long, low sand ridges. As soon as we came within range, a brisk skirmish fire was kept up for some time. While on this skirmish line I looked back across the river, and saw the bluffs covered with fleeing Mexicans. They melted away as dew before the morning sun, but we did not feel their loss.

The recall was sounded, our lines were rearranged with two 12-pound cannons on our right and a battery of four mountain howitzers on our left, commanded by Capt. McRae. Co. F, 7th U.S., was ordered to their support. We lay down behind the pieces while the artillery of both sides kept up a fire for some time. At last the rebels charged us, but were repulsed. Again they came on, this time in far greater numbers. We stood to our posts, the artillerymen standing to their guns as long as possible. We met the Texans at the muzzles of the cannon, but were overpowered by force of numbers.

I heard no orders, no shouting, no yelling. Everybody was busy fighting. We finally gave way, and found that the rest of our force had recrossed the river and were on their way to the fort.

During the fight over the guns it is said that Col. Canby shouted: "It is no use; save your lives if possible." It may be so, but I did not hear it. Capt. McRae was killed at his guns. Capt. Wingate, of the 5th, while on his way to help us, was shot and afterward died. His two companies did not reach us. As to our company (F, 7th U.S.) we went into battle with 60 men, and 18 of these were killed on the field or died a few hours after, 19 were wounded (many of whom never got well), and two were missing, making a loss of 39 out of 60. The loss was not nearly so great in the other parts of the field, but by our holding to our guns as we did, we saved our little force from total annihilation. There was but one man in Co. F without a bullet mark on his clothes or person.

On Feb. 22 the Texans sent in a flag of truce demanding a surrender of the fort. This was refused. They said they would take our fort as they did our battery, with revolvers and bowie knives. But they evidently thought better of it. They moved up the river, capturing Albuquerque, and were on the march for Fort Union, in the northeastern part of the Territory, when they were met by the two regiments of Colorado volunteers.—Lewis F. Roe, Co. F, 7th U.S., Knoxville, Ill.[38]

Sibley in New Mexico

Northern newspaper correspondents portrayed the conduct of the Texans during their year-long stay in New Mexico in the most unflattering terms, pillage and plunder being among the mildest language used. Some units of Sibley's Army of New Mexico occupied the territorial capital at Santa Fe for about two weeks but found little that was of use to them beyond a warehouse of goods intended for the Navajo Indians. During that time Governor Henry Connelly moved his office from the Palace of the Governors to Las Vegas, New Mexico, about 75 miles to the east. Upon his return we are told by the *Santa Fe Gazette* (April 26, 1862) that

Gov. Connelly is again installed in the Palace. Whilst he was absent some of the Texan officials occupied the venerable building but none of them attempted to exercise the functions of Governor. The only memento they left for our worthy Chief Magistrate was some of Sibley's proclamations and empty champagne bottles.

Reenlistment, Joining Sherman's Army, and the Beginning of the Atlanta Campaign, February–May 22, 1864

THE 50TH ILLINOIS VOLUNTEER INFANTRY, THE ADAMS COUNTY REGIMENT, ENTERED SERVICE ON SEPTEMBER 12, 1861, AND DID OCCUPATION DUTY IN MISSOURI DURING THE LATE FALL AND winter of 1861–1862. It gained the derisive nickname "The Blind Half Hundred" from the incidence of soldiers missing one eye as well as squint- and cross-eyed comrades. The name became a badge of pride.[1]

Then in February 1862, the regiment shipped out to join the attacks on forts Henry and Donelson on the Tennessee and Cumberland rivers. After these successes, it went into camp at Pittsburg Landing in southern Tennessee, where it suffered heavy losses at the Battle of Shiloh on April 6. Later that year, it was brigaded with the 7th and 57th Illinois Infantry regiments and found itself heavily engaged at the Battle of Corinth, Mississippi, on October 3–4. This affair reduced the strength of the 50th Illinois to twenty officers and 265 men.[2] By the end of 1862, the 39th Iowa Infantry joined the brigade, and these four regiments served together until the end of the war. Lewis Roe often made references to these other units.[3]

After Corinth, the 50th Illinois marched, maneuvered, went into camps, and occasionally skirmished with guerrillas in the northeastern corner of Mississippi until November 12, 1863, when it arrived at Lynnville in south-central Tennessee. At this point the regimental commander, Col. Moses M. Bane, was ordered to mount the men on mules, for what became a five-month stint as mounted infantry. By early December, the 50th Illinois found itself mule-borne, their mounts supplied partly by the army's quartermaster department and partly by raiding the countryside.

The troops lived well, thanks to well-filled granaries, smoke houses, and herds of cattle, sheep, and hogs.[4]

Under General Orders issued in June and September 1863, many of the original enlistees met the requirements for reenlistment as veteran volunteers. Some 340 members of the regiment received a discharge effective December 31, 1863, and on January 15–16, 1864, were mustered in again. The regiment then boarded a train and rolled into Quincy, Illinois, early on January 23, to a grand reception and a thirty-day furlough for everyone. The veterans encouraged recruits to join and fill up the ranks, and more than 200 new members followed after the 50th Illinois returned to Lynnville on March 5.[5]

Roe, as explained earlier, enlisted again and at this point his own introduction[6] to his 1864–1865 army journals resumes:

> [I] enlisted in Company "C" 50th Ills. [Veteran] Volunteer Infty. Feb. 10th 1864 to serve three years or during the war. I enlisted at Quincy, Ills. The 50th was then at Lynnville, Tenn. From Quincy [I] was sent to Camp Yates near Springfield, Ills. This was the worse hole I ever was in. Rain and mud continually, not much to eat, and what there was not fit for a hog. Several thousand recruits were crowded in a small enclosure. A great many died. After a few weeks we were transferred to Camp Butler, a short distance from Camp Yates. This place was in some respects better than Yates, but still far from decent—but we expected to endure privations and hardship, so there was not much complaining. While here we drew uniforms, and with new clothes and somewhat better rations, we got along very well.
>
> Here we remained for only about eight or ten days, until it came our turn to start for the south. Finally on a bright Sabbath evening our party, consisting of Lieut. [Cornelius F.] Kitchen and 12 recruits for the 50th, left Springfield by railroad for our Regt. I being an old soldier was placed next in command under the Lieut. Running eastward through Decatur [and the] State line, [we] took dinner at LaFayette, Ind., thence south through Indianapolis to Jeffersonville on the Ohio. Crossing the river into Ky. we put up over night at the Soldiers Home. Next morning on the rail again for Nashville. Arriving there, we were placed with about 2,000 other recruits in a building known as the Zollicoffer House. It was seven stories in height [and] had never been finished, only enclosed and studding and flooring put in.[7]

FIGURE 11. The Zollicoffer House [Maxwell House Hotel], Nashville, Tenn.,
early 1860s. U.S. National Archives, negative 165-C-942.

I shall not attempt to describe this place, only say that it was
very filthy, full of vermin &c. &c. Soldiers going home on furlough
and soldiers going to the front all stopped at this place, until transportation could be furnished. While here, they placed guards over
the doors with instructions to let none out, but the second day after
our arrival the 6th Iowa Infty. came up from the front and took
quarters in the Zollicoffer House. Being refused the liberty of passing out, they seized their guns, drove the guards away and passed
out when they wished. Instructions were now given to let the 6th
Iowa pass out but none other. So when one came to go out, the
guards asked, "What Regt?" If the answer was "6th Iowa" they were
passed out. As a consequence we all belonged to the 6th Iowa. I
have heard of Regts. decreasing in numbers very rapidly, but never
have I known one to gain in number so fast.

After remaining here a few days we were started south again by
railroad. Passing through Columbia [and] Lynnville, we found our

regiment in camp at Decatur Junction, a few miles from Decatur, Ala. Our Boys had been mounted on mules and were known as the 50th Ills. Mounted Infantry. Brother Edward and Cousin Luther Scarborough were here in the 50th.[8] Behold me then as a member of Co. "C" 50th Ills. Mounted Infty., otherwise known as the "*Blind Half Hundred.*"[9] After remaining a few days we were ordered to "Mooresville," Ala. Arriving at Mooresville, I commenced keeping a daily journal or record of events, from which I now copy.

Lewis Roe began his diary on April 3 at Mooresville, Alabama, as we will see. The regiment moved from there to Athens and then to Huntsville, Alabama, arriving finally at Chattanooga, Tennessee, after

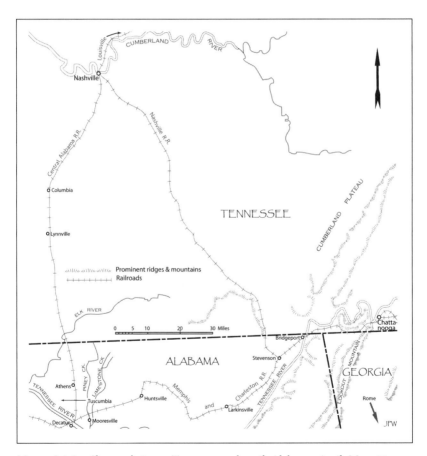

MAP 4. Joining Sherman's Army: Tennessee and north Alabama, April–May 1864. Courtesy of author.

dark on May 4. There they joined Sherman's Army and began their advance into Georgia—the Atlanta Campaign.

Roe's active involvement with this campaign lasted just two weeks: from May 9 through May 22, 1864. During this time, his regiment had minor roles in the battles of Lay's Ferry and Rome Crossroads on May 15 and 16, then marched south with the rest of the Army of the Tennessee to Kingston, Georgia. From a railroad junction there with

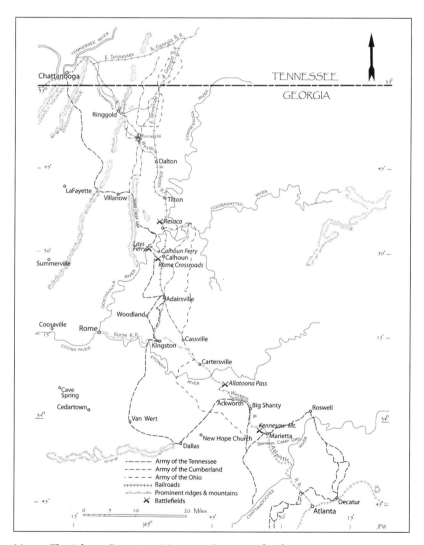

MAP 5. The Atlanta Campaign, May 1864. Courtesy of author.

the mainline Western & Atlantic, the Rome Railroad spur led west for some eighteen miles to Rome, Georgia. At Kingston, Roe's brigade was ordered to Rome, removing it from further participation in the Atlanta Campaign.

During the background research for this chapter, it became apparent that Lewis Roe's journal entry for May 15 gave details about the Battle of Lay's Ferry that went beyond anything included in the primary sources usually cited or in modern secondary accounts.[10] Was he an eyewitness or a participant? These questions led to a substantial effort to seek additional primary sources and eventually to enlist the aid of a local researcher as ways of evaluating Lewis Roe's account. Lay's Ferry is not commemorated in any way at the present time.

At the battlefield, just east of the Oostanaula River and several miles from Calhoun, Georgia, a key feature appears to have been the "large brick house" mentioned by Roe and others, including Brig. Gen. John Corse.[11] None of these narratives gave it a name. Roe called it a plantation, but he had probably never seen one, and this part of Georgia had few plantations. Two maps in the *Atlas to Accompany the Official Records* show a "Frick House" just southeast of Lay's Ferry, and author William Scaife labeled this the "George Frick House" in his work on the Atlanta Campaign.[12]

Records from this period show Frick and Frix as alternative spellings of a surname, and genealogical websites indicate that George Washington Frix, born in 1829, died on January 31, 1860, in Gordon County, Georgia. He had been a widower and had remarried in 1858; his new widow, Georgia, went to live with her father in Forsyth County, Georgia, by the time the 1860 Census was taken. His father, Michael Frix, and mother, Sarah, with two younger daughters, two sons, and a six-year old boy were all shown in the same household (#89) in the City of Calhoun, Georgia, where the 55-year-old Michael Frix reported himself as a farmer with personal property valued at $10,000 and real estate worth $8,000. Michael Frix (Frick) died on April 19, 1872.[13]

Gordon County, Georgia, courthouse records showed that Michael Frix deeded eighty acres of land in Gordon County, acquired originally when this area was part of Cherokee County, to his son George W. Frix as of February 16, 1857. This land, which apparently included the later battlefield, was only part of Michael Frix's property. Although the deed made no mention of any residence, we presume that George Frix

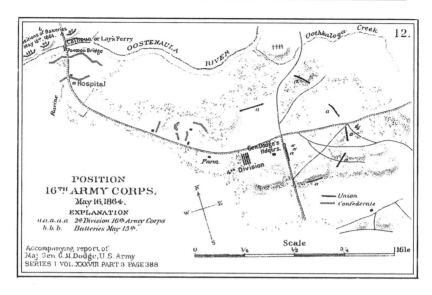

FIGURE 12. Positions at Battles of Lay's Ferry (May 15) and Rome Crossroads (May 16, 1864), Ga. From *Atlas to Accompany the Official Records of the Union and Confederate Armies* (2003) [1891–1895], plate 61 no. 12.

became the owner of a "large brick house" or plantation house on his property at this time. His father Michael and his father's household then moved to nearby Calhoun, Georgia, and managed the balance of his holdings from there.[14]

A possible explanation of why Lewis Roe and another soldier named George Cadman gave the accounts they did might run as follows. After February 1857, George Frix managed both his own property and his father's. When George Frix died on January 31, 1860, his widow held no vested interest in his real property. Michael Frix resumed managing both his own and his deceased son's properties. The large brick house stood unoccupied.

With the coming of the Civil War, the medical director of the Confederate Army of Tennessee, Dr. Samuel H. Stout, developed a hospital system that used stores, hotels, courthouses, private residences, and the like as hospitals, with frequent relocations as necessary. The recently abandoned Frix home would have been an excellent choice for one of Dr. Stout's hospitals. The map of the Lay's Ferry and Rome Crossroads battlefields by federal Maj. Gen. Grenville Dodge indeed shows a Confederate hospital at what is almost certainly the location of the Frix home, and the current landowner remembers "as a child playing in an old Civil War hospital that was on the property next to our farm."[15]

What happened in the late afternoon of May 14, 1864, is that part of Maj. Gen. James McPherson's Army of the Tennessee, including the 81st Ohio and the 66th Illinois infantry regiments, appeared suddenly on the west bank of the Oostanaula River at Lay's Ferry and attempted to establish a bridgehead on the east side. The Confederates on duty near the hospital, formerly the Frix house, were taken by surprise but recovered and resisted fiercely, taking heavy casualties. The Union commander on the scene, Brig. Gen. Thomas Sweeny, recalled his men and thereby allowed the Confederates to evacuate the hospital during the night of May 14–15, 1865.[16] Privates Roe and Cadman said that the plantation owner or a Confederate officer was killed at his doorstep here, an error identical to the claim that Cadman repeated three days later at another plantation. The identity of the person at Lay's Ferry is not presently known.

As to where the house/hospital lay on the battlefield, some description is needed. With respect to events on the 15th, one newspaper account spoke of "the house and outhouses" literally being perforated with round shot and shell from the Union artillery. A close estimate can be made from the report of Lt. Andrew Blodgett, who commanded Battery H of the 1st Missouri Light Artillery [Welker's battery] in support of the Union assaults.[17]

Initially, Blodgett went into battery with his Napoleons about 600 yards (or perhaps 400) north of the Oostanaula; later he moved one half-battery close to the river and gave the Confederates several volleys at 800 to 1,100 yards range. Cpl. Charles Wright of the 81st Ohio Infantry said that "The rebels, principally Wheeler's cavalry, were fortified about one-fourth of a mile from the river: a large brick house in our front was filled with their sharpshooters. They were dislodged by a single shot from Walker's [Welker's] battery, stationed on the other side of the river." Both Roe and the writer in the *Cincinnati Daily Gazette* confirmed that "the artillery got excellent range" and perforated the building. Lt. Henry I. Smith stated that the 7th Iowa Infantry's skirmish line "found the enemy's skirmishers about one-quarter of a mile from the river on the crest of the bluff, and promptly drove them back, routing them from in and about a brick farm house. . . ."[18]

FIGURE 13. Battle of Lay's Ferry, May 15, 1864, from a sketch by A. R. Waud. From print in the Allen L. Fahnestock collection, Peoria (Ill.) Public Library.

Under this battering, the entrenched Confederates gave way and were pursued by the 7th Iowa, 81st Ohio, and 66th Indiana infantry regiments, in company with units of the 66th Illinois Infantry (sharpshooters). As the Union skirmish line advanced, it was met by more rebels, who made a charge only to be blasted back by shellfire and renewed volleys of musketry, while the 7th Iowa made a "determined charge" on their left flank. Again the rebel lines gave way. After pursuing the Southerners for upwards of a mile, the men of the first and second brigades of the 2nd Division, 16th Army Corps, withdrew for the night and entrenched back in the vicinity of the Frick House.[19]

This reconstruction of the Battle of Lay's Ferry does not agree with any one of the official and unofficial accounts, but conforms best with the reports of some junior officers and others who were most directly involved.[20] It also fits well with the map of the Lay's Ferry and Rome Crossroads battlefields published in the *Atlas*, plate 61 #12. Most of the official reports on the actions of May 14–16 were not written until early September 1864, at the end of the Atlanta Campaign. Such a passage of time allows for lapses of memory and for any errors by officers who came to their commands subsequent to the fighting.

The purpose here has been to evaluate the reliability of Lewis Roe's account of the events of May 15. Brigadier General Sweeny sent his third brigade with Lewis Roe and the 50th Illinois upstream to Calhoun Ferry late in the afternoon of May 14. They were not recalled to Lay's Ferry until about the same hour on the 15th—after the day's fighting had ended. Roe's description of the events of May 15 was hearsay, rather than an eyewitness account. The "we" in his journal referred to the first and second brigades of his division. He didn't see any ladies in the windows, or the house being shelled, or the "Rebs" skedaddling. He wasn't there. He was keeping a personal journal, not writing history. When Pvt. George Cadman wrote to his wife on May 19, 1864, he also wrote from hearsay. Cadman's 39th Ohio Infantry arrived at the Rome Crossroads site as part of the 4th Division only in the early afternoon of May 16, having missed the Battle of Lay's Ferry altogether. Both Roe and Cadman repeated what they were told.

What Lewis Roe wrote is a perfect example of the situation that the editors of the *War of the Rebellion, A Compilation of the Official Records* series confronted early on and of why their editorial policy excluded personal documents. As early as 1882, Lt. Col. Robert Scott, who headed that project until his death, commented that "the experience of this office has demonstrated the utter unreliability of recollections of the war." In an interview, he cited two clear examples from his own experience with older officers.[21] What Roe and these veterans did was to project themselves into a situation that did take place, giving the reader or listener the impression that the narrator took part in the event. After the passage of years, they may have believed it themselves.

———

April 3rd, 1864.   Camp near Mooresville, Ala.

Detailed on Picket Guard this morning. There were 3 of us; Edward & myself and another. Our station was on the main road from Mooresville to Athens, one half mile north of Mooresville. One of us remains mounted while the other two pass the time as best we may. Thus we change every 2 hours during the day and night.

Apr. 4th.

This morning Edward & I thought we would like some milk for our coffee so when off duty we rode into town. Found some cows in a yard, milked our canteens full & returned to our post, made coffee &

had milk for the first time since we came south. Being relieved from guard about 9 o'clock, returned to Camp. Spent the day in cleaning my gun [and] fixing up our bunks. All the doors of our shanties have been taken from the houses of Mooresville & vicinity. It looks odd to see our rough board shanties fitted with nice painted doors. Such is war.

Apr. 5th. Tuesday.

A cold day. I hardly know how to pass away the time. We have no rations on hand, no "hard tack," no coffee or sugar or bacon, nothing to eat, but a wagon train has gone to Athens (15 miles away) for supplies. I had nothing but coffee for breakfast, boiled "swamp seed" (rice) for dinner, no supper. What if the guerrillas should pounce on the train and capture it? But it is well guarded and—well, we could live off the country for a few days.

I received my long expected letter from Louisa today. There is always a good deal of excitement in camp upon the arrival of the mail. Nothing cheers one so much as to get news from home.

Apr. 6th, 1864. Wednesday.   Mooresville, Ala.

Train with rations arrived safe. Another mail came in today, bringing me another letter from Louisa. A nice warm day. A scouting party was sent out today. It is said that they go to burn a ferryboat somewhere over the Tennessee River.

Apr. 7th. Thursday.

Our first company drill and dress parade took place today (dismounted). The weather is so nice these days that I suppose Col. [William] Hanna thought [that we were] having too much pleasure or enjoyment.

Apr. 8th. Friday.

The day is so pleasant and having nothing to do, Luther & I strolled through the woods, talked of home, cut our names on beechwood trees &c. Returning to camp, we found there was a rumor afloat that we were to be dismounted. I hope it will prove true. I don't like the mule brigade. I would rather be all cavalry or all infantry, [not] this half way business.

Apr. 9th, 1864. Saturday.   Mooresville, Ala.

The report now is that we turn over our mules tomorrow. The 25th
Wis. [Wisconsin] Infty. came through camp today. The rest of their
brigade has gone to Decatur. They were with Gen. Sherman on his late
expedition to Selma, Ala. On fatigue duty today building a bake oven.

Apr. 10th. Sunday.

Detailed on picket again today. My post is near Mooresville. All
of our horses & 100 mules were turned over to the 1st Ala. Cavalry
(Loyal) which came into camp today.²² I still keep my mule. Plenty
of milk again. We are ordered to Athens, Ala. tomorrow; Hd. Qrs.
of our Brigade.

Apr. 11th. Monday.

Moved out of our old camp. Ho for Athens is the word. Some on
foot and some muleback. I still retain my faithful grey mule. The 1st
Ala. Cavalry take our places. Encamped tonight in the beechwoods.
"There's a pleasure in the pathless woods," especially when on the
march. That is, when none intrudes.

1864.   Athens, Ala.

We are encamped on Big Piney Creek, 9 miles from Mooresville.
The planters are just beginning to plow, or rather their women slaves,
as the negro men have all run off. A planter's team was impressed to
carry the knapsacks of the footmen. Saw large quantities of cotton
lying in piles in the fields.

Apr. 12th. Tuesday.

Left camp quite early this morning, arriving at Athens about
11 A.M. Went into camp near the old fair ground. The rest of our
brigade are here—viz—57th Ills., 39th Iowa, 14th Ohio Battery.
Turned over the rest of our mules; farewell old grey. A detail has
gone back to Mooresville to bring up hospital stores and patients.

Apr. 13th. Wednesday.

Lying around camp all day. We have stretched our rubber blankets
and made our usual dog-houses. Every one seems to think we will stay
here some time, as Athens is the depot of supplies for "*left wing 16th
Army Corps*," to which we belong and will need a strong guard.

Apr. 14th, 1864. Thursday.　　　　　　　　　　　　　　Athens, Ala.

Had Regimental Inspection today. Received a letter from Louisa, also one from Mother, one from New York. Gen. G. [Grenville] M. Dodge is in command here.

Apr. 15th. Friday.

Our first brigade drill today; the 39th Iowa, 57th and 50th Ills. were present. A cold, blustering day.

Apr. 16th. Saturday.

Detailed with a foraging party today. Went out to Elk River at a planter's loaded with corn. Ed and I milked 6 or 7 cows and succeeded in getting 2 canteens of milk. We also killed a hog. After coming back to camp was detailed on camp guard for the night.

Apr. 17th. Sunday.

Attended church in Athens today. After coming back, orders were received to hold ourselves in readiness to march at a moment's notice. It is reported that a battle is going on at Decatur. We have taken down our dog-houses, rolled our rubbers and [are] ready.

Apr. 18th, 1864. Monday.　　　　　　　　　　　　　　Athens, Ala.

Did not move as expected. Reb Gen. [Philip D.] Roddey's force is reported 12,000 strong near Decatur.[23] The excitement yesterday was caused by his driving in our pickets at that place. We are now building log quarters. Everything looks as if we were to remain all summer. We have just heard of the Ft. Pillow massacre. Why will our Gov. enlist negros and not protect them? Government will certainly retaliate.

Apr. 19th. Tuesday.

It is reported that 30 deserters from the rebel army came into our lines at Decatur. Several prisoners passed through here that were captured in [a] skirmish at Decatur. A deserter enlisted in our Co. today. He was a conscript; made his escape about a month ago at Jackson, Miss. I traded my revolver for a watch, as we are now dismounted. I want as little to carry as possible. There is a good deal of excitement yet; many rumors.

Apr. 20th, 1864. Wednesday.   Athens, Ala.

Orders were issued for all persons to report at [the] hospital and be vaccinated. Refugees come through our lines almost every day. I had a talk with a family that came from the central part of Georgia. They say that great destitution prevails; that whole families will starve. One or two of these refugees were in the rebel army at Vicksburg when it was captured. They had great difficulty in getting in our lines. Brigade drill today.

Apr. 21st. Thursday.

On Picket today. Our post is on the Prospect road, 1 mile north of town. The 66th Ind. [Indiana], 52 Ills., a battery of 2nd Mich. Artillery passed on their way to Decatur. The 1st Mo. [Missouri] battery relieved the 14th Ohio, which was here. They too go to Decatur. We hear cannonading in that direction all day but suppose it is only practice. The negroes and citizens have been hauling wood past our reserve post all day. We levy a toll of a stick or two from each load to keep fire at night.

Apr. 22. Friday.   Athens, Ala.

Relieved from guard about 10 A.M. No news of importance. Brigade drill at 2 P.M.

Apr. 23. Saturday.

Lounging about camp all day. Hardly know what to do to pass away the time. Rec. [received] a letter from Louisa.

Apr. 24th. Sunday.

Attended church at 11 o'clock. A native preached. In [the] afternoon the chaplain of [the] 39th Iowa preached.

Apr. 25th. Monday.

Hard at work building quarters. Got our room finished and moved in. There are 16 in our mess now—viz—Sergt. Seiter, Scarborough, Corporal Hinckley, Privates Deer, Cooper, Birdsall, Stewart, Spicer, Cook, Robbins, Ward, M. Seiter, Jenner, Ed & I.[24] There are rumors of a move again. It is said that the 15th, 16th, 17th Army Corps will concentrate and form the left wing of an advancing army.

Apr. 26th. Tuesday.

We have all sorts of rumors today but as I cannot trace any of them to an authoritative source, no use to write them down. Brigade drill today.

Apr. 27th. Wednesday. Athens, Ala.

Battalion drill today. Broke the crystal of my watch while drilling in skirmish line. Attended prayer meeting at night. How different are the prayers of Soldiers. The burden of their prayers seems to be for our country and for dear and loved ones at home, that God would watch over, protect, and provide for them.

Apr. 28th. Thursday.

Detailed on a foraging expedition but afterward the order was countermanded. Orders were issued to be prepared to march at a moment's notice. Sent home all surplus clothing today. The box was sent by express to Mrs. Stewart of Payson. There are 1001 rumors afloat as to our destination. Some say Decatur, others Chattanooga, others Huntsville. Our whole brigade has marching orders.

Apr. 29, 1864. Friday.

On Picket. Our Post is south of town on the Huntsville road. I think we will move tomorrow, as the Officer of the Guard has just been around leaving orders to abandon our post at 3 o'clock in the morning. Some say we go to Corinth, Miss., as the R.R. through there is to be reopened. Afternoon—we were relieved at 4 P.M. The 3rd Ala. Colored troops took our places.[25]

Apr. 30th. Saturday.

Started out of camp about 8 A.M.; took the Huntsville road. The road was strewed with overcoats, blankets. Rained hard all day; roads very muddy. Camped on Limestone Creek, 11 miles from Athens.

May 1st. Sunday. Huntsville, Ala.

On the move again by 7 o'clock; rained all night, terribly muddy. No one knows much about mud until they see the Alabama article; red and sticky, oh, so sticky. Arrived in Huntsville at 2 P.M. at the same time that the 2nd brigade of our division came in from Pulaski, Tenn. It is reported that we start for Stevenson tomorrow.

May 2. Monday.   On the March

Left Huntsville at 1/2 past 6 in the morning. Marched through the principal streets, then took the road toward Stevenson, Ala. Huntsville is the most beautiful city I have ever seen. While here I met Warren McCroskey, one of my acquaintances of former years in Ills. He is a soldier belonging to an Iowa reg't. Our whole Division composed of the 1st, 2nd & 3rd brigades [is] with us. Gen. [Thomas W.] Sweeny commanding.

We are encamped on the side of a mountain. Have marched 18 miles.

May 3. Tuesday.

Our Reg't being in [the] rear today, we did not get started until near 8 A.M. Have been marching through high hills or mountains all day. Distance today 18 miles. Several boys gave out and came up in the night. I feel somewhat tired myself. It is rumored that we go by rail tomorrow.

May 4th. Wednesday.   Larkinsville, Stevenson,
                                                                          Bridgeport, Ala.
                                                                      Chattanooga, Tenn.

On the road again. We have marched 7 or 8 miles and are now at Larkinsville, Ala., a station on [the] Memphis & Charleston R.R. waiting to get aboard the train for Chattanooga. The report now is that heavy skirmishing is going on at Ringgold, Ga., just south of Chattanooga. 2 P.M. On the train—have passed through Stevenson and Bridgeport, Ala. Train after train are loaded with reinforcements for Sherman's Army.

South of Chattanooga.

11 P.M. Just arrived at Chattanooga and are encamped at the base of Lookout Mt. We felt our way in the pitch darkness to the banks of the Tennessee River, filled our cups with water, made coffee and as some were drinking, found that everybody's cup contained 3 to 6 maggots boiled. I threw my coffee away and concluded I did not want any coffee that night. The whole country is ablaze with campfires.

May 5th. Thursday.   Lookout Mountain

On the topmost rock of Lookout, I write these lines. I see now what [Maj. Gen. Joseph] Hooker's boys had to surmount in his famous battle "above the clouds." I can imagine how the boys clambered up the sides of the mt. in the face of the deadly fire of the rebels on the summit. Down there is where the rebel Pickets were captured the night before. There near the base is the 1st line of rifle pits. A little over half way up is the 2nd line. Then the final charge was made. "Brave boys were they."[26]

Several of our Co. started to climb Lookout. All gave up and went back except Luther S. and I. We finally reached the top and were well repaid for our trouble. A signal station is located here, also a photographer is here. He has pictures of different views of the mountain; of Generals, of groups of soldiers &c. About 4 P.M. we descended. Reached camp just in [time to] fall in for the march. Division after division passed and then we started.

Chickamauga Creek

Marched through the old battlefield of Chickamauga. Trees were knocked to pieces by shot and shell; everything bears marks of a hard fought battle. One of our boys found a skull; another an arm. Graves are scattered about in every direction. We are encamped on Chickamauga Creek, nearly west of Ringgold, Ga.

May 6th. Friday.

We made no move today. It is said that the main army is only 10 or 12 miles south of us. Well, we will soon form part of it. What is to happen will happen, I suppose. Sometimes I wish I knew. I do not believe this large Army will remain inactive very long. Have not heard from home for a long time. We are encamped in the thick woods, everybody giving their opinion as to what ought to be done; all are Generals.

May 7th. Saturday.

Started out of Camp at about 6 A.M. It was reported that the rebels were within 6 or 8 miles of here but we have marched 13 or 14 miles and met no opposition. We are encamped about 17 miles N.W. of Dalton. We are further south than our army has ever been. A woman told me we were the first Yankees she ever saw. It is expected that the great battle will take place near Dalton. I can form no idea of the size of our army. Our company on Picket tonight.

May 8th. Sunday.   Villanow, Ga.

Pickets called in early this morning and we started. We marched very cautious. It is evident that we are near the enemy. After a march of about 5 miles we reach the village of Villanow where we were joined by a large force of Cavalry under [Maj. Gen. Judson] Kilpatrick.

Near Resacca [Resaca], Ga.

We left our wagon train in Larkinsville where we took the cars; consequently we are short of rations. Ed and I ate everything for supper except a little meat. It is thought we are flanking the "Rebs" on the right. Encamped at the southern entrance of "Snake Creek Gap." Some skirmishing in our front today.[27]

May 9. Monday.   Snake Creek Gap, Ga.

Started shortly after sunrise. About a mile from camp we heard skirmishing in front. The 9th Ills. Mtd. Infantry were driven back. The 66th Ills. Infty (Sharpshooter) armed with the Henry Rifle deployed as skirmishers. Our brigade formed line of battle and we moved forward. The rebels were driven back with the loss of 2 left dead on the field, 3 wounded, 3 prisoners. Our loss was 3 or 4 wounded, including Col. [Jesse J.] Phillips, 9th Ills.[28]

We met with no more opposition until we were within 2 miles of the R.R. ~~Dalton~~ (Chattanooga & Atlantic) near the town of Resaca. Skirmishing commenced again. We drove them before us until near the town ~~of Resaca~~ when they opened on us with shot and shell, several of which exploded over our heads, but doing no harm. We were kept under fire until near dark and then fell back to "Snake Creek Gap." We are rather hungry tonight (Ed and I), having had nothing to eat since before daylight this morning, and then only a small piece of beef. Present time ~~12 o'clock~~ (midnight).

May 10. Tuesday.

Good news, good news. The rebellion is not ended, but our wagon train has come up and our haversacks are full again. Our Regt. was sent out about midnight to reinforce the Picket line. During the night there came up one of the hardest thunderstorms I ever saw. We were ordered back to camp. By laying the ends of 2 rails on a stump [and] getting on them, I managed to get some sleep.

FIGURE 14. Engagement at Snake Creek Gap, Ga., from a Theodore R. Davis sketch. From *Harper's Weekly*, June 4, 1864; collections of the Library of Congress.

May 11. Wednesday.   Snake Creek Gap

A cold, drizzly day. We are at Snake Creek Gap. This seems to be a passage through a low range of hills. I suspect we are flanking the rebel army on the right. I should think the Johnnies would have defended this pass, but we have met with little opposition. We have heard heavy cannonading in the direction of Dalton. Detailed on guard at brigade Hd. Qrs. Rec. a letter from Louisa.

May 12. Thursday.

Heavy artillery in the direction of Dalton. In the afternoon it became almost a continuous roar. There certainly must be a battle going on. We are very anxious. But we believe Sherman knows what he is about. The 15th Army Corps left here; they took the road towards Dalton. The 20th Corps (Gen. Hooker) came in tonight. Also 3 or 4 regts. of Kilpatrick's cavalry came in from the front. The Signal Corps have been flying signals all day.

May 13th. Friday.   Encamped in the woods

Awakened out of a good sleep early this morning with orders to be ready to start by daylight in light marching order without knapsacks. We got started about 8 o'clock; marched toward Resaca about 5 miles when skirmishing commenced. Our left came up with the enemy and the battle began. Our division being on the extreme right was not engaged. The 20th Corps did most of the fighting, although the 4th Div. of our Corps (16) was sharply engaged for awhile. Encamped in the woods in line of battle. Tomorrow I expect a hard fought battle. God give us victory.

May 14. Saturday.   Calhoun Ferry

Another day of fighting and the battle is not yet over. Our Regt. (50) has been lucky today, it has not been called into action yet. We were under artillery fire for a short time; lost 1 man wounded although Co. 'I' lost 6 men captured while skirmishing.

Early this morning the battle recommenced. Our brigade was ordered more to the right in the direction of Calhoun ferry over the Oostanaula River to throw a pontoon bridge over the, but failed owing to a strong force of rebs in possession of the opposite bank. The 2nd brigade of our division (2nd) suffered severely. Our Regt. was sent back to the rear on Picket tonight. There has been heavy cannonading and musketry toward Resaca all day.[29]

May 15th. Sunday.   Brick House near Calhoun Ferry

Still another day and the end not yet [in sight?]. How long, how long can this last? We moved still nearer to Calhoun Ferry. Our Sharpshooters (64th) [actually, the 66th Illinois Volunteer Infantry] followed by the 1st & 2nd brigades. After sharp firing, the engineers succeeded in laying the pontoon bridge. We rushed across, formed line of battle and moved forward, drove the rebels over a mile.

A large brick house stood ahead about 1/2 mile. The windows were full of ladies waving handkerchiefs and cheering on the rebs, but no use; we drove them back. They undertook to make a stand at the house. One or 2 pieces of artillery were brought to bear and again the rebs skedaddled were driven back. When we came up, we found the house empty. Several shells had passed through it, knocking shingles and bricks in all directions. The owner of the plantation lay dead in his yard. The ladies had disappeared. There were several dead rebels about the house and garden. We worked till near midnight throwing up breast-works. Several rebel dead lay among the flowers in the garden near the brick house. Truly it was "Death among the flowers."[30]

May 16th. Monday.   Retreat from Resaca

Another day has ended and the "Blind Half" has been compelled to retreat. This morning two brigades of our division 1st & 2nd started forward. Our skirmishers soon came up with the enemy [and] drove them steadily before, over a mile, when we came upon the main rebel army in full retreat along the R.R. We halted [and] held our ground for some time. The rebs made several charges upon a battery on the right of our brigade; came near capturing it, but it was withdrawn too quick.

The firing now became general on all sides except the rear. It was evident we were being surrounded. We were ordered to retreat, which we did for about 1/2 mile and took possession of a round hill and awaited reinforcements. The 15th Corps soon came up on the double quick. [We?] remained on the hill over night. Our loss in regt. 12.[31] The heavy cannonade on our ~~right~~ left the last few days was Sherman's attack on Resaca.

May 17th. Tuesday.

This series of battles are over. [Gen. Joseph E.] Johnston's army [is] in full retreat. The fight last evening was brought on by our running in[to] Johnston's army upon the flank. We remained in camp nearly all day. The 15th Corps has been passing our encampment since early in the morning. We remained in camp until nearly dark, then started forward in rear of [the] trains. Marched nearly all night until 3 o'clock in the morning. On to Atlanta is the word.

May 18th. Wednesday.   Adairsville, Ga.

Started from camp about 8 o'clock. We passed several lines of breastworks thrown up by the rebs. Marched until near noon, then lay over until night. Started again and marched until midnight, passing through Adairsville. We are on the right or west of the R.R. running from Chattanooga to Atlanta. It is reported that we have captured a whole brigade of Johnnies. Rec. a letter from Louisa.[32]

May 19th. Thursday.

Our march commenced about 11 A.M. Heard cannonading in front. Passed several dead horses. They show that our advance cavalry have quite heavy skirmishing. Several prisoners passed, going to the rear. Some of them say we can never "take Atlanta," others that "the Yankees can do anything." We are encamped in sight of Kingston.[33]

May 20th. Friday.   Kingston, Ga.

No move today. We are encamped with the 15th Corps, about 1 mile from Kingston. It is reported that our Div. goes to Rome, about 15 miles west of here. Reported that Johnston is throwing up fortifications on the south bank of the Etowah River, 20 miles south of here. If so, we will have a hard fought battle in a day or two. Kingston is at the junction of a branch R.R. from Rome with the main line to Atlanta.

May 21st. Saturday.

Still in camp near Kingston. Saw Michaël Fitzgerald, a soldier who served with me in Co. "F," 7th US Infty., and came home with me from N.M. He is now in the 35th N.J. Zouaves. The 4th Division of our Corps (16) has orders to be prepared for rapid marching. Our brigade has orders to move, but nothing has been said about *rapid* marching. Various are the conjectures as to where we are going. Some say to Vicksburg, others that we are going to flank Johnston out of his stronghold.

May 22. Sunday.   Rome, Ga.

Awakened out of sleep this morning with orders to get ready to march immediately. Got started about 7 A.M.; marched through Kingston, turned west on the road toward Rome. Only our brigade are along. Encamped 1 mile from Rome tonight. The 2nd Div. 14th Army Corps (Gen. Jeff C. Davis) are in Rome, they having driven the Rebs out a day or two ago.[34] It is reported that we are to relieve them.

A Skirmish at Rome Crossroads

After the engagement at Rome cross-roads, a captured "Reb" related to me his adventure with a soldier of the 66th Illinois, of the second brigade. This regiment was armed with 16-shooters (Henry rifles) and usually did more than its share of skirmishing. In this engagement, as usual, it was on the skirmish line. The "Reb" said he saw a "Yank" and at the same moment the "Yank" saw him, and each took to a tree.

Soon as thought he saw a chance for a shot and fired. "Then," he said, "that Yank just opened up and fired thirteen shots into my tree and the bark and dirt flew powerful; then he called out, 'Surrender or I'll fire a volley into you.' I certainly thought if he were going to fire a volley after those thirteen shots, I had better surrender. So I came out and he took me in. What kind of guns have you all got, anyway?"

Capt. James Compton, Company C, 52nd Illinois Infantry, first brigade, 2nd Division [16th] Army Corps, in his "The Second Division of the 16th Army Corps in the Atlanta Campaign," *Glimpses of the Nation's Struggle. Fifth Series, Papers read before the Minnesota Commandery of the MOLLUS* (St. Paul: Review Publishing Co., 1903); reprinted in *Echoes of Battle: The Atlanta Campaign*, ed. Larry R. Strayer and Richard A. Baumgartner (Huntington, W.Va.: Blue Acorn Press, 2004), 100.

CHAPTER SIX

Rome, Georgia, and the Battle of Allatoona, May 23–November 9, 1864

L EWIS ROE'S BRIGADE DID INDEED RELIEVE BREVET MAJOR
GENERAL JEFFERSON DAVIS'S 2ND DIVISION, 14TH ARMY
CORPS AT ROME, GEORGIA, AND FROM THEN UNTIL NOVEMBER
served as the garrison at this post. The 1860 Census had recorded 4,010
residents at Rome, nearly half of them slaves. Although the numbers
made Rome the second-largest city in northern Georgia (Atlanta was
the largest), by comparison it had less than one-third the population of
Quincy, the county seat of Roe's home county in Illinois. Other communities in this part of Georgia were much smaller.[1]

In 1860, on the eve of the Civil War, Rome prospered from a combination of trade, commerce, and manufacturing. Numerous farms
produced cotton, corn, wheat, tobacco, and other consumables, as Yankee foragers soon discovered. The city itself boasted a number of large
dry-goods stores and other establishments, while gracious homes of
brick and frame construction lined the streets. On February 14, 1860,
the city's streets and stores were lighted with gas for the first time. As
early as 1849 the Rome Railroad spur had linked Rome with the main
Western & Atlantic Railroad at Kingston, Georgia.

Steam-powered machinery at the Nonpareil Mills ground out
an abundance of flour and meal while the Noble Brothers Foundry,
opened in 1855, manufactured machinery of every kind, using iron
from the company's furnaces near Cedar Bluff, Alabama. The local
newspaper claimed 300,000 pounds of castings and almost thrice that
amount of pig iron transported over the Rome Railroad in the year
prior to July 1, 1860.[2] The town at this period was confined to the pen-
insula between the Oostanaula and Etowah Rivers.

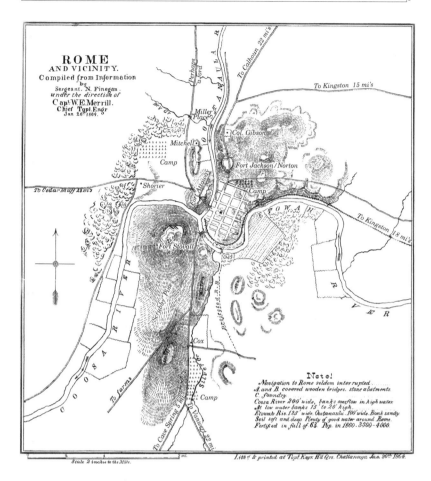

MAP 6. Rome, Ga., and vicinity, January 1864. U.S. National Archives, RG-77, CWMF N-38.

In the first year of the Civil War, Rome and Floyd County enlisted fifteen companies of soldiers and sent them off to join the fighting.[3] Rome began to turn out war materials for the as-yet distant battlefields. Through 1862, the Noble Brothers Foundry cast both bronze and iron field guns and delivered fifty-eight field pieces to the Confederate government, not counting six eight-inch siege howitzers cast for the State of Georgia. The Noble firm produced an estimated eighty-five pieces, but difficulties with obtaining materials, complaints of faulty castings, and disputes with the government ended the casting of cannons by 1863. A fire had burned the Noble Brothers gun carriage department as

FIGURE 15. The Noble Brothers Foundry & Machine Works, Rome, Ga. From George Magruder Battey Jr., *A History of Rome and Floyd County* (1969) [1922], p. 451.

well. Other small firms in Rome contracted to make cartridge boxes, haversacks, sword belts, and even buckets.[4]

A Soldiers' Aid Society enrolled hundreds of local women at the beginning of the war. Early in 1862, community leaders began to promote interest in the hospital situation, which initially led to citizens opening their homes to care for sick and wounded soldiers. The home-hospital program expanded until December, when Confederate medical authorities established five hospitals at Rome. These operated for about one year, until a scarcity of supplies and the threat posed by the Union victory at Chattanooga in late November led to the last hospital vacating Rome on December 8, 1863.[5]

Just once in the first three years of the war did fighting threaten Rome itself. Union colonel Abel Streight led four regiments of mounted infantry, about 1,600 men including his own 51st Indiana Volunteers, on a poorly planned raid eastward from Tuscumbia, Alabama. As the brigade marched across northern Alabama, it attracted rebel Col. Philip Roddey and his brigade and then Brig. Gen. Nathan Bedford Forrest's cavalry. They caught up with Streight on April 28, 1863.

From their first action at Town Creek, east of Tuscumbia, Streight and Forrest fought a running series of ambushes, skirmishes, rear-guard actions, and small-scale battles as Streight's brigade pushed east. After five days of near continuous fighting, Streight surrendered his

Figure 16. Rifled iron 6-pdr. cast by Noble Bros. Foundry, Rome, Ga. Piece is now in Naperville, Ill. Photo courtesy of Janet Hinck, Lombard, Ill.

1,466 worn-out troopers to Forrest at Lawrence's Spring, about twenty-four miles west of Rome. Forrest paraded his captives through Rome, where the people reviled the Yankees and gave the southern cavalrymen a hero's welcome.[6]

As the war continued, Rome experienced a crowd of refugees that may have peaked in the summer of 1863. By the end of the year, Union victories in Tennessee and the departure of the hospitals led many of these immigrants to move again. One visitor in February 1864 commented that Rome looked like "a deserted village."[7]

When Bvt. Maj. Gen. Jefferson Davis and his division from the Army of the Cumberland marched into Rome on May 18, one source later claimed that all but forty-two of the resident population had removed themselves. The bridges across the Oostanaula and Etowah rivers were burning, and departing Texan troops had looted the stores. General Davis quickly replaced the bridges with pontoons and found a considerable quantity of quartermaster, commissary, and medical supplies at hand, which he issued to his troops. He captured the Noble Brothers ironworks and machine shops "in good condition."

The enemy continued firing into the city from the south bank of the Coosa River until the 22nd, when the Union commander sent part of his first brigade across the river to disperse the rebels. Some of his soldiers had occupied themselves "pillaging day and night" while burning a few of the houses. Other stores, homes, and churches became store houses, hospitals, and an armory, as well as troop quarters and administrative offices.[8] The local newspaper, the *Rome Tri-Weekly Courier*, suspended publication after May 16, 1864.[9]

Such were conditions at Rome, Georgia, when Lewis Roe's brigade arrived there to maintain order and garrison the town. Even the displaced citizens must have seen the local situation as less than bleak, because Roe noted that they began coming back every day.

Other letters and diaries originated in Rome during the period of federal occupation. Best known is the diary of a local civilian, Reuben S. Norton, liberal extracts from which have been published.[10] The testimony of a Mrs. Ward before a U.S. Senate committee in 1883 is reminiscent and primarily concerned with living conditions and race relations.[11] A few letters by Pvt. George Drake, 85th Illinois Volunteers, and George M. Wise, 43rd Ohio Volunteers[12] add little, while Lt. Daniel Leib Ambrose of the 7th Illinois Infantry tells us that when his regiment arrived in early July, "Rome . . . is now converted into one vast hospital for the wounded and sick soldiers of the army of the Cumberland."[13] The entries for November 10–11, 1864, in Cornelius C. Platter's [81st Ohio Infantry] diary tell something of the destruction at Rome when Sherman's army abandoned the city.[14]

Pvt. Frederick Sherwood in Lewis Roe's own company sent ten letters to his mother between July and October, 1864; these were almost entirely concerned with family matters. However, he said in one that the local girls (he had been "stealing" their songs) were "getting so jealous of me they don't know what they are about."[15] Attitudes had changed considerably since George Drake wrote back on May 21 that "There are lots of ladies in this place [Rome] but they are awfully strong."[16]

The burning of Atlanta had a counterpart in the burning of all bridges, foundries, warehouses, mills, factories, depots, and other establishments in Rome that might be of use to the Confederates, this by order of Major General Sherman. Some, perhaps many, private homes and shops were burned as well when the federal forces evacuated the city

FIGURE 17. Rome, Ga., in 1864, at junction of Etowah and Oostanaula rivers. Photo courtesy of the Georgia Archives, Vanishing Georgia Collection, image flo 017a.

on November 10–11, 1864. Roe mentioned this destruction ("Rome is burning"), but there are more detailed accounts of the losses.[17]

Rome and all of northern Georgia lacked any authority after federal troops marched away. The gangs that Roe called guerrillas ran rampant; these consisted of deserters from both armies. Colquitt's scouts plundered people in the Rome area while Gatewood's scouts kept the country further north terrorized. It was June 1865 before federal authorities returned and established a firm military rule.[18]

———— ⬙ ————

May 23. Monday.   Rome, Ga.

Spent the day in running about the streets of Rome. It was quite a town before the war; must have had 3 or 4,000 inhabitants. Now many of the dwelling houses are empty. Stores all vacant except one drugstore. The stores were pillaged by their own troops.[19] I am told that they acted more like savages than civilized people. It is reported that our forces captured quite a number of bales of cotton, also a quantity of flour & meal & pork.

May 24. Tuesday.   Rome, Ga.

Rome is situated at the junction of the Etowah & Oostanaula
rivers. These unite & form the Coosa. Our brigade moved in[to] town.
Our Regt. (50) is to do Provost Duty. Our Co. ("C") is quartered in the
2nd story of a large brick hotel.[20] Several deserters from the rebel army
came in today. Also 2 of the 58 Ills. and 1 of [Col. William] Wilson's
Zouaves who were captured and made their escape.

7 plugs of tobacco per man were distributed, being the amt.
captured here. The 2nd Div. 14th Corps left here for the front, crossing the Etowah on pontoons. Col. [Abel D.] Streight's command
was taken about 20 miles west of here last year. They were kept
here overnight.

> Rome Georgia
> May 24th, 1864
> My Dear Wife,
>
> I received your letter of May 10th & also one from Mother of
> May 15th; rec. both last night. In Mother's letter she informs me
> that *we* have become *Parents*; that now I may call you *Ma* in earnest.
> Well, may God fit us for this new station in life; that we may prove
> ourselves true *Parents*; that our child may be brought up in the fear
> of the Lord. I am so glad to hear that you are getting along so well.
> I have felt a great deal of anxiety about you during the few weeks
> past & now, although I do not feel as anxious as before, still I shall
> feel very uneasy until I hear that you are entirely well. You must
> write very often, Dear Louisa, now, for you have *two* to write for
> now & I'll not forget that you are as anxious to hear from me as I
> am from you.
>
> You see by the heading [and] date of my letter that we are in
> Rome, Georgia. We may stay here some time as we are quartered in
> the city & doing Post Duty. Our Brigade are the only troops here.
> This place was captured by Gen. Jeff. C. Davis's Division, 14th
> Army Corps, on the 18th of May without much fighting. The Rebs
> skedaddled. It is a city of about 6,000 inhabitants. The rebels tore up
> & destroyed what they could before leaving & our men finished what
> they left. The stores have been turned inside out; everything of the

least value appropriated; but I am glad to say that with one or two exceptions the houses of those that remained in the city have been left untouched. But oh, the Flower Gardens; lots of them & all in full bloom. How I wish I could present you with a fine bouquet—Flowers of all sorts, sizes & colors. One who has never seen southern gardens can form no idea by reading my description.

On the 22nd our Brigade was ordered up here from Kingston to relieve the Division already here. There will be troops kept here for a long time, & we *may* stay. Still, I'm ready for whatever turns up. Our forces captured a printing press or rather 2 of them & the day after, a newspaper was published, called the Rome Weekly *Union*. I tried to get one of them & some Rebel papers (late), but they were all gobbled up before our Brigade came. I picked up several letters but none of a late date; I send one.

By the last Rebel paper published here I learn that Gen. Lee was driving every thing before him; that the flank movement we made on Dalton & in [the] rear of Resaca was just what Genl Johnston wanted; that he expects to annihilate our army; that the Yankees would have to wade in blood up to their knees before they entered Rome. But, O horrors; this paper was hardly dry before those hated Yankees; those Lincoln hirelings; those Northern vandals &c &c appeared just opposite the town.

I have not learned how much was captured. I have saw [seen] about 50 bales of cotton; 100 bags [of] corn meal. I cannot tell whether our Army has moved far from Kingston. It is reported that the Rebels will make a stand on the south bank of the *Etowah River* & I thought I heard cannonading in that direction today but am not certain. Col. Streight was captured 20 miles west of here & I am now writing within 2 rods of a house where lives a woman that *spit* in his face, so I am told.

I must close. Remember, Love, that my thoughts will ever be of thee & our little Darling. Keep up good spirits & all will be well. Remember, there's a good time coming & I believe it not very far distant. Tell Mother I answer her in a day or two as soon as I get stationery.

Yours
Lewis Roe

May 25. Wednesday.

On guard today; my post is in a hardware store. The owner has left for parts unknown. A large foraging party went out today. They brought in about 200 more boxes of tobacco, also a quantity of meat. One of our boys, [Reese] Carrigan, accidentally shot himself on this expedition. We are anxious to hear from the front or from Richmond. We know of nothing that happens outside of Rome. However, I am well contented to remain here, as I think we will for some time, as our brigade is all the troops here.

May 26th. Thursday.   Rome, Ga.

Relieved from guard at 9 A.M. Went in swimming in the Oostanaula, which many of us do every day and sometimes 2 times a day. The citizens of Rome are coming back every day. I suppose they have found out that the Yankees will not eat them. Our troops are building forts around Rome, which shows that we are going to hold the place.

May 27th. Friday.

Spent the day in lounging about town. Co. "B" our regt. has gone to Kingston for supplies. The soldiers of [the] 10th Mich. Battery are hauling cannon & muskets out of a deep well. The rebs threw them in before evacuating the place. Thus far they have taken out 3 pieces; one 10 lb. Rifle piece, one 12 lb. Brass (smooth), one steel Parrott piece, also several muskets.[21] They found a heavy piece under the floor of a foundry. Well, I hope to hear some news when Co. B returns from Kingston.

May 28th. Saturday.   Rome, Ga.

Co. "B" have come in but brought no mail. They say that a telegram came to Kingston, to the effect that our Army of the Potomac is near Richmond; that Jeff Davis and his cabinet have fled. It is reported that our Army is near Atlanta. I've heard heavy cannonading this morning. Rebel Gen. [Joseph] Wheeler succeeded in burning about 40 wagon loads of supplies.

May 28 [29]. Sunday again.

How different we spent this Sabbath from the 3 or 4 previous ones. Attended the Presbyterian church today. Heard the regular pastor [Rev. John A. Jones]; his subject was Peace. Very appropriate. He did not tell us what we should sacrifice for peace. We think we can realize the beauties of peace as much as he, or more perhaps. In the afternoon I heard the Chaplain of 39th Iowa; subject, Gratitude to God for late Successes. The chaplains of our Brigade have christened this church Union Chapel—services at 11 o'clock & at 3.

May 30th. [Monday]   Rome, Ga.

On fatigue today, building fortifications on Capitol hill. Reports are that Sherman has had another fight in the Allatoona Mts., but we have so many rumors. Gen. [William] Vandever is in command of Rome.[22] A small mail came last night and some papers today; none for me.

May 31st. Tuesday.

On guard. My post over [at?] the hardware store. More reports of heavy fighting toward Atlanta. It is said that Gen. Sherman has sent for transportation for 3,000 wounded. It is said that the remainder of our Div. 2nd lost heavily repulsing several charges.[23] Anxious to hear from home.

June 1st. [Wednesday]

After coming off guard, spent the remainder of the day in lounging about town. The 17th A.C. [Army Corps] from Vicksburg is expected through here every day. It is reported that we go to the front with them.[24] Well, if so, I am content, but I would rather stay here. They say that it is unhealthy at the front just now.

June 2nd. [Thursday]   Rome, Ga.

Orders were issued today forbidding soldiers leaving camp except to go to the river. These orders were given to prevent soldiers from ransacking dwelling houses. We rec. a large mail. I got a letter from Louisa, also one from Charley & Henry.

Friday, June 3rd.

Detailed on fatigue. We were unloading a train of corn & oats. It is reported that our forces entered Marietta yesterday. The 17th A.C., which was expected from Vicksburg by way of Huntsville, has not yet arrived.

Saturday, June 4th.

On guard today. My post is in the large Methodist church, now used as a magazine. Has been raining hard all day. The advance of the 17th Army Corps (Cavalry) came in ~~tomorrow~~ today; the remainder will be in tomorrow. Another mail today but no letter for me.

Sunday, June 5th.   Rome, Ga.

After coming off guard I attended church. Heard the chaplain of 39th Iowa. In [the] afternoon, the chaplain of the 57th Ill. (Collins) preached. A rainy, muddy day. The 17th Corps is encamped across the Oostanaula. There are only 2 divisions; the other 2 Div.'s are at Vicksburg.

Monday, June 6th.

The 17th Army Corps, [Major] Gen. Frank Blair commanding, passed through town today. In the afternoon I was detailed to go out with a party in the country to cut a load of clover. Had all the mulberries and raspberries I could eat. Would like to be on such a detail every day. Wheat is getting ripe; will soon be ripe.

Rome Ga., June 5th, 1864
My Dear Wife,

A rainy, wet Sunday morning. I am not yet relieved from Guard, but will commence a letter & finish sometime during the day. I received a letter from you a day or two ago. You were "sitting up in bed with our dear little *Mayflower* by your side."

How I would like to know how you are this morning. I hope God will spare our lives & that we may be permitted to meet you & our dear child, but still we must try to be resigned to his will, for we know that his "ways are above our ways."

You ask me to send you a pretty name for our little darling. Now, I don't want to influence you in the least in naming her. Don't you remember what I told you once? That you should have the naming of all the *Girls* and I of the Boys. However, I will send a few names, not that I intend you shall choose any of them, but merely to help you think. How do you like such names as Ella Louisa, or Emma Louisa, or Fannie Louisa, or Rosalind Louisa, or Rosa? I would like you to name her anything you think best. Whatever it is, I shall think it pretty.

You will write very often, I know. If we remain here, there will be a good chance to send letters. Do you get the *Dollar Weekly Times*? I wrote to have it sent to you. But I must close. Kiss our little "Mayflower" for me & accept one for yourself.

Ever yours,
Lewis F. Roe

When you write, mention the date of the last journal you receive.

Tuesday, June 7th.   Rome, Ga.

On guard again today. During the night, two houses were burned down. It is said that they were occupied by some women who spit in the faces of some of Col. Streight's command while passing through here as prisoners a year ago. Such acts are not right, but I am afraid I would do the same. It is supposed they were burned by some of the 17th Corps who were the prisoners at that time.

Wednesday, June 8th.

After coming off guard I went down to where those houses were burned, but could learn nothing more as to who burned them or why. Just before sundown, the report came that the rebels were advancing on the town. Our Regt. was ordered out on the double quick. 4 companies were sent across the river, with cavalry in advance. The rebs fired and then ran. The 4 companies recrossed and we marched back, leaving the cavalry as pickets. No one hurt. Probably it was only a few guerrillas hanging around to pick up stragglers.[25] We have a pontoon bridge across the Etowah [River], the rebs having burned the wagon bridge before leaving.

Thursday, June 9th.   Rome, Ga.

The scare about guerrillas has died away. Done nothing but lay around quarters. It is reported that Sherman [is] 5 miles below Marietta, near the Chattahoochee River. Rec. a letter from Louisa. Wrote to Frank.

Friday, June 10th.

On Guard again. This guard duty is quite heavy but we need not complain. We have shelter on most of our posts. Not as bad as picket duty. The 3rd Ky. Cavalry came in, bringing in 2 prisoners. They say that [Maj. Gen. Nathaniel P.] Banks has been driven back to New Orleans; that Grant has been whipped, but they acknowledge that things look rather blue hereabouts. They are probably some of the same tribe that caused such a rumpus the other night.

Saturday, June 11th.

After coming off guard I went in swimming, then made a set of chessmen. Beat Ed 7 games at checkers. 4 more prisoners today. That band of guerrillas will get themselves picked up.

Sunday June 12th.   Rome, Ga.

Attended church forenoon and afternoon. Preaching by Chaplain [Nathan G.] Collins (57th Ills.) & Chaplain [Peter T.] Russell (39th Iowa); our Chaplain [Matthew M.] Bigger (50 Ills.), is attending on the sick & wounded at Kingston. Co. "D" went out with a forage train, but ran upon a band of guerrillas and came back.

Monday, June 13th.   Raid toward Cave Spring

Our whole regt. with 2 companies of cavalry went out with the forage train. We went in a S.W. direction, toward Cave Spring. The day was wet and very muddy. The cavalry drove the rebels before them. We marched about 11 miles. Loaded the wagons within 3 miles of Cave Spring, mostly with wheat. We also took 85 head of beef cattle, 30 horses and mules, 15 sheep, 1 hhd [hogshead] of molasses, several hams. We also confiscated for our private use chickens, turkeys, geese, anything and everything that could be eaten. For my part I visited the mulberry and cherry trees, then the houses. In one I found a real no. 1 huckleberry pie. I filled my harbersack [haversack] with cornbread, my handkerchief with peas and lettuce. We got back about dark, having marched 22 miles through mud and water. We brought along 5 or 6 able-bodied negroes.

Tuesday, June 14th.

On getting up this morning I was so stiff and sore I could hardly navigate. Got breakfast and went back to bed again. At 9 o'clock I was awakened to go on guard. Several farmers came in today and took the oath. A great many deserters from the rebel army are in town. It seems to me that they ought not to have so much liberty. Some of them may be spies.

Wednesday, June 15th.   Rome, Ga.

The 57th Ills. went out with another forage train. Robt. Price came back to the company today. He left home 3 weeks ago. He saw my wife & Mother just before leaving; says they were well. I saw a N.Y. Herald that came by mail. The news from Grant was very encouraging. Wrote a letter to Mother.

Thursday, June 16th.

The 57th returned late last night, bringing in the usual quantity of forage. The cavalry which accompanied them were fired upon; 1 man wounded. They lost one supposed to be taken and shot by guerrillas. The 57th went in the direction of Coosaville, west of here. They brought 1 prisoner. Went to church this afternoon; heard the native preacher lecture on the 91st Psalm.

Friday, June 17th.   Rome, Ga.

Another small foraging party was sent out today. Detailed for guard but at inspection I was excused as my arms and accouterments were the cleanest. Flattering, isn't it; never happened to me before. Spent the day in reading a book I borrowed from a druggist downtown. It was an account of Capt. McClintock's expedition in search of Sir John Franklin.

Saturday, June 18th.

The foraging party brought in 4 prisoners. A barn belonging to the Presbyterian minister was burned last night. It is reported that there has been 2 days heavy fighting near Atlanta. We had a mail today but nothing for me. Col. [Moses M.] Bane has resigned and expects to leave for home in a few days.

Sunday, June 19th.

Attended church in forenoon. In afternoon our brigade (2nd) [3rd] were assembled to hear the farewell address of Gen. Bane.[26] Gen. Vandever now commands [the] brigade. Gen. Bane starts for home to-morrow.

Monday, June 20th.   Rome, Ga.

On Guard today. It has rained nearly every day for 2 weeks. A mail came in today; brought some papers but [no?] letters. I am quite anxious to hear from wife and "little one," but I trust that God will watch over them and give them strength to bear the trials of life. We still continue to go swimming every day. Lieut. [Cornelius F.] Kitchen (Co. "I") started for Pulaski, Tenn., with a lot of Contrabands. Also, a detail of men have gone to Chattanooga with a lot of prisoners. [Pvt. Henry C.] Morton of our Co. is one of the guards.

Wednesday [Tuesday], June 21st.   Rome, Ga.

Relieved from guard about 8 o'clock. Our Chaplain (Bigger) has just arrived from the front. He reports that everything goes on well. On last Sunday there was heavy fighting. How I pity the poor fellows, fighting all day and out on skirmish line at night. Truly, we have cause to be thankful that we are at Rome, where everything seems so peaceable.

The long-expected mail has arrived, bringing me a letter from Louisa. I had just finished reading it when the order came: "Co. 'C' fall in *double quick*" (time 9 o'clock at night). We were marched outside of the picket line and lay down for the night. Our Cavalry went still further. I suppose a few guerrillas have kicked up the rumpus.

Thursday [Wednesday], June 22nd.

Awoke this morning before the rest. Found a garden; picked a handkerchief full of green peas. Shortly after sunrise, the Cavalry came back; said they had been 7 miles out but saw no Rebs. So we marched back to town. Today 10 or 12 Rebs rode up to a house south of the Etowah and ordered the woman to leave as they were going to plant a battery to shell the ~~Rebs~~ Yanks out of Rome. Reports were brought in that the Rebs were firing on our pickets.

3 companies started out. A few volleys were fired; the rebs fled.[27] If we had a few more cavalry we could capture those fellows. Heavy cannonade heard in the direction of Marietta. Picked up a book called "Messiah Kingdom," which I am reading.

[Thursday,] June 23. Rome, Ga.

On Guard. 4 men on ~~guard~~ picket across the Etowah were captured by guerrillas. They belonged to Co. "B" of our Regt. 3 or 4 companies went out, but could find nothing.[28] The 1st Ala. Cavalry (Loyal) came in today. I'm in hopes we will capture a few of those prowlers now. We moved our qrs. farther up the street. Our old quarters are taken for a hospital. It is said that this place is to be made a general hospital for the Army at the front. By papers we learn that Grant has captured Petersburg and has R.R. communication from the south, with Richmond cut off.

Friday, June 24th. Rome, Ga.

Jayhawked a lot of books, which will keep me in reading for some time. I found them in a box in a lawyer's office. One book, the "Prince of the House of David," is quite interesting. It is said that the guards (of whom Pvt. Morton was one) who took [the] prisoners to Chattanooga are expected in tomorrow. Rec. a letter from Louisa.

Saturday, June 25th.

On guard today. It has stopped raining and is hot, very hot. No news of importance, but lots of rumors. Nothing that can be relied on.

Sunday, June 26th.

This morning the rebs made another attempt to capture a picket post of Co. "B," but they were badly fooled. Co. "B" captured 3 and killed & wounded 6, so they say.[29] Afternoon I went to church; heard Chaplain Collins (57th Ills.) give a lecture on the social condition of the South. The negroes think Chaplain almost a saint. After dark, 3 companies went across the Etowah and disappeared in the darkness. I suppose they have heard something about guerrillas. Henry Morton came back today.

Monday, June 27th. Rome, Ga.

Got up this morning but saw nothing of the rebs except one who came in and gave himself up. Says he was conscripted and sent to the rebel Army at Marietta. He made his escape there; got within 10 miles of us when he was again captured, but made his escape at Cave Spring. Shortly after sunrise we marched back to town. Heavy cannonading heard all day at the front. 500 sick & wounded were brought in on the R.R. today

Rome. Monday, June 27th, 1864
Dear Louisa,

I received your letter of June 14th on last Friday. I am so glad to
hear that you & baby are yet well. I also received the drawing of her
hand; what a little one it is.

So death is not found alone upon the battlefield. It has been
up there & has taken another of my uncles. Luther received a letter
informing him of his father's death the same mail I rec. yours. Of
course he feels bad & I hope it may be the means of bringing him to
consider his ways, but I'm afraid not. Aunt Ruth will have a hard time
with no one at home, but still I see hundreds of worse cases every day.

Family after family come in every day; women with 4 or 5
little children, begging for something to eat. Their husbands, some
have been conscripted, & they forced to leave home for the want
of something to eat. Some have been rich planters' wives. Only last
week, the guerrillas came within 5 miles of Rome. Stopped at a house
& threatened to hang the old man if he would not tell them where
the Yankee Pickets were. They took the old man off with them. The
woman and children started for our lines. As soon as we heard of it,
we went out, but could find nothing of them. On our way back we
overtook the woman & children. How she did beg of us to know if
they killed her old man, & still these things happen every day. No
wonder one's heart becomes hardened in the Army.

Yesterday Co. B had a skirmish & captured 3 Rebs. We were out
all last night. 1 came in & gave himself up. Henry Morton came to the
Co. yesterday. It was all humbug about the Rebels capturing 6 trains.

You must write often, my dear wife. Nothing I like so well as
to hear of loved ones at home. I wrote to Mr. Wagy [*sp.?*] about my
wheat. I have not yet received an answer. I must close. Kiss little baby
for me & remember that God will watch over & protect us.

Yours &c.
Lewis F. Roe

Tuesday, June 28th.

On guard again. We moved out of town today to make room for
the sick and wounded. Are in the east part in our dog-houses.

Wednesday, June 29th.   Rome, Ga.

Hard at work all day putting up board shanties. Very hot and sultry. The wounded from the front continue to come every day. They look very bad; covered with rags and dirt.

Thursday, June 30th.

Today is our regular muster, which occurs every two months. We have no company cooks now. Ed and I cook for ourselves.

Friday, July 1st.

Detailed to go out with a foraging expedition. Started about 5 A.M. Crossed the Oostanaula; marched about 15 miles to near Coosaville on [the] Coosa River. Drove a few rebs ahead of us for several miles, then they disappeared. Loaded our teams with corn & returned. The hottest day I ever felt.

Saturday, July 2nd.

On Guard. My post is over the Prisoners. In their talk they admit that their cause is hopeless and if Atlanta is captured, they are ready to give up. We have just heard that Lincoln has been renominated. The Army is almost a unit for them [him?].

Sunday, July 3rd.

After being relieved from guard, went to hear our Chaplain (Bigger) preach and in the afternoon a chaplain who came up from the front with the sick & wounded. Another foraging party went out today. Quite a no. of citizens can be seen on the streets every day now. When we came here there were none. Whether they are rebel deserters, spies, or refugees, I cannot tell. A mail today. Rec. a paper from home.

Monday, July 4th.

The nation's 87th birthday came in hot, very hot and sultry. A grand review of our whole Brigade by Gen. Vandever. No salutes were fired. We had on review two 64 pounders that we captured when we took the place.[30] This parading is not much fun for us [in] this hot weather, but then it is the 4th of July.

Tuesday, July 5th, 1864.   Rome, Ga.

On Guard again today. Guard duty seems to come quite often now. We have great news from Sherman. It is reported that he has compelled the rebels to abandon Kennasaw Mountain, driven them across the Chattahoochie River and captured 5,000 prisoners.

Wednesday, July 6th.

An expedition started today toward Cave Spring, a town 5 or 6 miles southwest of here.[31] Companies "F" & "I" of our Regt. (50) went along. They will probably have a fight with guerrillas as they are getting quite numerous around here lately. 6 rebel soldiers mounted came in and gave themselves up today.

Thursday, July 7th.

The expedition that went out yesterday has returned. They went as far as Cave Spring and as I ~~suspected~~ supposed had a skirmish with the Johnnies, killing 4 and capturing 5.[32]

[Friday, July 8th,] 1864.   Rome, Ga.

The lst Ala. Cavalry (Loyal) had a man taken by the rebs, who shot him at a house near Cave Spring. In return, the Cavalry shot a rebel prisoner and burnt his house. Such is war. The expedition brought back 80 negroes, 100 head of cattle, 30 horses. Loaded their train with corn & wheat; captured 5 prisoners, and 25 conscripts came in and gave themselves up. Our town is nearly full of deserters. I suppose a train load will be sent north soon.

Friday [Saturday], July 9th.

Four more deserters came in today. Another foraging party went out. Luther Scarborough and I went blackberrying. I gathered a pailfull. We expect to live on blackberry dumplings for awhile. Brother Edward has been detailed to take charge of a gang of negroes engaged in chopping wood. I tell him if he will pay attention and make the nigs work, he can secure a position as overseer after the war.

Sunday, July 10, 1864.   Rome, Ga.

Chaplain Bigger of our regiment (50th) preached in forenoon. In afternoon Chaplain Collins (57th) gave his 2nd lecture on the social condition of the South. The church was crowded. Several rebel deserters were there. Ed received a letter from Mother.

Monday, July 11.

On Guard. The 7th Ill. Infty. came in today. They were encamped across the Etowah River. Lieut. Kitchen arrived from the north; he says that it is false about so many trains being captured by the rebs. I am very anxious to hear from home. It has been several weeks since I rec. a letter.

Tuesday, July 12.

Our Company was divided into messes of about 10 each. Another train load of sick and wounded came up from the front. They say that the main part of the rebel army is across the Chattahoochie. Ed is still in charge of the negroes.

Wednesday, July 13, 1864.   Rome, Ga.

Ten prisoners were brought in by the 1st Ala. Cavalry (Loyal), one of them a colonel, another a conscripting officer. The town seems to be about full of rebel deserters. They are not under guard and can go about the city where they please. Rec. a letter from Warren. He was at Memphis & was well satisfied.

Thursday, July 14.

On guard. A general inspection took place at 2 o'clock today. Another train load of sick & wounded came in from the front. Rec. a letter from Louisa; also one from Father Smith.

Friday, July 15.

All of our prisoners of war and deserters were sent north today. Luther Scarborough was on the detail of guards. He will They will go as far as Chattanooga. The weather is very hot. I go in swimming in the Oostanaula almost every day.

Saturday, July 16, 1864.   Rome, Ga.

Done nothing all day but lounge around. Got hold of a book, Bayard Taylor's Travels in China & Japan. Quite interesting. Washed my shirts in [the] afternoon.

Sunday, July 17.

Attended church both forenoon and afternoon. Our Union chapel has been taken for a hospital. We have but one church for citizen and soldier. A citizen preaches in forenoon, our chaplain in afternoon. We hear rumors from the front every day. One is that Atlanta is captured. Rec. two letters, both from Louisa. Luther Scarborough came back today.

Monday, July 18th.

On Guard today. Rumors are still afloat that we have captured Atlanta. We can hear nothing definite.

Tuesday, July 19th, 1864.   Rome, Ga.

Drill commenced today. We drill one hour each day. The report now is that our brigade goes to the front, that Rome will be garrisoned by convalescents. The sick and wounded are doing well. They are kept neat and clean, being dressed in shirt, drawers, and long gown, sent by the Ladies' Aid societies of the north. But the poor fellows can't get anything nice to eat. I believe the doctors, hospital stewards, and attendants appropriate all the goodies.

Wednesday, July 20th.

Several refugees came in today from Van Wert, about 30 miles west [south] of here. The poor fellows were glad to get here; some of them fairly cried for joy. They say the guerrillas are plundering everybody. The 1st Ala. Cavalry rec. several recruits.

Thursday, July 21st.

The railroad between here & Kingston was torn up last night. A train was thrown from the track, but no one injured. A party of the 57th Ills. have gone in that direction. Our foraging party was fired into today. Well, more scouting expeditions will be the result.

Friday, July 22nd, 1864.   Rome, Ga.

On Guard again. The train which was wrecked night before last came in today. It is reported that Atlanta is ours. I can tell by the appearance of things that something unusual is happening at Atlanta.

Saturday, July 23rd.

A dispatch just from Atlanta says that Gen. [James B.] McPherson is killed. He was thought to be one of the best generals in Sherman's army. Who now will conduct the great flanking movements? His command was the 16th [&] 17th Corps. Our flags have been half-mast all day.[33]

Sunday, July 24.

Chaplain Bigger preached this afternoon. Rec. a letter from Bro. Charlie Read.

> Rome Ga. July 24th, 1864
> Dear Louisa,
>
> Sunday again & again I am seated at the same mess table writing this to you. Another week has passed since I wrote, & during that week great events have taken place. The rebellion is that much nearer to a close. Atlanta, the stronghold of the rebellion in the southwest, has been taken. The rebels have been driven from [the] mountains & hills. Hereafter our army can meet the enemy in the open field. We can hear of no particulars.
>
> There is no prospect of our leaving Rome. I expect we will remain here all summer. We are getting along first rate. Duty not very hard & plenty to eat. Today for dinner we had warm bread, stewed peaches, an apple cobbler, apple sauce, new potatoes, & fried bacon. We have apples, peaches & blackberries every day. Peaches are just beginning to ripen. Our foraging parties bring in chickens, geese &c.
>
> I went to church this forenoon. Rev. Mr. Kaufman, native of Rome, preached. He is not exactly secesh but nearly so. He goes about as far as he dares, for fear of an arrest. You must write often, my dear wife. Do you always have good health & does our little daughter keep well &c &c? Well, well, perhaps the time may come when I will have no need of asking so many questions. When I can see for myself.

I send you a leaf of the magnolia flower. When in bloom, it is nearly twice as large & perfectly white. I am expecting a letter every day from you. Kiss little baby for me & remember to write often.

Yours &c.
Lewis F. Roe

Monday, July 25.

On Guard again. 3 guerrillas were brought in. They were captured by the lst Ala. Cavalry (Loyal). There are several deserters & refugees in town. A train load will be sent north in a few days, I suppose.

Tuesday, July 26, 1864.   Rome, Ga.

Lieut. Kitchen, Co. "I," has resigned on account of ill health. He starts for home tomorrow. The nights have been quite cool for a week. Sleep with a blanket over us every night.

Wednesday, July 27.

We have just heard of a hard fought battle near Atlanta in which our Corps (16th) was ~~heavally~~ engaged. The rebels attacked our Army on the left of the lines east of Atlanta, but were driven back with heavy loss. The Johnnies must be getting desperate.[34]

Thursday, July 28.

A large train load [of] wounded from the front (Atlanta) came in today. Every building has been occupied as a hospital. 2 Rebel prisoners made their escape last night.

Friday, July 29.

Our foraging party had a skirmish with the guerrillas today. We lost 1 killed and one taken prisoner. We killed one & captured 6, one of whom was wounded.[35]

[Saturday,] July 30, 1864.   Rome, Ga.

We heard there would be battalion drill this afternoon, so several of us went down to the river (Etowah) to swim so as to escape the drill. But I wish I had stayed in camp and drilled, as while down to the river, I run a long splinter under my thumb nail, which pains me considerable. A rumor is in camp that we will be paid off in a few days.

[Sunday,] July 31.

Attended church this forenoon. In the afternoon there was a very heavy rain; almost washed us off of our hillside. Report says the Paymaster came in last night.

Monday, August 1st.

The 44th U.S. Colored Regt. moved on this side of the Oostanaula today. This is the 1st Black Regt. I ever saw together.[36] Rec. a letter from Bro. Warren, also one from Louisa.

Tuesday, August 2nd.

The Paymaster has come and [the] Co. Clerks are busy making out their payrolls. Rec. a letter from home containing a proclamation from President Jackson [sic] in regard to disunion.

Wednesday, August 3, 1864.   Rome, Ga.

I did not sign the payrolls with the Co. today. In my case there is a mistake. On the muster rolls of the Co. I am marked as a recruit, with only a recruit's bounty instead of a veteran's. My discharge from the Regular Army is gone. I gave it to the recruiting officer at Quincy. He said I would get it when I rec. my 1st installment of bounty at Springfield, Ills. At Springfield they told me they knew nothing of it. I then wrote to the Adjutant Gen. of Ills. at Springfield to search the pigeon holes of his desk for the lost discharge and to rectify my enlistment papers. I don't expect to see my discharge again, but I'll bother the authorities all I can.

Thursday, August 4th.

This is the day appointed by the Pres. as a day of fasting and prayer. I am on Guard. Services were held in the church. Chaplain Bigger spoke, also a Mr. Stewart, one of the few who have always remained loyal. Gov. Stone of Iowa was here a few days ago to look after Iowa wounded soldiers.

Friday, August 5th, 1864.   Rome, Ga.

Our mess being without a cook, I volunteered my services. My lost discharge came tonight from Springfield with a new Descriptive Roll, so that puts me all right again on the money question. But I can't draw any pay this time as the pay rolls have gone to the Paymaster. Well, I am better satisfied now that I have my old discharge.

Saturday, August 6.

We have just rec. the news of the mine explosion at Petersburg. A wet, rainy day. Ed & I will have to sleep in a wet bed tonight as our shanty leaks badly. Well, we're used to it.

["A few leaves are here lost"—Lewis Roe's note]

Sunday, August 14.

Did not attend church today. Rained very hard in [the] afternoon. Maj. [William] Hanna, commanding Regt., has gone to ~~Huntsville Ala~~. Report is that Rebel Gen. Wheeler has torn up the R.R. between here and Chattanooga. Anyhow, we have no mail from the north today.

Monday, August 15.   Rome, Ga.

There is some excitement in Camp. It is said that the rebels have captured Adairsville, a station on the R.R. between here and Chattanooga. The 39th Iowa & 57th Ills. of our Brigade left for the scene of action. The 1st Ala. (Loyal) returned from a scout. They went down the Coosa to Cedartown, bringing back 15 or 20 prisoners. Our mail came in today, bringing a letter from Louisa.

Tuesday, August 16.

Have heard nothing further from the raid, although there is a report that the R.R. was torn up near Resaca.

Wednesday, August 17.

Two flags of truce came in today. I could not learn their object. A deserter told me there was a camp of 700 rebels about 8 miles west. If so, I expect we will have lively picket firing for some time.

Thursday, August 18.

Have heard nothing from the 39 Ia. & 57 Ills. But the 44 U.S. Col. went after the rebel camp I spoke of yesterday; drove them back. In their retreat, they met our Cavalry, when they scattered in all directions. An order for Luther Roe's discharge came today.[37]

Friday, August 19, 1864.   Rome, Ga.

Pickets firing most of the day. The Rebs drove in a party of the 7th Ills., capturing 2 or 3 of our men. I understand they captured a Lieut. of the 7th and shot him in retaliation for one of their no. shot last night.[38]

Saturday, August 20.

On Guard today. This afternoon 12 of us Guards were detailed to move a family from town out in the country. They had to give up their house for a hospital.

Sunday, August 21.

6 Companies of the 50th [Ills.] Regt., Co. "C" being one of them, were sent on an expedition after guerrillas. We crossed the Etowah and were there joined by 6 companies of the 7th Ills. We marched up the river in an easterly direction 10 miles. Saw no rebels.

Monday, August 22.

Started back toward Rome about 9 A.M. Marched sometimes on one road, then on another. In about 16 miles, we reached Rome. I suffered severely on this trip, was quite unwell. Have a slight fever.

Tuesday, August 23.   Rome, Ga.

Lay abed most of the day. Yesterday's trip was rather hard on me. Have heard nothing from the 57th Ills. and 39th Iowa, which left here on the 15th. Report says they are guarding trains on the Chattanooga and Atlanta R.R. A party was sent out after peaches for the Regt. Edward was one of the no. Returned at night with a wagonload. Rec. a letter from L[ouisa].

Wednesday, August 24.

On Guard. My post is in the large rolling mill the rebel Gov. erected here at the commencement of the war.

Thursday, August 25.

A large mail came in today. Luther S., Luther Roe, Edward & I received our share. I am about over my spell of sickness, brought on by exposure in the march the other day. It rained all day. I slept in my wet clothes.

Friday, August 26.

Two of the 7th Ills. while beyond the picket lines were gobbled up by guerrillas. Why will our boys run the pickets for the sake of a few peaches, chickens &c.? There is danger of being shot by rebs & our pickets. Risk too great.

Saturday, August 27.   Rome, Ga.

I understand a train was thrown from the track and about 50 rods of track torn up. 2 soldiers shot, but the guerrillas were driven off. The rebels seem to be making every effort to destroy the R.R. in Sherman's rear.

Sunday, August 28.

Edward & the rest of the non-vets are quite anxious to know when they can go home. Their time was out some time ago. Luther Roe has gone to Chattanooga to pay over his bounty. I suppose he will rec[eive] his discharge when he returns.

[*No entry for Monday, August 29*]

[Tuesday,] August 30.

We have just heard of a raid on Memphis by the Reb Forrest. I see it stated that the 137 Ills. lost 11 killed, 13 wounded, 75 missing. I am afraid that Bro. Warren is killed or a prisoner. He belonged to Co. "B" of that Regt.[39] A rumor has it that Atlanta has been captured, but I cannot trace it to any authentic source.

Wednesday, August 31.   Rome, Ga.

A lot of sick and wounded started for the north. We are anxiously waiting for the news of the Chicago Rep[ublican] Convention. There are but few McClellan men in the Army. I am quite anxious to know whether Warren came off safe in the attack on Memphis by the Rebs.

Thursday, September 1st.

Well, the 1st of Sept. finds us still at Rome. We can count ourselves fortunate the past summer here, almost in sound of cannon around Atlanta and still never engaged in battle, and still many of the boys would like to be at the front. On Guard again. My post is over the captured cotton.

Friday, September 2nd.

Good news. Good news. Today while on drill a dispatch was read to us that Atlanta was captured. Our troops entered it at 4 o'clock this morning. We have had no mail from the north for 2 or 3 days. I suppose the Johnnies have again torn up the R.R.

Saturday, September 3rd.   Rome, Ga.

Atlanta is ours. Captured with lots of prisoners, artillery &c. Well, what now will be done; are we to still hold on to old Rome?

Sunday, September 4th.

Yes, Atlanta is ours. We also hear that Ft. Morgan, Mobile Bay, has been taken. Rec. a mail from the North. In a letter from Bro. [at] home I learn that Bro. Warren came out of the Memphis fight all right. A rebel Captain and 15 deserters came in and enlisted in the 1st Ala. Cavalry (Loyal).

[No entry for Monday, September 5]

Tuesday, September 6.

Detailed to go to Chattanooga as guard over some Rebel prisoners, but just before we went aboard the cars, the order was countermanded.

Wednesday, September 7th.   Rome, Ga.

Our scouts had quite a skirmish with the guerrillas about 10 miles from here, killing 2 [and] wounding 5. One of our scouts was killed and 2 wounded. Our Regt. intends to send soon for the Henry repeating rifle, a very nice gun, cost 48 dollars.[40] I hardly know whether to send for one or not. If the Regt. has them, I would like one.

Thursday, September 8.

Still no news from the North. They say that Rebel Gen. Wheeler has done a great deal of damage to the R.R. Luther S. and I went down to the Etowah; got a skiff & spent the forenoon in rowing.

Friday, September 9.

On fatigue. I heard the Adjt. of the Post say that he thought we would stay here all winter. Hope we will.

FIGURE 18. Rome, Ga., in 1864, view looking ENE from south side of the Etowah River. Photo courtesy of the Georgia Archives, Vanishing Georgia Collection, image flo 017b.

Saturday, September 10.

On Guard. Mail came in. Rec. a letter & paper from L[ouisa] and a letter from Warren. I am glad to know he is safe.

Sunday, September 11.

We have no more meetings as the churches are used as hospitals. It is reported that the hospitals are to be removed from here.

Monday, September 12.

The Non-Vets time expires tomorrow. All of our rebel prisoners and deserters were sent north yesterday.

Tuesday, September 13.   Rome, Ga.

The non-vets have not started home yet, although they are relieved from duty. The 44 U.S. Infty. (Colored) left for Dalton. I rec. Louisa and our baby's picture today.

Wednesday, September 14.

On Guard. 4 rebel deserters and 2 prisoners came in today. The deserters were in the last fight below Atlanta. The Paymaster, Hospital Dept., came in today.

Thursday, September 15.

This morning a large foraging party went across the Etowah. They loaded with corn about 5 miles out. Just as the last wagon was being loaded, the rebs charged on the train. Our boys formed behind the fence, gave them a couple of volleys, and they fell back. The wagons were placed in advance and hurried into Rome. The Rebs followed to within 2 miles. They had 2 pieces of artillery. As soon as we heard of it, the alarm was sounded. The 57th Ill. [and] 39th Iowa, which only came home from the Wheeler scout yesterday, and 7th Ills. started across the Etowah. Our Regt. remained under arms, also about 1000 convalescents were armed, but the rebs were driven back with the loss so far as known of 2 ~~wou~~ killed, 3 wounded, 5 taken prisoners. Our loss was only 1 wounded.[41] Rec. a letter from L[ouisa].

Friday, September 16.

The excitement has died out. Things move on in the usual way. The Rebs have vanished. We have been at work all day, building shanties. Signs indicate that we are to stay all winter. The boys say that building barracks is a sure sign of leaving. We left Decatur Junction & Athens, Ala., just as we finished our shanties. The non-vets have not gone yet. They are waiting orders.

Saturday, September 17.   Rome, Ga.

On Guard. No news of importance. The 7th [Ill.] Inft. went out to strengthen the pickets. Moved in our new quarters today. So I suppose we will leave soon, as usual.

Sunday, September 18.

I believe I have got hold of the truth about our late scare. About 800 rebels from [Gen. John B.] Hood's Army were sent to Cave Springs (10 miles S.W. of here) to conscript persons and arrest deserters. They heard that we were evacuating Rome and started to take quiet possession, but running across our forage trail, concluded that "Prudence was the better part of valor" and retreated. 6 companies, "C" included, went over the Etowah to reinforce the pickets tonight.

Monday, September 19.

The sick and wounded are being paid today. Many will be discharged for disability.

Tuesday, September 20.

A mail in today. Luther Roe rec. his discharge today. Received a letter from Mother. L[uther] Roe started for home.

Wednesday, September 21.   Rome, Ga.

All quiet on the Etowah. Not a shot has been fired by the pickets for some time. Have the guerrillas left our vicinity or are they planning some new mischief? Rec. a letter from Louisa, also one from Frank Read. 8 deserters came in today from the Rebels.

Thursday, September 22.

On Guard today. News of a victory gained by Gen. Sheridan over [Lt. Gen. Jubal A.] Early in the Shenandoah Valley, Va. The good cause seems [to be] marching on.

Friday, September 23.

Some of the boys have organized a Negro Minstrels show. They are to make their first appearance tonight.

Saturday, September 24.

It has been quite wet and rainy for several days. I slept quite cold under one blanket. 6 or 8 more deserters came in yesterday and today.

Sunday, September 25.   Rome, Ga.

News of another victory by Sheridan. He seems to have got the Johnnies on the jump. The thing is winding up. I prophesy that by the next 4th of July the war will be over.

Monday, September 26.

Four companies of our Regt. went over the river to cut and haul wood. I suppose those of us who remain will have more duty to do until they return.

Tuesday, September 27.

I was surprised this morning to find that our whole Division (4th div. 15th A.C.) had arrived from the front.[42] They came by R.R. One Division of 4th Corps (Newton's) have gone north toward Chattanooga. It is reported that Forrest, Wheeler, & Roddey have joined forces, intending to cut our "Grub line," which may account for the movement of troops north. "Something is in the wind."

Wednesday, September 28.

All sorts of rumors; will not write them down as I can trace none of them to a reliable source.

Thursday, September 29.   Rome, Ga.

No mail has come in for a day or two, so we must conclude that the R.R. has been tapped. The Non-Vets started for home today. They march to Kingston, thence by R.R.

Friday, September 30.

Gen. Van Derveer [Brig. Gen. William Vandever] has been relieved from command of our Div. (4th) and [Brig.] Gen. [John M.] Corse takes his place.[43] Wheeler, Roddey, [and] Forrest must be causing considerable trouble, as more troops arrived from the front.

FIGURE 19. Bvt. Maj. Gen. John M. Corse. Photo courtesy of Iowa State Historical Society.

Saturday, October 1st.

I like the change in commanders. Rebel deserters are now placed under guard. None are allowed to come inside our lines unless they are willing to go north. No one is allowed to pass out.

Sunday, October 2nd.

The 9th Ill. Mounted Infty. came in this morning, bringing in a lot of prisoners. Drill has been ordered again.

Monday, October 3rd.

No drill today. Too wet and rainy. We have had no mail for some time. It is reported that the Rebs have torn up our R.R. in the rear.

Tuesday, October 4th.   Allatoona Pass

On guard today but was relieved at noon and ordered to prepare 3 days' rations in harver-sack [haversack]. On returning to camp we found all sorts of rumors afloat. From the best we can learn, it seems that the rebel Army has succeeded in escaping from Sherman and is moving north. There is trouble in the air.

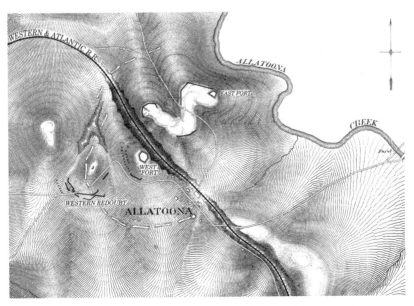

Figure 20. Allatoona Pass and vicinity at the time of the Confederate attack, October 5, 1864. U.S. National Archives, RG 77, CWMF N-103–1.

Wednesday, October 5th.   Allatoona Pass

A terrible battle has been fought and thank God we are the
victors. A portion of our brigade, consisting of the 12th, 7th, 50th Ills.,
2 companies of 57 Ill. and 39 Iowa were loaded *on* and *in* a R.R. train
last night at 8 o'clock and ran with lighting speed to Kingston (20 miles),
the junction with the main line running from Chattanooga to Atlanta.
Turning south, we ran through Cartersville, stopping at Allatoona,
30 miles south of Kingston. We were stationed on a side hill, facing
south on the east side of the R.R. cut.

At about 3 A.M. the firing along the picket lines became quite
severe. Soon the batteries opened and the battle was on. Our line was
withdrawn from the side of the hill to the crest. At about 8 o'clock there
was a lull in the attack. A flag of truce was seen approaching. They
came to demand a surrender. Gen. Corse, commanding our forces,
refused and the fight was on. We were surrounded. About this time
we were ordered into the earthworks on the west side of the pass. We
moved down the hill, crossed the R.R. and up the hill on the west side
under a heavy musket firing. The rebels made repeated charges, but
were finally repulsed [at] 9 o'clock P.M. with great loss. After it was
over, the nearest dead rebel lay 30 ft. from our works.

FIGURE 21. The Allatoona Pass, looking north. George Barnard photograph.
    U.S. National Archives, image 165-SC-29.

FIGURE 22. Fort at Allatoona Pass, west side. George Barnard photograph.
U.S. National Archives, image 165-SC-28.

Our Co. "C" lost in killed James Spicer, Terrill Proctor and David
Robbins. Quite a number were wounded, some of whom died afterwards. I have been unable to find the total loss of the Regiment. The
remainder of the day and night was spent in picking up the dead and
wounded of our men and rebels. I was wounded in [the] left shoulder
and went on train of wounded back to Rome. Numbers of the worst
wounded were left at Cartersville.[44]

[*No entries for October 6 through October 8*]

Sunday October 9th.   Rome, Ga.

Rome seems almost like home. I lay abed most of the day. The
remainder of our wounded were brought in. There are reports that
the rebels are advancing on this Place. It is said that Hood's whole
army is this side of the Chattahoochie River; that they will make
desperate efforts to cut the Railroad & thus compel Sherman to
evacuate Atlanta.[45]

Rome Ga. Oct. 9th, 1864
Dear Louisa

I still live & I almost consider it a miracle that I am still alive & well. A great battle has been fought & thank God we are the victors. There were not large numbers engaged on either side, yet all say that it was the hardest-fought battle of the campaign. I have passed through it with only a scratch on my left shoulder, the bullet cutting through my clothes & just grazing my shoulder, making only a very slight wound.

On the afternoon of the 4th, our brigade, consisting of 8 companies of [the] 50th Ills., 9 of the 7th Ills., the 12th Ills., 8 companies [of the] 39th Iowa & 2 of the 57th Ills., altogether amounting to about 1,000 men, were ordered to be ready in a moment's notice with 3 days' rations. We got aboard of the cars & started about 8 o'clock at night. We believed there was some disturbance along the R.R., but we didn't know where. I was detailed as one of the color guard. We whizzed along at lightning speed through Kingston. Turning south, we passed through Cartersville & stopped about 12 o'clock at night at Allatoona, 30 miles south of Kingston. We were told that the rebs had torn up the R.R. between that place and Kennesaw, 12 miles from there. We stacked arms & lay down, but before 5 minutes, the Pickets commenced firing on every side. We were kept awake the whole night in this way & occasionally a bullet would whistle uncomfortably us [sic]. There were two earthwork forts, one on each side of the Railroad. By sunrise on the morning of the 5th, we were ordered up in the one on the left hand side [i.e., east] of the R.R. The rebels planted a battery within 1/2 a mile of our fort & commenced shelling.

The shells flew thick & fast, but only wounding 2 of our Regt. About 10 o'clock we were ordered over to the works on the right of the R.R. Half of our regt. with the colors found room on the inside; the remainder took shelter in the ditches just outside of the fort. I went in with the colors, but afterward jumped over the works in the ditch. 2 brigades of rebels undertook to charge the fort. The bullets flew like hail. The rebs got within 100 yds., but had to retreat. Again they charged, & again fell back. Once again they charged. Our men fell on every side. I was standing up in the ditch taking aim when a ball passing through my clothes just breaking the skin, leaving a mark about 3 inches in length & 1 in width on my left shoulder. I am only a little stiff in my shoulder.

After I was struck, I jumped back inside of the fort & went to loading for others. After a while, I took my place at the works & fired as fast as I could load. The 3rd time the rebs charged, they came within 30 yds. of the fort, but our fire was too hot for them. They threw away their arms & scattered in every direction. The battle was over & our "flag was still there." We captured over 300 prisoners, exclusive of wounded, & I think their loss in killed & wounded will amount to at least 1,000. Ours will be 6 or 700. We had only about 1,500 men, while prisoners say that their force amounted [to] between 6,000 & 8,000. It was French's Division of Stewart's Corps that we were engaged with. Gen. Corse was wounded. The highest in rank after the fight was over was a captain.

We lost very heavy. Our loss in the regt. is 14 killed, 87 wounded. The no. engaged was 260. Total loss in the regt. 101. The loss in the company was 3 killed, 11 wounded; total killed & wounded 14. No. engaged of our company, 36. Those killed were James Spicer, Terrill Proctor, & David Robbins. The wounded were Lieut. [Samuel W.] Starrett, Lieut. [Charles M.] Tarr, Jacob Seiter, Slater Lewis, Anson [sic; Ansel] Lewis, William Carter, Gideon Hadley, James Kelly, John Jenner, Raymond Martin, and Jerry [Jeremiah] Browning.

We buried the dead there & brought the wounded back to Rome. I do not know when I can get this letter through, as we never get any more mail and I suppose the mail does not go from here there [sic]. I expect you will hear all sorts of rumors concerning our fight. We left 3 regts. to garrison Allatoona & came back to Rome last Saturday. There may be a good deal of fighting along the R.R. this winter, but you know that's what I enlisted for.

Yours ever,
Lewis F. Roe

Monday, October 10th.

We have very cold nights now, almost cold enough for frost. About 10 o'clock we were ordered out in line as it was said that the rebs were advancing. We stacked arms but were not again called on, but I expect we will be before morning. The 23rd Army Corps is said to be within a few miles of here. Details have been at work, throwing up breastworks in town all day & piercing the brick houses for musketry.

Tuesday, October 11th.   Rome, Ga.

Awakened this morning about 3 o'clock with orders to be ready to fall in by daylight. We formed into line at that time; stacked arms, broke ranks, with orders to be ready at a moment's notice. We all expected a battle before night, as it is well known that nearly the whole of the rebel Army of the southwest is encamped near here. I hate to go into a fight; the thoughts of my wife & child make a coward of me, but I know that my life is in God's hands & that "He doeth all things well." I try to be content.

Wednesday, October 15th [12th]

We went foraging this morning about 14 miles [*torn*] Calhoun road northeast of here. Loaded our wagons with corn but I loaded my harversack with [*torn*] & sweet potatoes. Besides, I had all [*torn*] & persimmons I wanted to eat. [*torn*]alry had quite a skirmish. They [*torn*] Rebels a mile or two. Sherman [*torn*] all of his army [*torn; several lines missing*]

Thursday, October 13th.

Awakened this morning about 3 o'clock with orders to be up & ready to march by 1/2 past 4 with 2 days' rations. Our Brigade started at the appointed time; crossed the Etowah & took the road toward Cave Springs. When out about 3 miles we commenced skirmishing with the rebs. They had 2 pieces of artillery & so did we. They would plant their battery on every hill & shell us until we got close up to them or would be silenced by our guns. We kept up a constant skirmish fire; they falling back & we advancing in this way. We drove them near 8 miles. It being near sundown, we returned to Rome. It was a "*forced reconnaissance*" to find out the strength of the enemy in that direction.

We only lost 10 or 12 wounded in our brigade. Our Regt. lost none. It was a hard day's work for us. We marched in line of battle over 5 miles over hills, through brush, over f[*torn*]. The 23rd [Army] Corps had a little fight too, across the Oostanaula, capturing 2 pieces [of?] artillery & 50 or 60 prisoners, about [*torn*] miles from here.[46]

Friday, October 14th.   Rome, Ga.

Most of the Army have gone towards Resaca & this afternoon I heard heavy cannonade in that direction.

Saturday, October 15th.

There are several reports abroad [*torn*] the rebels were whipped at Resaca [*torn*] that they have captured Dalton. An expedition started across [the Oostanaula] they had quite a skirmish [*torn*] rebels, capturing Gen. W[heeler's Adjutant?] & Inspector General [and] brought in 20 prisoners.[47]

Sunday, October 16th.   Rome, Ga.

It is a beautiful Sabbath day. The Sundays seem much more pleasant than other days. Heard cannonading in the direction of Dalton. Everything quiet here. It *is said* that Gen. [George H.] Thomas is at Chattanooga with 50,000 recruits.[48]

Monday, October 17th.

Busy all day hauling brick to build chimneys to our shanties. The nights are getting so cold that it is quite uncomfortable without a fire. It is reported that Dalton has been captured.

Tuesday, October 18th.

Detailed on two days' picket. My post is on the Cave Spring Road. This afternoon our cavalry have been skirmishing with the Rebs [in] advance of our picket post.

Wednesday, October 19th.

Last night the Rebs tried to capture a Picket Post next to ours, about 150 yds. distant, but did not succeed. The night was quite dark. They tried to crawl up on their knees & hands. Our boys saw them & fired. They jumped up & ran through the brush as if Sherman's whole army was after them. No news from anywhere.

Thursday, October 20th.

Kept up a sharp lookout last night. Was not troubled on our post but they kept [up] a firing on other posts along the l[ine]. Relieved from picket about 10 A.M. Slept the remainder of the [day].

Friday, October 21st.

Another mail has come [*torn*]. I got 3 letters, 2 from L[ouisa; *torn*] from Warren. We learn [*torn*] elections in Indiana, Ohio [*torn; line missing*].

*[Dated Rome Oct. 22nd/64 at top of page, but no
journal entry for that date.]*

Sunday, October 23rd.

Started for Rome again about 8 o'clock, arriving there by 3 this
afternoon. A large train of wagons has come from Sherman's army
in here for supplies. He is about 30 miles down the Coosa River. It is
reported that our Brigade will leave here soon.

Monday October 24th.

Got up this morning before daylight as our regiment was
ordered out on a foraging expedition, to start at 6 o'clock. Crossed
the Oostanaula & took the road leading to Summerville. Loaded the
wagons about 10 [miles from?] Rome with corn. I filled my haversack
with sweet potatoes. Got back to Rome about sundown. Gideon
Hadley, Private of our company, died today of wounds received
at the battle of *Allatoona*.

Tuesday, October 25th.

Another large train of wagons from Sherman's army came in today
for rations. Private John Jenner of our company died this morning &
was buried in the afternoon. I had charge of the funeral escort. He died
of wounds received at the battle of *Allatoona*. The 14th Ohio battery
came in this afternoon.

[Wednesday, October 26th]

Detailed on guard but was sent back, [there?] being too many. Our
wounded [*torn*] to be sent further north. Lieut. [Charles M.] Tarr [*torn*]
resigned & Lieut. [Samuel W.] Starrett goes home [*torn*] furlough.

[Thursday, October 27th]

[*torn*] a wet rainy day. . . . night lost 12 [*torn; lines missing*]

Friday, October 28th.   Rome

Walter Hinckley, substitute for a drafted man, joined our company today. There are reports about our whole army moving toward
Savannah, but I don't believe it.[49]

Saturday, October 29th.

Considerable excitement through town today. Gen. Sherman is here & other generals of lesser note. Nearly all of the sick & wounded have been sent north. It is well known that the 14th Army Corps goes to Chattanooga. The 2nd Cavalry Division has just passed through, going east. There is a big move on foot. Sherman probably knows what it is. I'm sure I don't.

It is reported that the Rebels are crossing the Tennessee River at Eastport [Mississippi]. All sorts of rumors afloat. Probably none of them true. Mounted Guard; was on the left & again [I] had the good luck to be sent back to the company, there being too many corporals detailed.[50] The 14th Corps has ~~just~~ come in. They are encamped across the Oostanaula River.

Sunday, October 30.

Turned over my [gun] & accouterments to another substitute that joined our company. I am [on] Daily Duty as company clerk. Chaplain Bigger preached the funeral sermon of those of our boys that fell at Allatoona. Also, Col. Hanna took leave of us. He goes home on leave of absence. The 23rd Corps is here.

Monday, October 31st.

Muster day. Our Regiment is out now. There is a review of the Division. I am left here to do some writing as I had no gun or "*Kit.*" Troops have been passing through here all day. Where they are going is a mystery to me. Col. Hanna said we would leave in a few days. Well, I am ready.

Tuesday, November 1st.

Another day has passed away & we are still here, although everybody thinks we will leave. Troops have been passing through all day. Our Corps (15th) are at Cave Spring, 16 miles southwest. 2 large 8-inch siege howitzers were blown up today.[51] That looks something like evacuating the place. All who are not able to march are ordered to report to the Doctor in the morning. Where we are going is still a mystery.

Wednesday, November 2nd.

Another day has gone & we are still at Rome. The last of the 14th Corps passed through to-day. The "Eternal City" is now deserted; only our Division remains. All the hospitals have been moved; commissaries too. Doors swing open. All those not able to march reported to the Doctor.

Thursday, November 3rd.

The weather has been wet & drizzly for the last 3 days. A bad time for starting out. We are all prepared. Will probably start somewhere either north, south, east, or west tomorrow.

Friday, November 4th.

Our Brigade was paid off today. I received 185 dollars. It is reported that we leave next Monday. A mail came in yesterday. I hope I will hear from home again before leaving.[52]

Saturday, November 5th.

Still here at Rome. There is some mystery about this move. They have kept the grist & saw mills running all day. That looks like staying here. But they blew up 1 or 2 pieces of artillery. That looks like evacuating. I am beginning to think we will not go at all. I sent $170 dollars home to Louisa by Slater Lewis. He goes home on furlough. Received a letter from her tonight.

Sunday, November 6th.

Crowds of citizens are down to the Depot waiting for transportation north. It is reported that the Rebs tore up about 1 mile of track between here and Chattanooga. No train today.

Monday, November 7th.

Heard news of a battle between Hood & Gen. Thomas in which the rebels were defeated. The battle took place near Decatur, Ala. Wrote a letter to Father Smith.

Tuesday, November 8th.   4 miles from Rome, Ga.

Election day. Our Regt. (50th Ills.), 66th Ind., [and] 12th Ills. went out foraging. I (as Co. clerk) did not go. Saw the 7th Iowa vote. It was about 1 in 12 for McClellan. I think this day will decide the fate of our Republic. Will we remain a free and united people or will Disunion & Discord triumph? I hope it may turn out a great victory for the Union. Hurrah for Old Abe.

Wednesday, November 9th.

A wet, rainy day; no signs of moving. We may stay here all winter. The 39th Iowa only gave 2 votes for the Copperhead Party yesterday. The 81st Ohio is the strongest Copperhead regiment in our Division. It was nearly equally divided.[53]

At Home in Rome

Shortly after Lewis Roe's brigade occupied Rome, Maj. William Hannah caused the regimental and U.S. colors to be displayed over the sidewalk in front of the 50th Illinois Infantry headquarters, so that all might have the privilege of passing under them. Some twenty-nine years later, the editor of the regimental history credited comrade J. A. Hoops, formerly of Company G and on guard duty at the time, with the following:

> The headquarters of the Fiftieth Ill. Veteran Volunteer Infantry on the 30th day of May, 1864, was in a building located on the south side of Maine street, Rome, Ga., just at the foot of an incline as we went east. Immediately over the sidewalk were suspended our regimental flags, while on the opposite side of the street were displayed in like manner, the colors of one of the other regiments in our brigade.
>
> About 2 o'clock p.m., on the above date the undersigned was posted as a sentry in front of our regimental headquarters, and a part of the instructions was that all citizens passing to and fro on the walk, should go directly under the flag. At the hour above mentioned, two ladies came down the walk, one was quite matronly, probably thirty-five or forty years of age, while the other was a dazzling charmer scarcely out of her teens, and endowed with a superabundance of vivacity, vim and vindictiveness far above the requirements of the occasion, and was the spokeswoman of the

pair; when near the flag they came to a HALT, LOOKED, first at it, then at the sentry, and with evil eye and restless nerves gave utterance to the following questions:

"What have you'uns all got that dirty rag hung over our sidewalks for?"

Reply—"We place our flag there so that the fair ladies of the south may have the honor of passing under their national emblem."

Young lady—with gnashing teeth, clenched fist, and a countenance that bid defiance to all Yankeedom—"We'uns all want you'uns all to understand that we'uns belong to the confederate states of America, and we'uns won't go under your Yankee flag."

Reply—"You will go under your country's flag or stand here beneath its folds while we remain in your city."

Young lady—"We'uns all will show you'uns all that Lincoln's dogs can't come down here and tyranize over we'uns."

Whereupon she left the sidewalk and attempted to pass around the flag, at the same time hurling the following epithets at the flag and its supporters: "You Lincoln hirelings, you Yankee dogs, we won't be thus insulted; you can't make us go under that detestable thing. We'uns would get down on our knees and crawl through the mud of our streets, before we'uns would do it."

By the time they had passed over the gutter, intending to go around the flag, the sentry presented them the point of his bayonet and commanded them to go back on the walk and pass under the flag, or consider themselves under arrest; (at this time the Colonel's orderly, Charley Hubert, came out from headquarters and assisted in trying to get them to pass under the flag and go on their way in peace), but they would not, and the young lady declared she had spit in the face of Col. Streight when a prisoner in their city, . . . and would treat likewise any and all yanks that came in her way, whereupon she endeavored to execute her threat, but feeling the sharp point of a bayonet in her flesh, withheld her spittle, but continued her wrathful utterance until placed under arrest and taken into headquarters, where they listened to just such a lecture as only Major Hanna could administer.

Having been properly admonished were again ordered to pass under the flag; they reluctantly obeyed, and were released from arrest. They again began their abuse of the flag, the Union soldiers, the government, and all connected with it, resulting in again being placed under arrest and ordered to walk the beat with the sentry then on duty for the remaining part of the two hours, passing under the flag every time they went up and down the beat. Having repented of their folly they were released from arrest, and thanking the sentinel in good humor, went their way, wiser for their experience and with more respect for the Boys in Blue.

From Charles F. Hubert, *History of the Fiftieth Regiment, Illinois Volunteer Infantry*, pp. 426–28.

This story apparently had a considerable circulation at the time; another version with Maj. Gen. O. O. Howard in place of Major Hanna and sans location or the vernacular language, is found in Frances Thomas Howard's *In and Out of the Lines* (New York: Neal Publishing Company, 1905), 124. Mr. Robert Anglea of Rome, Georgia, points out that there are good reasons for thinking that this story has been editorially enhanced if not made up. There is no Maine Street in Rome and never has been; the main street in the city runs north-south and to be on the south side of the street would place one at the south end of the city. The dialect used is not a vernacular of Georgia or Alabama, but was used in rural Appalachia. "You all" would be appropriate for the Rome area and is still used.

CHAPTER SEVEN

The March to the Sea, November 10–December 14, 1864

IN THE TWO MONTHS FOLLOWING THE CAPTURE OF ATLANTA, SHERMAN PLANNED HIS NEXT CAMPAIGN. THIS EVOLVED FROM A PROPOSAL TO STRIKE OTHER INDUSTRIAL CITIES IN GEORGIA TO marching to the coast, while leaving Maj. Gen. George Thomas in Chattanooga to counter what would become Confederate General Hood's invasion of Tennessee. General Ulysses S. Grant, initially reluctant to have Sherman turn his back on Hood, finally agreed with his western commander's proposal to "make Georgia howl."[1]

For his March to the Sea, William T. Sherman mustered some 62,000 troops, organized as a Left Wing and a Right Wing. The Left Wing had the 14th and 20th Corps under Maj. Gen. Henry W. Slocum, while Maj. Gen. Oliver Otis Howard led the 15th and 17th Army Corps in the Right Wing. Howard's command still bore the name Army of the Tennessee; the Left Wing came to be called the Army of Georgia. Maj. Gen. Peter Osterhaus led Roe's corps, the 15th.[2]

George Thomas retained the 4th Army Corps, and Maj. Gen. John Schofield still commanded the 23rd Army Corps, the Army of the Ohio. Together with two divisions drawn from Missouri, they held the line in Tennessee. Sherman, who also had Brig. Gen. Judson Kilpatrick's 5,000 cavalrymen, now faced only the 3,500 horsemen under Confederate Maj. Gen. Joseph Wheeler plus whatever opposition the Georgia militia might offer.[3]

The 50th Illinois began its march at a camp four miles east of Rome, Georgia, on November 10. This division (4th Division, 15th Army Corps) under Brig. Gen. John Corse joined Sherman the next day at Kingston, Georgia. Early on the 12th, this part of the army set off with "Weather superb, roads mostly good." Only those fit to travel accompanied the

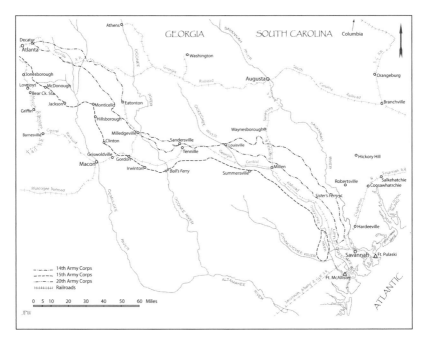

MAP 7. The March to the Sea, November–December 1864. Courtesy of author.

campaign; the sick, wounded, nonveteran volunteers, and others had been sent to the rear (to Chattanooga).[4] Everybody moved out on the 13th. The 15th and 17th Corps departed from a place south of Marietta, Georgia, known as Smyrna Camp Ground; the 14th Corps from Cartersville (south of Kingston), and the 20th Corps from Atlanta. Kilpatrick and Sherman made their departure from Marietta.[5] Lewis Roe never actually saw Atlanta; his corps passed around to the right (west) of the burning city.

Only Sherman knew the destination of his columns, and he initially had the Left Wing make a deliberate feint, toward Augusta, Georgia, then turn south and converge at Milledgeville, at that time the state capital. The Right Wing appeared to be heading toward Macon but then veered east in the direction of the rail junction at Gordon, south of Milledgeville.[6] Despite Sherman's secrecy and deceptions, the *Chicago Times* broadcast his plans to march through Georgia on November 9. Almost before it began, the South knew what was coming.[7]

The columns moved along in rough alignment and within supporting distance of one another. Always in contact, they followed the sparse roads and at times cut through fields and forests. Kilpatrick's cavalry, shadowed by Wheeler, served as a shield to the Right Wing as far as Griswoldville, then moved east to screen the Left Wing's movements as it advanced to Savannah. Sherman himself traveled with the Left Wing as far as Tennille Station, then with the Right Wing and the 17th Corps.[8]

Lewis Roe and the 15th Army Corps continued east from Gordon to the Oconee River crossing at Balls' Ferry, thence toward the Ogeechee River by way of the Louisville Road. The 4th Division marched through a wilderness along the southern side of a tributary and then the Ogeechee itself all the way to Savannah. The 2nd and 3rd Divisions took a parallel route as much as a dozen miles to the south.[9] Roe's comment, "Into the swamp again," pretty much said it all.

The March to the Sea is easily followed on the excellent maps in a recent title.[10] Roe apparently never saw Sherman himself on this march, although the general's entourage joined Brigadier General Corse's 4th Division for part of the day on November 27.[11] For most of the infantry, the March to the Sea was a figurative walk in the park, although a very muddy one at times.

Actual fighting was minimal and mostly involved the cavalry units. On November 16, two brigades of Kilpatrick's command had a lively skirmish with Wheeler at Lovejoy's and Bear Creek stations, southeast of Atlanta.[12] The fighting that Roe reported on November 19 appears to be unrecorded, but November 20 saw Kilpatrick's second brigade skirmishing again and forcing Wheeler back toward Macon. The next day, the only real battle during the Savannah Campaign began when the 9th Michigan Cavalry destroyed a railroad train at Griswold Station and reduced a pistol, soap, and candle factory and the town of Griswoldville to smoldering ruins.[13]

On November 22, the Battle of Griswoldville saw three brigades of Georgia militia, primarily old men and boys, charge the battle-ready second brigade of Major General Osterhaus's 1st Division, 15th Corps, only to be shot to pieces.[14] Roe, who was in the 4th Division, took no part in this battle.

The Right Wing spent its days slogging through swamps and building corduroy roads; the 15th Corps alone constructed almost twenty-seven miles of corduroy roads in the Savannah Campaign. By December 9, the 4th Division faced the rebel batteries between the Atlantic & Gulf Railroad and the Savannah Canal, about a dozen miles southwest of Savannah and perhaps eight miles from Fort McAllister. This fort, a relatively small but important earthwork, stood on the south bank of the Great Ogeechee River as the principal Confederate fortification blocking access toward the coast and the Union fleet.[15]

What happened next was that Sherman needed to open communications with the Union naval forces offshore more than he needed Savannah. Capt. William Duncan with a sergeant and a private of the 10th Illinois Cavalry floated down the Great Ogeechee in a dugout, past the Confederates in Fort McAllister, and in three nights and two days slipped out to sea. There the gunboat USS *Flag* recovered them and delivered both the message and the messengers to the Union naval commander.[16]

The heavy guns at Fort McAllister all faced the river, while on the landward side the works stood exposed. General Howard now pushed his 15th Corps to the Ogeechee River and outflanked the Confederate outer defense line, leaving Fort McAllister vulnerable.

On December 12, Brig. Gen. William Hazen's 2nd Division, 15th Corps crossed the river upstream at King's Bridge and turned eastward to approach the fort from the rear. Hazen's brigades assaulted the fort late on the afternoon of December 13, and in fifteen minutes the federals poured over the walls to capture the position. Union casualties totaled 134 killed and wounded, mostly from the explosions of a new Southern weapon—torpedoes. These were upended artillery shells with contact fuses, buried along the lines of approach. Step on one and it exploded, with disastrous results. Lewis Roe may have been a witness, but he had no role in the taking of Fort McAllister.[17] The capture of Savannah itself now became just a matter of time.

Much has been written about foraging and property destruction during the March to the Sea, foraging being officially sanctioned pillaging of food supplies for men and livestock from the countryside. Sherman's Special Field Orders No. 120 on November 9 made this official policy: "The army will forage liberally on the country during the March."[18] From the standpoint of Sherman's army, this worked wonderfully well. One private with the 17th Corps wrote later that "Our daily bill of fare consisted of fresh pork and chicken, cornpone and

FIGURE 23. Sherman's foragers on a Georgia plantation. From Rossiter Johnson, *Campfires and Battlefields* (1967) [1894].

chicken, sweet potatoes and chicken, and for a change we always take a little more chicken."[19] Only near Savannah did food supplies run low. The army's droves of beef cattle actually increased in number; the draft animals were in good condition, and both the artillery and cavalry ended the march with more animals than when they began.[20]

After the destruction at Rome, Cassville, Kingston, Cartersville, Marietta, and Atlanta before the march got underway, the deliberate burning of houses and farms may not have been a widescale problem. But any public or government facilities, including cotton gins and grist mills, were destroyed without hesitation.[21]

The losses in Sherman's army totaled just 1,888 men killed, wounded, missing, or captured, for a loss rate of 3 percent. Twenty-nine had been killed or mortally wounded in action and 196 wounded. Health of the men had also been outstanding with only thirty-two deaths from disease reported. One such took place in Roe's own 50th Illinois, the only casualty suffered by that regiment in the Savannah Campaign.[22]

Thursday, November 10th.

It is now 2 o'clock and we are ordered to move at 3. I cannot tell
where we are going. Some say north & others south. Good Bye to Rome.
May God watch over me through this trip. Encamped tonight about 4
miles from Rome. I write these lines by the light of our first campfire, so I
shall call this Camp No. 1. Rome is burning. I do not know whether it was
set afire by order or not. I have no idea where we are going to.[23]

Camp No. 2. Friday, November 11th.   Near Allatoona

Encamped 4 miles south of Kingston on the R.R. so we are going
south. The old yarn has again sprung up that we are going through to
the coast. Heavy frost last night, but we have plenty of rails. The whole
country is lit up with our camp fires. Saw an old negro who did not
know his own age. Says he was in Charleston when taken by the British.
He was born in Africa. Passed the 14th Corps at Kingston. The mail
came up with us tonight, but no letter for me. I will write one. Probably
I can get to send it when we reach Atlanta.

Camp No. 3. Saturday, November 12th.

One mile south of Allatoona. Went over our old battlefield. Rebel
graves are on each side of the road. They were buried just where they
fell. Gen. Sherman passed us today. The 14th Corps are coming in our
rear. In sight of Kennesaw Mountain. Marched about 16 miles.

Camp No. 4. Sunday, November 13th.

Near Marietta. We march in single file by the side of our train
to protect it from any sudden attack of the enemy's cavalry. Passed
through Acworth and Big Shanty. All intercourse with the north is cut
off. The 14th Corps are busy tearing & burning the R.R. I don't suppose
Sherman will let the grass grow under our feet, but will move south as
fast as possible.

Camp No. 5. Monday, November 14th.

Chattahoochie River. Passed through Marietta. It has been a very
nice city, about as large as Rome, but now it is nearly all burnt down;
only a few houses remaining. The railroad is torn up; every rail heated
& bent, some of them wound around trees. We passed line after line of

earthworks. The country is pretty well dug up & while bullets were flying so thick here, we were enjoying ourselves at Rome. We are within 8 miles of Atlanta.

Camp No. 6. Tuesday, November 15th.

4 miles southwest of Atlanta. Went around to the right of Atlanta. Passed over lines of breastworks, rifle pits, forts &c. &c. Saw where our main line was within 50 yds. of the Rebel line. The bushes were completely chawed off with bullets; not a twig left untouched. Laid over for 2 or 3 hours within sight of the city, then started forward again on the Macon Road. We got our last mail today & I rec. a letter from Louisa.

Atlanta was burning all day & tonight the light of the burning city makes our camp light enough to read by. I understand the Depots, Warehouses and all foundries, Public buildings are to be destroyed. Thus the Gate City, the stronghold of the South, is destroyed.

Camp No. 7. Wednesday, November 16th.

6 miles southeast of Jonesborough. Tired, very tired. We have marched long & late; marched steady from sunrise until 8 o'clock tonight. Heard cannonading to our right. Probably at Jonesborough. I have learned that our expedition consists of the 14th, 15th, 17th and 20th Corps, about 50,000 men & 10,000 cavalry under Kilpatrick.[24] It is said that there are about 10,000 rebels, state militia, ahead of us. I had rather easy times until yesterday as I had no gun, but I picked up one & will have to march in ranks hereafter.

Camp No. 8. Thursday, November 17th.   Jackson, Ga.

Within 2 miles of Jackson. Another hard day's march is over & we are about 22 miles further in Dixie. Passed through McDonald [McDonough] today. Passed the 1st & 2nd Divisions of our Corps (15th) lying in camp. Several of our boys fell out; they could not keep up. We are only about 45 miles from Macon; about day after tomorrow I expect a fight. We are in a very rich country. Forage in abundance, such as sweet potatoes, chickens, &c.

Camp No. 9. Friday, November 18th.

We made a night's march, laid over all day & started just at dark. Laid over to let the 17th Corps & train cross our road. Got into camp about 1/2 past one o'clock. Several of the boys fell out. I was very tired & sleepy but managed to keep up. Most of them eat too many sweet potatoes, chickens &c. while lying over.

Camp No. 10. Saturday, November 19th.

[On] Ocmulgee River. Rained last night after we came into camp. We got up this morning, wet and nasty. My blanket was very heavy but we only marched about 5 miles. We are waiting for the 17th Corps to cross the river. It has rained all day & the roads are very muddy. 30 or 40 prisoners passed us today. They were captured by our cavalry.[25] The advance of our army had quite a fight to secure the crossing of the Ocmulgee. We cross on pontoons for which we have a special train of wagons to carry them.

Camp No. 11. Sunday, November 20th.

Near Monticello. Our regt. in advance today. We floundered along about 12 miles & encamped. 3 of us went out foraging. I got 3 chickens, a chunk of dried beef, & a canteen [of] molasses. A very muddy wet night; passed most of the night in roasting chickens. 5 companies of our Regt. are on guard tonight in town. Continued in a day or two. Lewis F. Roe

Camp No. 13.[26] Monday, November 21st.   [Hillsboro]

Rained all night & all day. Mud knee deep. Our regt. was in [the] rear today. We had a terrible time before getting into camp. Several of the boys threw away their knapsacks. I managed to carry mine through. Got into camp about 9 o'clock at night. After dark it blew hard & turned quite cold. Our blankets were soaking wet; no sleep that night. I thought many times of home & wished myself there often. We are encamped at Hillsboro. No supper; wind blows so very hard can build no fires.

Camp No. 14. Tuesday, November 22nd.   Clinton, Ga.

Near Clinton. Got up all in a shiver this morning. Thawed out my blankets [and] threw a piece of fresh meat on the coals for breakfast. After my fast was broke, we started out on the Macon Road & tonight we are only 10 miles from the city, so we may expect a fight tomorrow. We only marched about 9 miles today. Our pontoon train got stuck in the mud. Wagons broke, soldiers laughed, teamsters swore, & so it went. Finally we went into camp, leaving the teams to get out themselves. I foraged some sweet potatoes. Some say that our Cavalry was repulsed at Macon & that our advance is fortifying.

Camp No. 15. Wednesday, November 23rd.

Started again at daylight. Passed through Clinton; turned off of the Macon Road. It is said that we are going to Gordon, the junction of the Milledgeville Road.²⁷ The 39th Iowa & our Regt. were in advance. We took the wrong road & marched about 5 miles out of the way. I hardly know the location of our camp tonight. Clear & cold.

Camp No. 16. Thursday, November 24th.   Gordon, Ga.

Marched only 7 miles today. Crossed the R.R., which we found torn up & burning. Our troops have possession of Milledgeville but not of Macon. Our Company on picket tonight. The 3rd Division is here. Most of the town of Gordon was burnt; all except [the] dwelling houses. Had a talk with an old Planter; said he was a strong rebel, that our men acted inhuman in taking every thing from him. He asked us for something to eat. He thought [that] the rebels were better soldiers than us. I admitted that 1 of their men could whip 10 or 12 of our men, but we could beat them eating; that we was agoing to eat out the State of Ga.

Camp No. 17. Friday, November 25th.   [Irwinton]

Left camp about sunrise, marching in a southeast direction. Passed the 2nd Division of our Corps; went through Irvington [Irwinton]. We are encamped about 6 miles southeast of that place. I think we must be near the Oconee River. Saw the 1st Division, 17th Corps, about 1 mile to our left. The country we are passing through is not as good as that a few days ago. Filled my haversack with sweet potatoes. Got all the persimmons I could eat.

Camp No. 18. Saturday, November 26.   [Oconee River]

The drums awoke me about 4 o'clock. We started forward again.
A march of about 6 miles bought us to the Oconee [River]. Found the
17th Corps there. They had quite a lively skirmish this morning to lay
down their pontoons.[28] Our Division crossed first & advanced about
8 miles [to] where we are encamped tonight. Expect we will have a
skirmish nearly every day now as the Johnnies are getting quite thick
in front. Saw Gens. [Oliver O.] Howard & [Peter J.] Osterhaus.

Camp No. 19. Sunday, November 27th.   [East of the Oconee]

This is the Sabbath, a day set apart for the worship of God.
Probably my folks have been to church today while I have been
engaged in a far different occupation, that of tearing up and burning
the Macon [Georgia Central] Rail Road. We commenced at the Oconee
River bridge & burned eastward about 15 or 20 miles. The last mile post
was marked 136 miles to Savannah. We used the fence rails on each side
of the road to heat the iron rails [and] as levers to pry up the R.R., turn
it over, knock off the iron rails, pile up the R.R. ties, set them afire, then
put the iron rails on top. They will get red-hot in the middle [and] the
ends will drop down, leaving the rails crooked and useless.

Camp No. 20. Monday, November 28th.

Forward again by daylight, but our route has been through a poor
country inhabited only by the "Poor white trash." Our road ran through
a continual forest of tall pines with scarcely an opening.

Camp No. 21. Tuesday, November 29th.

Tired & worn, I throw myself down on the grass & try to write my
journal by the light of our campfire. We have marched about 25 miles
today through swamp & over corduroy roads. A great many of the boys
are too tired to cook their sweet potatoes. I am very tired myself but
never was known to be too tired to eat.

Camp No. 22. Wednesday, November 30.   Summerville

All wet & daubed with mud, I again scribble in my little book. We
are 17 miles further in the swamps of Georgia & looking at the corduroy roads we have built. I think we have made good progress. I was
out foraging today. Kept on the left flank of the column, about 2 miles

FIGURE 24. The Fate of the Rail Fence. From *The Century Magazine*,
October 1887, p. 918.

from the road. Brought in a ham, a hand basket full of sugar, canteen of
molasses, quart of salt, & my Harversack full of sweet potatoes. Passed
through a small collection of log shanties called Summerville. I should
think Swampville would be a more appropriate name. It is reported that
Savannah has surrendered to Gen. [John G.] Foster.[29] I wish I could
hear from home; hear from America. We have not heard who our next
President is yet. The pontoon train has gone forward. I suppose we are
near the Ogeechee River.

Camp No. 23. Thursday, December 1st.

Another bad day's march; about 12 miles through swamp, as usual, but tonight the country appears a little better. Perhaps we *will* get through after a while. I believe our whole Corps [15th] is here. Our camp fires extend several miles.

Camp No. 24. Friday, December 2nd.   Along the Ogeechee

Into the swamp again, but that is nothing. Now, it would be something if we were out of them. One of the boys saw an alligator. Our route is down the Ogeechee [River]. I think the 20th & 14th Corps crossed above & are probably tearing up the R.R. [toward] Millen.

Saturday, December 3rd.

We rested today. Soap was issued for the 1st time since leaving Rome & we had a wash. Inspection at 2 P.M. I have heard cannonading in advance. Other parts of the Army may be engaged. I have heard various rumors of peace. God grant they may be true. With peace & a good Government, it would almost be a heaven on earth. I know that peace must soon come. The Confederacy is a mere shell. I have not seen a dozen men at home that are able to bear arms. All are in their armies & those armies on their frontiers & they become less & less every day.

I have strayed away from camp this afternoon & am seated under one of these monstrous pines that grow here. I feel in a thinking mood. I wish I could look away up in Illinois & see how my wife & child are getting along. God in his mercy has thus far watched over me & kept me in safety & I feel that he will also take care of them & then when this cruel war is over, I know that there will be joy & happiness in one family at least.

This is a cruel war; at least things are done which are cruel, by some of our boys, & were they known at home, would forever disgrace them. Our officers are not to blame. Every house that we pass has a guard placed over it & none are allowed to enter, but some will straggle or pillage & destroy, break open trunks & drawers & often destroy what they do not want. Such conduct is mean & none but a mean, unprincipled villain will do it. We have orders to take everything outside that can be eaten, but nothing more.

I often wonder what or where we are going to. I have a pocket map, & from our position it would seem that we were going straight to Savannah. I suppose Sherman will lay siege to that place. Some think we will pass above there & land at Charleston. We are confident of success wherever we go. The boys have all confidence in Sherman. They think he can do almost everything & our Division almost worships Gen. Corse ever since Allatoona. He has an ugly scar across his cheek which he rec. there. He works like a pioneer; takes hold of the wagons with the boys, & helps get them out of mud holes; carry logs to build corduroys.

I must stop scribbling & go back to camp. Perhaps they may have orders to move before this. I expect to see the "Briny Deep" in 4 or 5 days. Lewis F. Roe

Camp No. 24. Sunday, December 4th.   Still along the Ogeechee

Our Company was on Picket last night. We were not relieved this morning until the Regiment [50th] had been gone an hour or more. A rapid march of about 5 miles brought us up with them. Found them building a Corduroy Road across a swamp, but tonight I think we are about out of the swamp as we are on a good road and in a settled country. Our road is about 2 miles west of the Ogeechee and running parallel with it. We could see the smoke of the burning railroad all day, on the other side of the river. The 14th and 20th Army Corps are over there.[30]

Camp No. 25. Monday, December 5th.

Several Rockets were thrown up last night from Gen'l Howard's Head Quarters. I do not know whether they were trying to signal to the coast, or to some other part of the Army. As we passed the old camp of the 1st Division [15th A.C.] we saw that they had thrown up breastworks last night. So there must be "*Johnnies*" about.

Tuesday, December 6th.

No move in our Division today. We are again in the swamps. I wish we could get out of them. Still, there is one advantage in using this swamp water. It does not take much coffee to color it. I should think it would be impossible to carry on a summer's campaign here. I am in hopes we'll be farther north by the time the hot months come.

Camp No. 26. Wednesday, December 7th.

We have had a bad, wet day. Commenced raining just as we left camp & has been raining ever since. Marched about 10 miles; the 1st brigade of our Division went 2 miles farther & threw a pontoon bridge across the Ogeechee. They had been skirmishing with the "rebs" nearly all day, but finally succeeded in laying the bridge. Report says that there are 40,000 Rebs at Savannah. If true, there is work ahead. There is considerable cannonading going on now at the river.[31] I expect we will be called on before morning.

Camp No. 27. Thursday, December 8th.   Crossing of the Ogeechee

Crossed the Ogeechee this morning and started forward, our Brigade & our Regiment in advance. Skirmished with the "*Johnnies*" some, but they fell back rapidly, leaving their rifle pits & breastworks. The 1st and 2nd brigades captured 1 piece of artillery and about 20 prisoners yesterday.

Today they [the Johnnies] fell trees & dug pits in our road. Pshaw, do the Rebs expect such work will amount to anything; we removed them in far less time than it took them to cut them. Nearly half of the command have been employed with axes clearing the road, but in spite of the rebs, we have marched about 16 miles and tonight we are encamped on the canal which runs west of Savannah into the Ogeechee. Went in swimming today. The water was quite warm. Gen[s]. Howard & Corse were with us today.[32]

Camp No. 28. Friday, December 9th.

Our Brigade being in advance yesterday, was in [the] rear today & had to guard the wagon train. The 1st & 2nd Brigades went forward, driving the rebs about 5 miles & encamped. We came up with the wagon train. Threw up breastworks.

Camp No. 28. Saturday, December 10th.   [Near Savannah]

The ball has fairly opened. Our brigade and our Division [4th of 15th A.C.] was the first on the floor. We drove the rebels back about 3 miles this morning when we came upon their main line of works surround[ing] Savannah, which are in plain view. There is a swamp about 1/2 mile wide between us & them. We formed in line & opened on their forts with 2 batteries. The cannonading was quite heavy all day. Several shells came over our Regt. but did no injury. Their fire was directed towards our batteries. At night we moved back just out of range & encamped.[33]

Camp No. 29. Sunday, December 11th.   [8 miles S. of Savannah]

Rained very hard last night; wet everything. Our blankets were in a puddle. Got up about 2 o'clock and built a big fire. At 7 we fell in line. Our Division was relieved by the 1st & we fell back about a mile & went into camp. Our batteries keep up a constant pounding. Heavy cannonading on our left.

Today is the Sabbath. I wonder what our folks are doing at home? Are they still well or not? I wish I could hear one word only. Tonight it is clear, but the wind blows quite cold. Our skirmishers keep popping away, whether they see anything to shoot at or not. I saw several ricefields today. I can hardly tell where we are, but think we must be about southwest of the city, by the milestones. I see we have 8 miles of ground to fight over yet. The swamp between us and the works of the enemy is flooded every day with tidewater from the ocean, but I do [not] know how far away the ocean is; can't see it. We are on a large, travelled road running south from Savannah. Across the swamp in our front it is graded up above high water, but it is swept by the enemy's cannon. The swamp is impassable. Gens. Howard, Osterhaus & Corse are with us.

Monday, December 12th.

We have made no move yet. Our skirmishers are crawling up closer & closer to the rebel forts. Our batteries keep pounding away day & night. 8 prisoners that were taken from the 39th Iowa at Allatoona last October made their escape from the rebels & came in today. They escaped on the 25th of last month & have been hiding in the swamp ever since. They say that our lines extend entirely around the city from the Savannah River above the city to the river below; that our Corps is on the extreme right.

Our foraging party was within view of the coast. They saw Ft. McAllister at the mouth of the Ogeechee. Heavy cannonading on our left. Part of our Division moved up within short range & threw up some breastworks. I suppose our turn will soon come.

Tuesday, December 13th.

Still lying in camp listening to the music of our cannons. It is one constant roar. The 2nd & 1st Divisions moved farther toward our right, toward Ft. McAllister. I was up in a tree a good while looking at our skirmishers. They would rise on their knees, fire, & fall flat; then creep closer, fire, creep forward until they got within a short distance of the fort, then a charge and the fort was theirs. Tonight the report is that Ft. McAllister is taken.[34]

Wednesday, December 14th.   [Still S. of Savannah]

The report about Ft. McAllister is confirmed. We have taken it with 600 prisoners & 20 guns. It is nearly quiet on our front, but the left of the lines are waking up. The taking of Ft. McAllister has opened the "cracker line" to the fleet and a large wagon train has gone to Ft. McAllister for supplies. The fact is, we are getting very short of grub. I have been puzzled many times to know where to get enough to eat. But I suppose we will receive supplies soon.

Wrote a letter home; don't know when I have a chance to send it. Went out on the skirmish line but saw no Johnnies. Saw & tasted the tide water from the Ocean. Most of the ricefields about here are covered with tidewater during the day.

When Sherman Marched Down to the Sea.

Our camp fires shone bright on the mountains,
That frowned on the river below.
While we stood by our guns in the morning
And eagerly watched for the foe.
When a rider came out from the darkness
That hung over mountain and tree.
And shouted "Boys, up and be ready,
For Sherman will march to the sea."

Then cheer upon cheer for bold Sherman
Went up from each valley and glen,

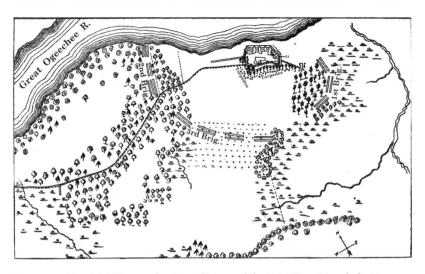

FIGURE 25. Fort McAllister at the time of its assault by Brig. Gen. Hazen's division, December 13, 1864. From *War of the Rebellion, A Compilation of the Official Records of the Union and Confederate Armies*, vol. 44.

And the bugles re-echoed the music
That came from the lips of the men.
For we knew that the stars in our banner
More bright in their splendor would be,
And that blessings from northland would greet us
When Sherman marched down to the sea.

Then forward, boys, forward to battle
We marched on our wearisome way,
And we stormed the wild hills of Resaca;
God bless those that fell on that day.
Then Kennesaw, dark in its glory,
Frowned down on the flag of the free.
But the east and the west bore standards,
And Sherman marched down to the sea.

Still onward we pressed till our banners
Swept out from Atlanta's grim walls
And the blood of the patriot dampened
The soil where the traitor flag falls.
Yet we pause not to weep for the fallen,

Who slept by each river and tree.
But we twined them a wreath of the laurel,
As Sherman marched down to the sea.

Oh, proud was our army that morning
That stood where the pine darkly towers.
When Sherman said, "Boys, you are weary,
This day fair Savannah is ours."
Then sang we a song for our chieftain,
That echoed o'er river and lea.
And the stars in our banner shone brighter,
When Sherman marched down to the sea.

CHAPTER EIGHT

Savannah, Georgia,
December 15, 1864–January 26, 1865

SAVANNAH WAS THE OLDEST AS WELL AS THE LARGEST CITY IN GEORGIA IN 1860, WITH A POPULATION OF 22,292, ABOUT TWO-THIRDS OF WHOM WERE FREE WHITE CITIZENS AND ONE-THIRD slaves. The community lay on a bluff surrounded by tidewater marshes and rice fields crossed by swamp-bordered creeks and rivers. Roads and railroads radiated from the urban area along five narrow causeways. In the decade before the Civil War, commerce and agriculture combined to make Savannah an enormously wealthy community. The railroads carried more than four million bales of cotton from the interiors of Georgia and South Carolina to ships waiting at Savannah's wharves, including 500,000 bales in 1860 alone. The surrounding country produced almost 26 million pounds of rice in 1860; more than the rest of Georgia combined. Southern yellow pine by the millions of board feet also left Savannah as timber and sawn lumber. Flour and rice mills, several foundries, sawmills, cotton presses, and other industries contributed to the wealth of the town.[1]

The Civil War ended all of this, with the Union occupation of Port Royal and Hilton Head Island in South Carolina, only thirty miles distant, followed by the bombardment and capture of Fort Pulaski at the mouth of the Savannah River. This virtually blocked access by the sea after the spring of 1862. Sherman's advance in December 1864 cut off approaches to the city by road and railroad, save the Union plank road to Hardeeville in South Carolina, which he thought lay beyond his immediate reach.[2]

Grant, as commander-in-chief, originally intended to send Sherman and his army by ship to Virginia to finish Robert E. Lee. By mid-December,

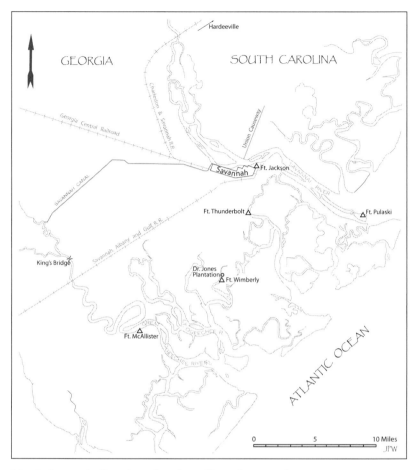

MAP 8. Savannah, Georgia, and environs, December 1864–January 1865.
Courtesy of author.

Grant had rethought this and in a letter of December 16 the army's chief of staff told Sherman "that this whole matter of your future action should be left to your discretion."[3]

Sherman had already begun placing rifled siege guns where they could bombard the center of Savannah. On December 17, he demanded the surrender of the city under threat of the "harshest measures" if he had to resort to an assault. The Confederate commander, Lieutenant General William J. Hardee, refused the demand; he already had authority to save his troops and material rather than sacrifice all in a drawn-out resistance.[4]

Even before the loss of Fort McAllister at the southern end of Savannah's defenses, preparations to evacuate Hardee's command were underway. Confederate general P. G. T. Beauregard arrived and directed the construction of a series of pontoon bridges across the Savannah River, using plantation rice-flats, to allow a withdrawal into South Carolina. When Hardee telegraphed Beauregard for more help, the general returned to push the work to completion on the 19th. Sherman had no way of knowing what Beauregard and Hardee were up to when he made his demands.[5]

Maj. Gen. Henry Slocum, commanding Sherman's Left Wing with the 14th and 20th Corps, could have thwarted the whole escape plan. He proposed on the night of December 15 to cross an entire corps to the South Carolina bank of the Savannah River, threaten the enemy's flank, seal off that side of the city, and be in a position to shell every part of it. Sherman, however, had an attack of the hesitations. As late as December 20, while Sherman was out with the fleet or at Hilton Head, Slocum was told that there were no new orders. Only a thin line of pickets and a screen of cavalry lay between him and the Union Causeway, the single remaining escape route. That day, Sherman's heavy guns carried shot and shell to all parts of the enemy's works.[6]

On the night of December 20–21, Hardee led his troops across the Savannah River and escaped along the Union Causeway to Hardeeville, South Carolina. Beauregard's aide, Col. Alexander Chisolm, wrote in later years that "This was one of the neatest achievements of the war."[7]

FIGURE 26. Pontoon bridge on the Savannah River, which the Rebels crossed during the evacuation of Savannah on the morning of December 21, 1864. W. T. Crane sketch, reproduced from *Frank Leslie's Illustrated Newspaper*, January 1865, in collections of the Library of Congress (negative LC-USZ62–31274).

Sherman, embarrassed, had clearly made a mistake. Hardee left behind all of his heavy ordnance and ammunition, large amounts of cotton, rice, and other stores, and a city virtually undamaged. The mayor and other city officials surrendered the town to federal officers around 4:30 a.m., and Sherman's men occupied Savannah later in the morning of December 21.[8]

During November and December, Southerners were being told that the Union forces had retreated from Atlanta with their broken columns falling back across the Tennessee River. Now this same army marched into Savannah while the citizens watched through curtained windows. "'Why, torment their lying hides!' said an old Union man of Georgia: 'they tell us Sherman's army is falling back; at the same time the durned fool rebels are retreating so fast that you could play checkers on their coat-tails.'"[9]

Most of the residents stayed home and incidents of burning or looting were almost nil. Sherman seized the stocks of cotton, rice, and all other subsistence stores. For the remainder of the month, a major problem continued to be removal of obstructions in the Savannah River. Trade and commerce were strictly limited.[10]

While Lewis Roe was not impressed by Savannah, Pvt. Myron Loop of the 68th Ohio thought it the most beautiful place it had been their fortune to visit.[11] The soldiers discovered one feature in Savannah that affected them deeply; this was a one-acre tract enclosed by a strong, high palisade, the work of Col. G. F. Wiles of the 78th Ohio Veteran Volunteer Infantry (17th Army Corps) and his command. Within the enclosure rested 300 or more of their fallen comrades, their names unknown, laid out in trenches, without coffins, victims of the prison camps in Savannah.[12]

The 50th Illinois evidently made their camp about one and a half miles southeast of the city, under the shelter of a large embankment in a line of Confederate earthworks.[13] When ordered to build houses, or shanties as Roe called them, the boys naturally turned to foraging for materials. They found a plentiful supply of lumber and other "fixins" at Dr. Jones's plantation, about nine miles south of Savannah. Dr. George F. T. Jones, the owner of Wormsloe Plantation, used the two-story timber dwelling there as a country home. Roe listed some of the damages to Wormsloe; Jones also lost his library with 1,300 books and manuscripts. The Confederates had erected Fort Wimberly, a large earthwork,

Figure 27. The Mansion at Wormsloe ("Dr. Jones' plantation"), Isle of Hope, Ga. Courtesy of Hargrett Rare Book and Manuscript Library, University of Georgia Libraries.

nearby. The house, much enlarged and remodeled after the Civil War, remains private property, while the bulk of the former plantation is now Wormsloe Historic Site, administered by the State of Georgia.[14]

Sherman's army may have been in "splendid order" but his men were hungry, in spite of plenty of meat and sweet potatoes. Rations were not regular and foraging continued. This extended to oysters from the Savannah River and coastal flats when the tide was out.[15] Rice was in abundance, but hulling and cleaning this kept the soldiers occupied just to get enough to eat. Private Loop described this process, which ended with the rice and a good-sized chunk of Georgia beef boiling in a camp kettle to make a rice soup. The troops lived thus until December 18, when coffee and hard tack, bacon, and beans, took the place of rice and beef.[16]

With no Confederate forces remaining in this part of Georgia and the natives content with the occupation, the army enjoyed a month of peace. As one soldier said, "I wish I could think of something interesting to write."[17]

Camp No. 29. Thursday, December 15th.

Our Regiment was ordered out on a foraging expedition. Crossed the Ogeechee at Kingsbridge; crossed the Gulf R.R. Encamped about 12 miles west of the river. They [the Guard here] were expecting a boat load of supplies at Kingsbridge.

Friday, December 16th.

Continued our march this morning. About 11 miles travel brought us into a rich country where there was plenty of forage. We got about 300 bushels of sweet potatoes, about 40 wagon loads of corn, & the boys loaded themselves with chickens, sugar, molasses &c. We then commenced our return. Encamped on the same ground we did last night.

Camp No. 30. Saturday, December 17th.   Return from foraging

Started again this morning by daylight. Met the 1st Division, 17th Corps, going down to Ft. McAllister. Saw several steamboats at Kingsbridge. Got into camp about 8 at night. There was a large mail waiting for us. I received 4 letters; 2 from Louisa, 1 from Luther Scarborough & 1 from Charlie Smith. Not much of importance transpired while we were gone.

Camp No. 31. Sunday, December 18th.

We moved camp about 100 yds. to our left & built Dog Houses [log shanties]. I was kept busy all day writing for the Company. Preaching at 2 P.M. but I could not find time to attend. Drew a box of *Hard Tack*. The first we have seen for over a week. I tell you they were good. A few sweet potatoes are good, but I have had enough of 'em tonight. No more thank you.[18] I suppose communication with the north is fairly opened. Lewis F. Roe.

Camp No. 32. Monday, December 19th.[19]

Have been writing for the company but found time to build a Doghouse and write a letter to Louisa, as the first mail left for the north this afternoon. Cannonading quite brisk, but not much fighting with small arms. Heard heavy firing in the direction of the city. Think it must be our fleet.

FIGURE 28. Savannah, Ga., looking upstream along the Savannah River, January 1865. George Barnard photograph. U.S. National Archives, image 165-SC-49.

Tuesday, December 20th.

Our batteries were awake early this morning even before I got up. Our skirmishers keep up their part of the tune. There has been an advance of a few hundred yards. Our advance is within easy range of the rebel fort. Our boys watch the port holes [embrasures] and when the Johnnies try to use their cannon, they throw in a shower of lead, making it rather sickly work for the Rebs. "The Union Cause is gaining ground." Wrote a letter to Luther Scarborough.

Camp No. 33. Wednesday, December 21st.   We enter the city

"*Savannah is ours*." We marched into the city about 7 o'clock this morning; found all their forts evacuated, leaving all their heavy guns behind. The Rebels crossed [the] Savannah River in the night. It is thought that they may meet Gen. [John G.] Foster's forces. I have not learned the amount of our captures yet; saw about 200 prisoners. The noise we thought was cannonading yesterday must have been caused by the Rebs blowing up guns [&] ammunition preparing to evacuate. Encamped 1/2 mile south of the city.

Thursday, December 22nd.

Went all over town today. We captured several large warehouses filled with cotton, 200 pieces of Artillery, [and] 3 Steamboats. The rebels blew up an Iron Clad [CSS *Savannah*] to prevent us taking it. The citizens appear very well pleased with the change. They say that Wheeler's cavalry plundered everything before leaving. Moved camp nearer the river. A very cold night; froze a little. Wrote a letter to Louisa.

Friday, December 23rd.

We are ordered to build houses. It is thought that the Army will stay here some time. Steamboats came up from the fleet today. Received a letter from Louisa. We are encamped on the R.R. The boys take a [railroad] car, load it with lumber, & push it down to camp, then use the lumber to build our shanties. Citizens are beginning to come out on the streets again. I suppose they have found out that the Yanks will not eat them.

Saturday, December 24th.

A Grand Review came off today of our Corps, by Sherman. I do not know how it happened, as Sherman is not noted for Reviews. Only the Army of the Potomac knows how to review.

Sunday, December 25th.   Savannah

Christmas Day. No pies or Chicken-fixins for dinner but only a little mush & sugar. Our rations are not very regular yet. Attended the Presbyterian church in town both forenoon & afternoon. Rev. Mr. Axon, the regular pastor, preached.[20] At night Chaplain Bigger of our Regt. preached in camp.

Monday, December 26th.

Saw the 1st Schooner today. Ships have not come up the river yet as there are too many obstructions, but they are busy removing them.

Tuesday, December 27th.

The 14th Corps was reviewed today. Heard that Gen. Thomas had gained a great victory over Hood at Nashville. "Surely the Union Cause is gaining ground."

Wednesday, December 28th.

We hear that Jeff Davis has gone to Europe, but of course it is a yarn. Vessels of large size are beginning to come up the river. As I write this, there is a large vessel of 3 masts just coming in sight. It is 10 miles from Savannah to the mouth of the river.

Thursday, December 29th.

The Citizens held a meeting today to see what position they should take, now that they were under the "Old Flag." They passed a series of resolutions, accepting of the President's Amnesty, declaring themselves in favor of Peace &c. We are building quarters.

Friday, December 30th.   Savannah

The Old Year is drawing to a close. Time flies fast, but not as fast as I would wish. I long for the time when Peace shall triumph over war. For the time when I can rejoin my wife and friends at home. I feel hopeful that the time is not far distant.

Saturday, December 31st.

The last day of the year. The Muster Rolls have kept me quite busy for several days past, also various other Papers, Rolls [and] Returns, so I have no time to run about. Capt. [Henry E.] Horn our Regimental Commander has resigned & gone home. Capt. [Horace L.] Burnham of our company now commands the Regiment. Capt. [Timothy D.] McGillicuddy, who has commanded the Regt. since Allatoona, has resigned.[21]

Sunday, January 1st, 1865.

New Year's Day. I remained in my shantie all day & wrote a letter to Louisa. Quite a cold day for this country. I have been thinking over my wanderings; thinking of the places I have spent my New Year's days for a few years past. 1865 in Savannah. 1864 with my wife in Adams [County] Ills. 1863 Fort Union N.M. 1862 Fort Craig N.M. 1861 Fort Craig N.M. 1860 Fort Bridger U.T. 1859 Fort Bridger U.T. 1858 Gilson, Ill.

Out of the last 8 New Year's days, I have only spent 1 at home. It seems my fate or Destiny to ramble in that way. How I would like to drop in at home tonight. Well, Perhaps the time will come soon. I ought to be thankful to God for his care over me & mine during the Past year. If I am living the next New Year's, where will I then be? Perhaps at Home.

Monday, January 2nd.

Well, another day in the new year has gone. I went out in the country about 8 miles for lumber to finish our shanties. The plantation [Wormsloe] was owned by a Dr. Jones,[22] who left when the Yankees came. He left most of his property. We found nearly a hundred negros (slaves) in their quarters. Dr. Jones has a very large house and [it] was richly furnished, but now the furnishing is gone. I regret to say that somebody destroyed lots of valuable furniture; marble top stands, tables, bureaus. This I think is wrong. The things destroyed did no good to the rebel cause and ought to be let alone. I got for our shantie a door, window & table.

Tuesday, January 3rd.   Savannah

Last night I went up to town to go to the theater. There being none, I went to church & probably spent my time as well or better than if I had attended the theater. I spent the day in putting the finishing touches on our shantie. We are comfortably fixed now. I have no idea how long we remain.

Wednesday, January 4th.

The 17th Corps have received marching orders. 1 Division left today. They embarked on board transports at Fort Jackson. I understand the whole Corps will leave tomorrow. Where they are going, no one can tell.

Thursday, January 5th.

The remainder of the 17th Corps left today. I suppose other Corps will follow in a few days. I have just heard that our fleet & land forces are fighting at Wilmington, N.C. Perhaps our Army will join them. Lewis F. Roe.

Friday, January 6th.[23]   Savannah, Georgia

Our whole regiment was on fatigue today, building breastworks close around the city. I suppose that a small force will garrison it.

Saturday, January 7th.

We had a grand review of our Corps (15th) today by Gen. Sherman. We did very well, so they say. Gen. [John A.] Logan was there, having

FIGURE 29. Gen. Sherman reviewing his Army in Savannah, January 1865. Sketch by
W. Waud. Collections of the Library of Congress negative LC-USZ62–161.

just arrived from the north.[24] We drew new clothing today, which we
were badly in need of.

Sunday, January 8th.

It is rumored that the 1st Division of our Corps starts tomorrow
for Beaufort [South Carolina]. The ships down at the wharf, 10 or 12 in
number, have all their colors flying, probably in honor of the battle of
New Orleans in 1812. Attended the Independent Presbyterian church
in town. The meetings are attended by a very few old men and several
soldiers, but no ladies.

Monday, January 9th.

I have nothing to do nowadays but to hear reports and I hear
Plenty of them. They have it now that our Division [4th] will remain
here. The 1st Division have not left here yet, but expect to go tomorrow.
They expect to go to Fort Thunderbolt & there embark for Beaufort,
South Carolina.

Tuesday, January 10th.

Went out to Dr. Jones' Plantation about 8 miles from here for lumber to build a kitchen. Neglected to take our Rubbers [ponchos or rubber blankets] & got a bad wetting, the rain poured down in streams. We walked back 8 miles in just 1 3/4 hours. Pretty tall walking, we think. Saw 2 great big animals in the river, about as large as a horse. I guess they were porpoises; none of us knew.[25] The 1st Division has gone.

Wednesday, January 11th.

A cold, windy day. Lt. Col. [William] Hanna & Lt. [Samuel W.] Starrett came to the Regt. today. They were home on leave of absence. They came by way of New York. Ansel Lewis joined us from [the] Gen. Hospital at Nashville. Heard Q.K. Philander Doesticks P.B. lecture.[26] 2 conscripts joined; there are about 200 on the road here.

Thursday, January 12th.

Kilpatrick's Cavalry was reviewed today by Sherman. Secretary of War (Stanton) was there, also Gen. [Montgomery] Meigs, Q.M. General. The Cavalry presented a very fine appearance; about 6,000 in number.

Friday, January 13th.

The 2nd Division of our Corps has left. 2 Divisions of the 20th Corps left some days ago & the whole 17th Corps went over a week ago. I have all of the Company writing done & will probably do duty in the Co. in a day or two.

Saturday, January 14th.

Nothing of importance to write about today. The citizens have opened their stores. Things look quite business like.

Sunday, January 15th.

Our whole Regiment was at work on the breastworks. Received a letter from Louisa. No news about moving.

Monday, January 16th.

The 14th Corps have orders to start out tomorrow. I suppose the Army will move on Charleston. I think it very likely our Division will stay here. Gen. Corse has been made Brevet Maj. Gen. for bravery at Allatoona.

Tuesday, January 17th. [*Misdated January 16 in original notes.*]

1 Division of the 20th Corps started today. I succeeded in getting a New York Herald today, the 1st northern Paper I've had for a long while. Some of the merchants have got in a supply of goods from the north.

Wednesday, January 18th. [*Misdated January 17 in original notes.*]

The Division that left yesterday had to come back last night. A large bridge that had to be crossed was torn up by the heavy flood. This will delay our move a day or two. The 14th Corps has not gone yet. It is well known now that we will leave in a day or two. Our Regt. of Engineers have gone to repair the broken Bridge. Lewis F. Roe

Louisa, you need not expect any more letters from me for some time as we will start tomorrow probably. LFR

[*Editor's note: The journal entries from January 19–26, 1865, are taken from Lewis Roe's second notebook. His original journal from this period evidently has not survived.*]

Thursday, January 19th.

The troops that started yesterday returned ~~returned~~ last night. A barge [pontoon?] bridge over the Savannah R. was torn up by the heavy flood. This will cause a delay. But the rumor now is that Sherman's whole Army will soon be on the move. This is as it should be.

> January 19th, 1865
> Dear Louisa
>
> Here I am with knapsack on my back & harversack full of hard-tack, ready for another campaign. Our Division is out in the street, waiting for our turn to cross the pontoon bridge over the Savannah River. As we were near the Christian Commission rooms, I thought I would drop in & write, as in all probability my last letter from Savannah. It is quite a wet & chilly morning & my fingers are so numb that I can hardly write.
>
> It is thought that we go to Charleston; at all events we will soon be in that "hot bed of treason," South Carolina. All of Sherman's Army is on the move. This place will be held by a portion of the 19th Corps, just arrived. We are glad that our 4 Corp. [Division?] remains

together. Look for us pounding away at Charleston in about a week.
Every body is confident of success & we think we can almost see the
end of the Rebellion. Continue to write, directing your letters via
Savannah. I will write again whenever there is an opportunity, but it
may be sometime.

Good by, my dear wife; kiss our little one for me.
Yours & c
Lewis F. Roe

Friday, January 20th [*misdated January 19 in second notebook*]

Started on another campaign, but returned at night to our old
camp. I understand that there is about 50 miles of corduroy road to be
built. The almost incessant rain is the cause of all our troubles, I expect.
It is reported that Charleston is evacuated.

Saturday, January 21st [*misdated January 20 in second notebook*]

Had our knapsacks packed ready to move at a moment's notice, but
tonight it is said we will remain here several days, as the country on the
other side of the river is flooded. It has been raining for the last 2 days.
Provisions given by the northern cities to the poor of Savannah are
coming in every few days.

Sunday, January 22nd [*misdated January 21 in second notebook*]

Still wet and raining, but the 14th corps started up the river,
through mud and water. 2 Div. 19th Corps came in; they are to remain
here. Went to church today. Heard a first-rate sermon. Heard of the
capture of Ft. Fisher, N.C.[27]

Monday, January 23rd [*misdated January 25 in second notebook*]

2 of our boys whose time of service has expired left for home today.
Drill has commenced again.

Tuesday, January 24th.   Savannah

A very cold day; the coldest day I have felt. Ice froze 1/2 an inch
thick last night, which is very unusual for Savannah. No signs of a
move as yet. Still we are expecting orders every day.

Wednesday, January 25th.

Still continues clear and cold. There are reports afloat that we start tomorrow. The Quartermaster and Hospital Dept. have orders to move tomorrow. We are ready and anxious to start.

Thursday, January 26th.

There seems to be no let up to the cold weather. We made another start for Beaufort, S.C., or some other place today, but only got as far as town when we were ordered back.

Oysters on the Half-Shell

Charles D. Kerr accompanied Sherman's campaigns through Georgia and the Carolinas as the Adjutant of the 16th Illinois Infantry, 14th Army Corps. In later years, he contributed a well-written and accurate overview of their experiences to volume 1 of the Minnesota MOLLUS series, *Glimpses of the Nation's Struggle* (St. Paul, Minn., 1887), 202–23.

Kerr recalled that their "one month's stay in the vicinity of Savannah was simply delightful. . . . The succulent oysters brought to each regiment by wagon-loads from their bed in the [Ossabaw] sound, where they had lain undisturbed for years, will never be forgotten.

"Listen to the *menu* from my diary of Sunday, January 1, 1865, and pity the poor soldier: 'Dinner for headquarters' mess. Oyster soup, oysters on the half shell, roast goose, fried oysters, roasted oysters, rice, raisins, and coffee, with condensed milk, of course. A little top-heavy as to oysters, but we don't complain.'"

Up Through the Carolinas, January 27–March 27, 1865

LATE IN 1863 THE UNION AND CONFEDERATE WESTERN ARMIES SETTLED INTO "WINTER QUARTERS" TO REORGANIZE AND RE-EQUIP FOR A NEW ROUND OF FIGHTING IN THE SPRING. ONE year later President Lincoln pushed his generals to keep the war going without a break. Army chief-of-staff Maj. Gen. H. W. Halleck put it this way in his letter of January 1, 1865, to Sherman.

> It is useless talking about putting any of our armies into winter quarters. It is not necessary, and the financial condition of the country will not permit it. Those troops not required for defense must move into the enemy's country and live on it. There is no alternative; it must be done.[1]

Sherman had scarcely arrived in Savannah when he started planning his next campaign. This he outlined in letters to generals Halleck and Grant. His army would strike north to Columbia and Camden, South Carolina, breaking up the railroad system while ignoring Charleston, South Carolina, and Augusta, Georgia. Continuing beyond, he would reestablish contact with the fleet at Wilmington, North Carolina, then move on to Raleigh. This would force Robert E. Lee to react. It was a perfectly elegant strategy and one that gained immediate acceptance. He optimistically told Grant in his letter of December 24 that "I expect to be ready to sally forth again" in about ten days. He soon moved the date back to January 15.[2]

General Sherman still had four army corps. Maj. Gen. O. O. Howard retained command of the 15th and 17th Army Corps—the Army of the Tennessee and the Right Wing. As of January 8, Maj. Gen. John A.

Logan assumed command of the 15th Corps. The Left Wing, or Army of Georgia, consisted of the 14th and 20th Corps, all under the same commanders who had taken them to Savannah. Bvt. Maj. Gen. Judson Kilpatrick had just fewer than 4,500 cavalrymen present for duty. In all, almost 64,000 experienced campaigners awaited their trek up through the Carolinas.[3]

January 15 came and went; getting troops in place and marshaling supplies took time. The men began to move during the second week of January. The Right Wing—the 17th and most of the 15th Army Corps (some 24,600 men without Bvt. Maj. Gen. John Corse's 4th Division)—went about fifty miles by sea from Savannah and disembarked at Port Royal Island on the coast of South Carolina, then marched inland to a place called Pocotaligo. Sherman had transferred his headquarters on January 9 to Beaufort on Port Royal Island and later moved to Pocotaligo. The navy had to move the means of transport as well—wagons, ambulances, and pontoon trains—and as many as 20,000 animals. Storms at sea delayed the arrival of materials, virtually all of which had to come by ship. Sherman said his supplies sometimes came by daily driblets. The army would move out when the wagons were loaded. While the wagons would carry foodstuffs to meet immediate needs, the assistant adjutant general for Lewis Roe's division issued a masterfully worded field order that said in effect—waste not, want not, and don't neglect to forage.[4]

By January 28, the two corps positioned between the Salkehatchie and Coosawhatchie rivers were ready to march northward along parallel roads, and Sherman expected to start on Tuesday, January 31. He had been waiting to hear from his Left Wing, the 14th and 20th Corps, with about 29,300 troops under Maj. Gen. Henry Slocum, who had departed Savannah on January 20. The 1st and 3rd Divisions of the 20th proceeded up the east side of the Savannah River. Very heavy rains prevented Roe's own 4th Division of the 15th Army Corps from crossing at Savannah, and they took the west side of the river instead. Everyone met about thirty miles upstream at a place known as Sister's Ferry. On February 4, the troops on the western side of the river finally crossed the mile-wide stream to unite the Left Wing.[5]

Sherman started anyway on February 1 and a courier from the 20th Corps caught up with him at Hickory Hill, a planter's house on the Coosawhatchie River, eighteen miles along the way. His aide,

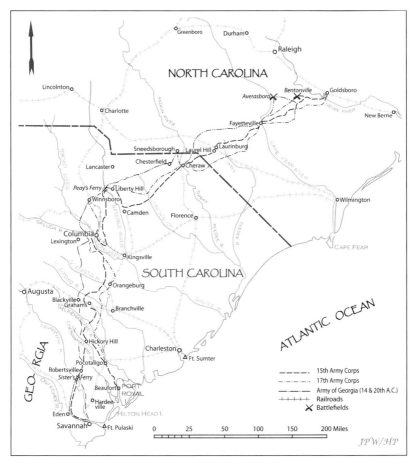

MAP 9. The Carolinas Campaign, February–March 1865. Courtesy of author and
Holli Pope.

Maj. Henry Hitchcock, wrote that only Sherman and very few others knew even the general outlines of their campaign or that its initial
objective was Columbia.[6]

The Left Wing made uneven progress for the first week. Lewis Roe's
journal and brief references in *War of the Rebellion, A Compilation
of the Official Records* show that his 4th Division, 15th Army Corps
moved independently, basically following in the trail of the 14th Corps.
The expectation was that the 4th Division would rejoin its own (15th)
Corps at Hickory Hill, about twenty-six miles east of the river.

The Right Wing advanced as far as the South Carolina or Augusta and Charleston Railroad on the 7th and spent the following day tearing up tracks, burning ties, and twisting rails. That same day part of the Left Wing caught up at a point called Graham's Station, and the next two days turned into a binge of destruction along a forty-mile stretch of the South Carolina Railroad. Many towns were burned as well. Lewis Roe and the 4th Division joined with the rest of the army after this orgy of railroad destruction had been pretty well completed. He was wrong about Branchville, where the enemy sat waiting as Sherman passed to the west instead.[7]

The Southern mindset had held that his destination(s) must be Charleston or Augusta. To encourage this line of thinking, the Left Wing and Kilpatrick's cavalry threatened Augusta, bottling up the defenders there, then struck north in the direction of Lexington, South Carolina, where they skirmished several times before feinting east and camping a few miles west of Columbia on February 16. As Wade Hampton wrote later, "It would scarcely have been possible to disperse a force more effectually than was done in our case."[8]

Roe's division had made its own way after leaving Sister's Ferry on the 5th, following existing roads as far as Hickory Hill. The troops kept on the trail of the 17th Corps until the evening of February 10, when the division came to Lee's plantation on the South Carolina Railroad and camped for the night. Brevet Major General Corse rode another four miles ahead to the Corps headquarters. There, according to a newspaper correspondent,

> Tonight [February 10] a small man, with a keen, lustrous eye, and the features of a brave and tireless soldier, with a ugly scar from a bullet wound on the left cheek and ear, threw himself into a chair at General [John A.] Logan's headquarters, exclaiming with a fervor that evidenced how intensely in earnest he was, "Thank God, Logan, I'm here at last." The glare of the camp fire lit up the bronzed features of the hero to Allatoona, General Corse.[9]

The Right Wing continued to have an interesting time of it as the troops headed northeast towards Orangeburg. There the 17th Corps proceeded to demolish the railroad northward for twelve miles. The 15th Corps remained in reserve a few miles to the west, where three

brigades of the 2nd Division skirmished with the enemy while crossing the North Edisto River. The 4th Division (Roe's) stayed in reserve.[10]

Once across the river the troops entered the turpentine country,
as Lewis Roe called it. For generations the southern longleaf pine had
been a source of naval stores; the pine resin, pitch, and turpentine
essential for the operation of wooden sailing ships. The pine woods
either caught or were set afire, and while Lewis Roe's journal implies
that the fires were horrific, the *Cincinnati Daily Gazette*'s correspondent penned a much more vivid account:

> I witnessed to-day more destruction of property than has been
> wrought on any other day of the campaign. Stored away, some
> distance out in the pineries, the troops found nearly a thousand
> barrels of turpentine. This was fired at once. The prodigious column
> of smoke that rose majestically toward the heavens and canopied
> the country for miles and miles, mangling the pitchy blackness with
> the lighter smoke ascending from the burning trees of the pineries,
> actually shut out the sun rays, and left the army in a murky, dirty
> darkness. The trees all thick with resinous drippings were fired by
> the soldiers as the column passed through, and this entire dense
> forest of pines, when I entered it, was swimming in suffocating
> smoke, and hot with the crackling, roaring flames. The dry brush
> and leaves took fire, the dead pines blazed, and the forest seemed
> but a vast temple of nature, with columns of fire supporting an arch
> of verdure.[11]

Not one of the official reports in the *War of the Rebellion, A Compilation
of the Official Records* volume that covers the Carolinas Campaign
mentioned this destruction in turpentine country.

In contrast with the bright prospects for the Union cause at the
beginning of 1865, the Confederacy stood in disarray. General Hood
resigned command of his Army of Tennessee on January 13, even as surviving units began making their way east to the Carolinas. Two weeks
later, a native South Carolinian and forceful cavalryman, Maj. Gen.
Wade Hampton, transferred back from Virginia. With his promotion
to lieutenant general on February 16, he held command of all 6,700
Confederate cavalrymen opposing Sherman.[12]

Following his retreat from Savannah in December, Lieutenant
General Hardee took up his command of the Department of South

Carolina, Georgia, and Florida at Charleston, South Carolina. General Beauregard, also at Charleston for a time, led something called the Military Division of the West, which evidently included everything from Augusta, Georgia, to the west. The Southern forces were "much divided," as another general put it. They had been falling for one after another of Sherman's feints and deceptions. Beauregard's orders for rear guards to destroy all bridges, trestles, and railroads when possible, had simply helped to cut the Confederates' own lines of retreat and supply, much as Sherman's men were doing intentionally. The rebels' near-obsession with burning baled cotton to keep it out of Yankee hands would soon lead to a disaster.[13]

On February 16, President Davis appointed Beauregard to command all of the troops operating in South Carolina. That day both Beauregard and Wade Hampton were in Columbia, but they did not organize a resistance. Somehow the two Confederates avoided meeting, and after skirmishing and an artillery exchange, resistance there faded away. The city's mayor rode out at about 11 a.m. and surrendered Columbia to Col. George A. Stone of the 25th Iowa Infantry. A correspondent for the *New York Tribune* noted that on their entrance into the city, "the women rushed frantically into the streets with bottles of whisky and basins of whisky, and cups of whisky, and whisky in every sort of vessel." The mayor demurred on this behavior, but the governor reportedly said, "No, let the damned Yankees drink it and get drunk." And so they did. Lewis Roe's journal omitted a few such details.[14]

After Sherman entered the city, he ordered all arsenals, warehouses, railroads, depots, "machinery useful in war," and other property of use to the enemy destroyed, while sparing private homes, schools, asylums, etc. Many accounts described the burning of Columbia in great detail, including that all of the cotton had been moved into the streets with the bales torn open. One correspondent said that some of Major General Wheeler's men, the last Confederate troops to leave town, set fire to the cotton initially. Arriving federal soldiers apparently put it out, but a strong gale on the evening of the 17th rekindled the embers. Burning tufts of cotton flew in all directions, and many of the soldiers again attempted to extinguish the flames, but by the following morning about one-third of Columbia had been turned into a blackened ruin. Major General Logan's 1st Division of his 15th Army Corps had provost duty that night, but "the citizens had so crazed our men with

FIGURE 30. Ruins in Columbia, S.C., No. 2. George Barnard photograph. From *Photographic Views of Sherman's Campaign* (1977) [1866], plate 55.

liquor that it was almost impossible to control them. . . . Some fiend first applied the torch and the wild flames leaped from house to house and street until the lower and business part of the city was wrapped in flames."[15] And as his journal shows, Lewis Roe was an eyewitness.

Thus far Sherman's strategy had worked extremely well. Beauregard, Hardee, and Hampton had marshaled resistance at places Sherman had no intention of visiting, such as Augusta and Charleston. Jefferson Davis belatedly realized that divided commands were not a good way to fight a war. On February 6, he did what he should have done long before; he confirmed General Robert E. Lee as general-in-chief of the Confederate armies.[16]

Lt. Gen. James Longstreet, Lee's most trusted Corps commander, knew about the shifts of command in the making, and he sent Lee a well-timed recommendation that Joe Johnston be restored to command of the Army of Tennessee. When Lee finally acted on this recommendation, he found Johnston at a place ironically named Lincolnton in western North Carolina. On February 22, Johnston received orders to assume command of the Army of Tennessee and all of the troops in the Department of South Carolina, Georgia, and Florida.[17]

General Lee ordered Johnston to concentrate all available forces and drive back Sherman. This order came much too late. Sherman's army had already captured Columbia, South Carolina, and the city largely lay in ruins. Charleston had been ignored, and one day later that city's garrison evacuated it without a fight.[18] Sherman and Johnston, however, would meet in battle one more time.

The Union troops completed their work at Columbia as the Left Wing and Kilpatrick's cavalry continued north to the Greenville and Columbia Railroad and ripped up these tracks on the 19th. This infantry-cavalry combined force then headed straight for Winnsboro, South Carolina. The rest of the army resumed its march on February 20, and in two days the Right Wing advanced some forty miles to a crossing named Peay's Ferry on the Wateree River. The Left Wing crossed farther upstream while Kilpatrick's cavalry ranged north as far as Lancaster, South Carolina, near the North Carolina border. The two infantry wings then turned east to threaten the railroad town of Camden, South Carolina, but bypassed it instead, leaving a detachment from Brevet Major General Corse's second brigade to destroy the government stores there. Until the 26th, the army met no opposition. Beauregard believed that Sherman would continue north toward Charlotte and so had his men out of place, as usual.[19]

At Lynch's Creek, the Right Wing encountered a swollen stream and flooded lowlands to either side, too deep to ford. The infantry divisions waded across on the 26th, when the first brigade in Corse's division clashed with Maj. Gen. Matthew Butler's division of rebel cavalry. Corse's men pushed the enemy back after heavy skirmishing and held onto the crossing. The wagon train that bore the army's supplies had to wait until March 1 when the water subsided enough for two plank bridges to be constructed by the 15th and 17th Corps respectively. The Left Wing meanwhile had fallen far behind. Perhaps as some small compensation, Major General Howard noted that "We found the country at this point very rich, plenty of provisions for the horses and men."[20]

As the architect of this campaign, Sherman more than anyone was aware of what such delays were costing him. He learned, probably through prisoner interrogations, that he no longer faced just Gen. P. G. T. Beauregard and lieutenant generals W. J. Hardee and Wade Hampton, but his old nemesis from the Atlanta Campaign, Gen. Joseph E. Johnston as well. This put a different complexion on matters, as Sherman took the trouble to explain in his report of April 4, 1865. Johnston could be expected to make good use of any delays to gather his scattered army, and Sherman had ample reason for exercising "extreme caution" when he continued eastward toward Goldsboro, North Carolina, then about six days away.[21]

Two days after leaving Lynch's Creek, the Union 17th Corps pushed into Cheraw, South Carolina. They had a fierce skirmish, fighting through the town with the fleeing Confederates, who set fire to the bridge there across the Great Pee Dee River. With Cheraw secure, Sherman arrived on March 4, and except for the 14th Corps, the rest of his army filtered in over several days.[22]

Cheraw lay at the terminus of a railroad spur that led up from Florence and Charleston, South Carolina. Earlier the Confederates had run everything north to Cheraw, including twenty-five artillery pieces, thousands of small arms, immense quantities of ammunition and stores of provisions, some 44,000 pounds of gunpowder, and even a large amount of vintage wines. Maj. Gen. Frank Blair subsequently distributed the latter to other Union officers "in fair proportions." The business district and public buildings were ransacked and burned, although private residences largely escaped.[23]

A terrific explosion on the morning of March 6, described by Roe, had some interesting consequences caught by the regimental historian. . . .

> Shells and solid shot, grape and canister rained all over the city. One of the boys, sitting by the fireside entertaining a young lady, was surprised by a shell passing through the side of the house and between them, burying itself in the brick of the chimney.
>
> At the camp of the Fiftieth, one-half mile away, the sergeant-major was engaged in washing his clothes, he was suffering with a severe chill at the time; the Chaplain was standing near, when suddenly the air was full of shrieking missiles and a 12-pound shell struck the fire between them and went bounding on. The sergeant-major was cured of the ague at once, while the Chaplain, not knowing what was up jumped into the air and then made good his escape.[24]

Such pyrotechnical displays were becoming a predictable feature of Sherman's campaign.

Cheraw lay only about seven miles south of the North Carolina line and the 20th Corps had actually camped near Sneedsborough, North Carolina, on March 4–5, before turning south to rejoin the other Corps. On leaving Cheraw and crossing the Great Pee Dee River, Sherman directed his army northeastward toward Fayetteville, North Carolina, distant some sixty miles. Lieutenant General Hardee retreated before this oncoming host, skirmishing with the 14th and 17th Corps, which reached Fayetteville on the 11th. By now, many soldiers had become shoeless. General Hampton captured the camp of one of Kilpatrick's brigades in a surprise raid, but the Union horsemen rallied and drove him off.[25]

From his camp near Laurel Hill Church, Maj. Gen. O. O. Howard had sent two scouts bearing dispatches through the lines to Wilmington, North Carolina, on March 7. They slipped past the enemy and arrived at the coastal city two days later. As a result, the day he arrived at Fayetteville (March 12), Howard was surprised by the whistle of an army tug, the *Davidson*, which had ascended the Cape Fear River bearing a little sugar and coffee, a few shoes, and a quantity of oats, but unfortunately no mail or even newspapers. More vessels followed. This first contact of Sherman's army with the outside world in forty-four days was clearly a morale-booster for the troops.[26]

Before the war, Fayetteville had been the site of a U.S. Arsenal. Sherman now leveled and burned the arsenal buildings there and broke up every piece of machinery. Captured ordnance included twenty-six cannons, more than 2,000 muskets, and thousands of rounds of small-arms ammunition. The steamers returning to Wilmington carried the thousands of refugees, white and black, who had been following the army since Columbia.[27]

Sporadic resistance still reflected a lack of coordination on the part of the Confederate command. However, by March 10 General Johnston had resumed his efforts to concentrate his forces ahead of Sherman. As of March 17, he had a little over 15,000 infantry, 900 artillerymen, and some 4,000 cavalry at hand. The two sides were roughly equal in cavalry, but otherwise Johnston could scarcely match one of Sherman's Corps in strength.[28]

At Fayetteville, major generals Howard (Right Wing, 15th and 17th Corps) and Slocum (Left Wing, 14th and 20th Corps) changed their order of march and acted on intelligence findings to organize four "light" divisions in each wing. These would travel with reduced wagon trains bearing munitions, leaving rations to be carried in the soldiers' haversacks. Howard selected the four divisions in Major General Logan's 15th Corps, with Corse's division in the lead. The army passed March 12, 13, and 14 at Fayetteville, then moved out from the Cape Fear River on March 15. Corse's men, with Lewis Roe and the 50th Illinois, reached the South River that afternoon and forced a crossing after a severe skirmish. The next day they skirmished again and then slogged along in rain and waded through waist-deep swamps before arriving at the Goldsborough road.[29]

A dozen miles to the north, on the same day, the federal Left Wing came up against Confederate Lieutenant General Hardee's Corps, some 6,500 strong, blocking the direct Goldsborough road. Fifteen hundred of Wheeler's cavalry joined him. They fought most of the day against Major General Slocum's four "light" divisions and Kilpatrick's cavalry in what was called the Battle of Averasborough. Sherman had accompanied Slocum's column. The Right Wing meanwhile had its hands full "wallowing along the miry roads" and worked its way well to the east before it finally heard about the battle that night.[30]

Sherman thought that the enemy would make no further opposition to his progress, and he shifted from Slocum's to Howard's wing on the 19th. He found the 15th Corps badly straggled for fifteen miles along the New Goldsborough Road. The 17th Corps and the wagon trains were making their own way along a parallel road about five miles to the south.[31]

Johnston considered that he had won the Averasborough contest. He redeployed Hardee's corps with substantial reinforcements, so that he had around 15,000 men poised on either side of the Goldsborough road on the morning of March 19. They skirmished with the advance of the 14th and 20th Corps, and at 2:15 p.m., Johnston ordered his two wing commanders to launch their assault. The Battle of Bentonville continued into the night with Johnston's Confederates contending against Slocum's force of about 20,000 men, and ended in a draw for that day. Casualties on both sides were heavy. Lewis Roe's division and the 15th Corps took no part in this fighting.[32]

That night Sherman, who was ten miles east of the battlefront at Falling Creek Church, received word that Slocum had held the line, but he could be in serious trouble and needed reinforcements to face at least 45,000 enemy troops. General Sherman quickly ordered the 2nd Division of Roe's Corps to retrace its steps and then turn north to join Slocum's forces, which it did by 6:30 a.m. on March 20. Early that same morning, the 1st, 3rd, and 4th Divisions of the 15th Corps left their camps near Falling Creek Church and moved north a few miles to Cox's Crossroads, then bore left and west down the Goldsborough Road toward the battlefield. Scarcely a mile along, they clashed with Butler's cavalry, after which the 7th Illinois (part of Roe's brigade) had lively work with their sixteen-shot Henry rifles in keeping up a running fight. By noon, the 15th Corps "could distinctly hear the musketry in General Slocum's front."[33]

Three regiments from the 1st Division were ordered forward while the rest dug in. One regiment, the 25th Iowa, linked up with a regiment from the 2nd Division and the two units then had "pretty warm work" with the North Carolinians in their front. Major General Blair's 17th Corps came up in mid-afternoon and skirmishers from the two wings finally met about 4 p.m., reuniting Sherman's army. Lewis Roe's version of the day's events was accurate but very much on the sparse side.[34]

In contrast, Roe's journal entry for March 21 offered as detailed and accurate an account of the Battle of Bentonville as one could ask for. The regimental history and Lieutenant Colonel Hanna's report told even more about the 50th Illinois' actions.[35] The regiment held its place in the line of battle all day, pushing its skirmish line into the enemy's rifle pits, then retreating, only to rush forward and then retreat another time. This see-saw fighting continued into the night with the regiment losing only two men killed and fifteen wounded. By 3 o'clock the following morning, the enemy had evacuated their whole line of works.[36]

The 7th Illinois and part of the 50th Illinois followed the retreating rebels as far as Bentonville, then returned to their old camp. Sherman issued a congratulatory letter to his army on March 22 just before he started off for Goldsboro, about twenty-five miles distant. The army followed, and on March 24, most of the regiments crossed the Neuse River and marched through Goldsboro. Sherman reviewed them there, as Lewis Roe noted in his last journal entry.

The March 26 paragraph in the regimental history said that the 50th Illinois had been out fifty-eight days from Savannah. This was almost a month longer than the Savannah Campaign, and the men had marched about 200 miles farther, across much less hospitable terrain.

In Georgia, the army had mostly traveled parallel to the river systems, whereas in South Carolina, it must have seemed that the troops were crossing one river or swamp after another until they reached Columbia. Beyond Columbia, the regiments passed over hilly country for a few days until Sherman redirected the march toward the east, after which they faced flooded river crossings or worse almost daily. One officer noted that from mid-January to the end of the campaign, it rained on twenty-one days.

The flooded rivers and impassable roads were a major problem for the wagon trains as well. Pioneer corps, consisting of detachments drawn from each division, reconstructed bridges and made corduroy roads so that the trains could pass. Pontoon trains, with eighty-five or more wagons, were also a permanent feature of each wing.

Reading the reports of the campaign generates an awareness and finally an admiration for the efficiency and speed with which everything was done. Nothing slowed this army; bridges across flooded rivers were rebuilt within hours, and miles upon miles of corduroyed roads were laid down, using poles, pine saplings, and fence rails. In some cases, these were pinned down underwater so that the army could maintain an average pace of eight to ten miles a day. Sometimes torpedoes had been placed in segments of submerged roads; removing these required special care.

Officers in some of the corps developed an interest in statistics, and Bvt. Maj. Gen. Alpheus Williams estimated that his 20th Corps corduroyed at least 275 miles of the roads traveled by the trains, while burning some 500 cotton gins and presses. Major General Logan's 15th Corps reported corduroying 101 miles, while his 4th Division (Corse's) built thirty-one bridges. Bvt. Maj. Gen. John Geary, 2nd Division, 20th Corps, wrote the best single account of how Sherman's army accomplished these feats of construction.[37]

The men themselves were seemingly made of iron. Sherman's medical director, Dr. John Moore, reported a very small number of sick soldiers in the Carolinas campaign, a fraction over 2 percent in an army of 65,000. This was much less than if they had been in garrison. Those who died of illness, if any, were so few that no specific tabulation for them was made. Casualties—those wounded, killed, and captured or missing—totaled only 3,939 in all for the Left Wing, Right Wing, and Cavalry Corps. Using Dr. Moore's figure of 65,000 as the strength of the command, the casualty rate amounted to only 6.06 percent. More than half of these resulted from the two battles of Averasborough and Bentonville.[38]

Once arrived at Goldsboro, the soldiers waited to see what Uncle Billy would do. He promptly took the railroad (which had just been rebuilt) to the coast and thence by steamer to City Point, Virginia, where he conferred with President Lincoln; generals Grant, Meade, and Ord; and others, then returned to Goldsboro within a week. In his absence, trainloads of clothing, shoes, food, and full supplies of everything arrived for the troops, "and all things were working well." The 50th Illinois received two sacks of mail and eighty-five recruits. For two weeks, the army would rest, refit, and recuperate in its camps around Goldsboro.[39]

⊶⊷

January 27th, 1865[40]

Camp No. 1. We are off on another campaign, but where are we going? Of course, we expect we will cross the river into S.C. [South Carolina]. Well, she needs a taste of war, and when we get over the river, she'll get it. Left Savannah about 8 o'clock this morning, and tonight are encamped on the Ga. Central R.R. Some think that as we did not cross the river at Savannah, we are going to Augusta. The 2nd Div. 20th Corps and ours (4th Div. 15th Corps) were the last to leave Savannah. It has been quite a cold day, but we are in the big pine woods and have big fires and are all right. Our Brigade (3rd brig. 4 div. 15th C.) built a mile of corduroy road today.

January 28th.   Camp near Eden, Ga.

Camp No. 2. We marched about 8 miles today and built a good deal of Corduroy Road. On train guard today, which is an irksome job, helping wagons out of the mud. We go a short distance, probably half a mile, when the train gets stuck in the mud. Teamsters swear, officers get uneasy, &c. Happy the soldier who has a large stock of patience. About dark we come floundering in, looking and feeling a good deal worse for wear. The next time our brigade is on train guard I hope we will be out of the swamps. But where are we going; that's what we want to know. Tonight we are encamped near Eden, a station on the Ga. Central R.R.[41]

FIGURE 31. Making Corduroy Road. From Charles F. Hubert, *History of the Fiftieth Regiment, Illinois Volunteer Infantry* (1894), p. 347.

In camp 30 miles above Savannah Ga.

Jan. 30th, 1865

My Dear Wife

 I am on Camp Guard tonight. It is now 11 o'clock & I have to sit up until 12 to post the next relief, so I think I'll try & write you a few lines. An orderly came round & said to "have your letters ready by 7 o'clock tomorrow."

 Well, I suppose your first question would be, what are you doing out here in the Swamp? I don't know what we are doing or where we are going to. All I know about it is, we left Savannah 4 days ago & have been floundering along through mud & water until we have come this far out. Of the 30 miles from here to Savannah, there must be at least 10 miles [of] Corduroy roads built. If ever I get settled in America, I shall run for roadmaster, for I believe I understand road making first rate.

 They say it is only 4 miles further to the Savannah River, where we will cross over in South Carolina, & I guess it is the truth for I heard several boats whistle. They say that our train is to load there with provisions & then start out on a grand campaign. Others say we are going to a place called Coosawhatchie on the Charleston & Savannah R.R. a few miles from Beaufort & there fit out. Some say our campaign will be against Augusta, others say Charleston, others say Branchville. I expect to find myself near Richmond soon.

Our Division & the 2nd Division 20th Corps only are along. The remainder of the 15 & the 17th Corps went by water to Beaufort. We are to lay over here tomorrow. The marching is not hard, but we march about a mile, then stack arms & build a road over the swamp. My shoulders are a little sore though, as we have to carry a pretty big knapsack. Perhaps it would interest you to know what is in it. It has 1 woolen blanket, 1 rubber blanket, 2 shirts, 1 pr. Drawers, 1 pr. stockings, a Bible & a likeness of a certain woman & her baby, skein of thread, some writing materials. That with 3 days rations in my harversack [and] 40 rounds of ammunition in my Cartridge Box make quite a respectable load.

These nights are rather chilly, but we build up big fires of pine knots & logs & get along first rate. We do not get any sweet potatoes yet, but expect to as soon as we get over the river. In one of my letters to you, I said that I had rec. a letter from "*Bill.*" That was a mistake of the Printer; it was Charley Smith I rec. a letter from. I cannot send it home as you want me to because it is destroyed. The last letter I rec. from you was mailed on the 8th of this month.

I hope you & our little Carrie will keep well. I am in hopes this war will soon be over & I can come home once more. Every thing looks as if the end of the rebellion was nigh; then what a great & glorious time over these United States. You must write as often as you can. I'll get your letters I guess. Direct to 3rd Brig. 4th Div. 15th A.C. Sherman's Army via New York. I think we will keep open communication with Augusta [*Roe probably meant Savannah*]. Good night. Kiss our child for me.

Yours &c.
Lewis Roe

January 29th.   Springfield, Ga.

Camp No. 3. Still between the 2 rivers; Savannah and Ogeechee. About the only question discussed by the boys is where we are going to? If we are going in S.C., why don't we cross the river? Some of the boys put it in this way; that we are going to flank it; that is, march around its head waters. We march very slow; only about 10 miles today. Encamped near Springfield.

January 30th.   Sister's Ferry

Camp No. 4. We made another march of about 8 miles today. Passed through Springfield, also passed the 2 Div. of 20 Corps. We are encamped about 3 miles from Sister's Ferry over the Savannah River. Several boats are at Sister's Ferry; they came up from Savannah. I suppose they are loaded with supplies. I understand that we have quite a number of empty wagons in our train. Sister's Ferry is 30 miles from Savannah. On Camp Guard today. Wrote a letter to Louisa.

January 31st. February 1st.

Camp No. 4. No move today. We sleep a good part of the day. Built Dog houses today. The weather is somewhat warmer; warm enough to [be] out in our shirt sleeves. Chaplain Collins, 57th Ills., lectured at night. A large attendance.

February 2nd.

Gen. Corse, Div. commander, reviewed our brigade (3rd, 4th Div., 15 Corps). It is reported that we join our Corps (15th) at Hickory Hill, 40 miles away.

February 3rd.   On Savannah River

A pontoon bridge has been put across the river. A fatigue party was detailed to go over to build roads; also another party was detailed to go out foraging. Luckily, I escaped both details. It has been a rainy, wet day. I am anxious to leave. Saw an account of a big fire in Savannah.

Saturday, February 4th.[42]   In the Blackwater Swamp

Camp No. 5. Encamped at Sister's Landing. We remained in camp until about 4 o'clock P.M. A march of 3 miles brought us to the river. The 20th Corps crossed the river at about 1 o'clock. Crossed on

Pontoons. We reached the river and commenced crossing about dark and such a time as we had. There were two pontoon bridges; one for the trains and another in which the pontoons were placed end to end for the troops to cross on. As we came on this bridge, the pontoons would tip from side [to side], making it quite difficult for anyone to stay on the bridge at all. But there were torches at intervals. So we cross over. The bridge was about half a mile in length.

Now we cross the wide Savannah River bottom fully a mile wide, over a narrow causeway, wide ditches on each side filled with water and frogs. I have heard frogs before, but last night the frog concert was almost deafening. The night was pitch dark, but in time we came to the bluffs (which were only sand ridges) and encamped. We reached camp about 9 o'clock at night in the thickest fog I ever saw. Passed the 14th Corps & 2nd Div. 20th Corps.[43] Well, here we are in South Carolina. The first state to rebel. The boys talk about making the State howl, and they will. Day's march 8 miles.

Sunday, February 5th.

Camp No. 6. We lay with our knapsacks packed all day, expecting to move at any moment. Meanwhile, our Div. train was loading with provisions shipped up from Savannah. We made no move until about 5 o'clock P.M. About dark we came to a corduroy road built by troops who were in advance of us. We stumbled over this corduroy as best we could in the dark. It was about 3 miles in length, coming into camp about 9 o'clock in a place without wood or so dark that we could not find any. So we lay down wishing for the morning. It is reported that Sherman's Army will be reinforced by 2 Corps, the 4th & 23rd Corps from Tennessee. Encamped near Hardeeville.[44] Day's march 8 miles.

Monday, February 6th.   Robertville [Robertsville]

Camp No. 7. Roused up very early this morning; swallowed break-fast in a hurry & started out. Our march was through a fine country. The rebels have cut trees across the roads & obstructed them in every conceivable way. In the afternoon it commenced raining. Went into camp about dark. We have a wet, bad time. Day's march 15 miles.

Passed through Robertville today. Every house was burned; only a ~~house~~ church left standing. Burned by troops in advance. Builded [*sic*] a good deal of corduroy roads.

Tuesday, February 7th.   Hickory Hill

Camp No. 8. Got up all in a shiver. Everything wet; could hardly start a fire. Got breakfast; marched about 1 mile to a rail fence & waited for the train to pass. We built large fires & dried our blankets. About 2 o'clock we started a march of 4 miles; 3 of them over a swamp brought us to Hickory Hill. Our Corps was here 3 or 4 days ago, but have left in advance of us. Rec. mail. Got 2 letters; 1 from Louisa & 1 from Mother. Day's march 5 [miles].

Wednesday, February 8th.

Camp No. 9. We overtook a train of the 17th Corps that had been to Beaufort with wounded. The 17th have had a fight in front; had about 150 wounded.[45] It is said that our Corps (which left Savannah long before we did and went by sea to Beaufort S.C.) is only 20 miles ahead. The boys [foragers] got several hogs & some smoked meat today. Day's march 12 miles.

Thursday, February 9th.   Salkehatchie Swamp

Camp No. 10. Passed the late battlefield of the 4th Division 17th Corps & Wheeler's men. The "Johnnies" had fortified one side of a deep swamp. Our men had to wade it and drive the rebs from their position. The rebs had fortified the oppo. side [of the river]. One brigade of the 17th plunged in the swamp, waded within musket range in front and kept the Johnnies busy, while 2 brigades crossed the swamp further to the right, thus coming upon their flank. Soon put them to rout. We went into camp behind the old rebel works, to wait for the train to come up. It is said that we are only 25 miles from Branchville. I cannot tell where we are, but it must be near the Combahee River, west of Charleston.[46] Day's march 5 miles.

Friday, February 10th.

Camp No. 11. Just one year ago today I reenlisted for 3 years. Today 1/3 of my time is out. I am in hopes that I will have only a few more months longer to serve. I am very tired tonight, having marched a long ways. It is said that we are only 5 miles from the R.R. running to Augusta. It is also rumored that Branchville has been taken. Day's march 22 miles.

FIGURE 32.   Storming the Salkehatchie River. A. R. Waud sketch, from *The Century Magazine*, October 1887, p. 925.

Saturday, February 11th.

Camp No. 12. Left camp early this morning; crossed the railroad which we found torn & burning. Crossed the R.R. [the Augusta branch of the South Carolina Railroad] at Graham's Station, 20 miles west of Branchville. Came up with our Corps. Crossed the South Edisto River. The "Johnnies" had a line of works thrown up to prevent our crossing, but they were easily flanked out. Day's march 16 [miles].

Sunday, February 12th.   [Orangeburg]

Camp No. 13. Crossed the North Edisto River about 5 miles west of Orangeburg. The 17th Corps is going up that R.R., tearing it [up] as they go. Today we passed through the turpentine country, which was all on fire, making the sky black with smoke. It was dangerous driving the Ordnance train through the burning timber. One wagon was burned up.[47] Passed the 1st Division. We are only 20 miles from Columbia. Day's march 16 miles.

Monday, February 13th.

Camp No. 14. Several Johnnies came in & gave themselves up today. Went out foraging; got some bacon, potatoes & lard. We appear to have got out of the swamp & have been marching through a fine, rich country. It is said that we are going to Wilmington. Day's march 10 miles.

Tuesday, February 14th.

Camp No. 15. Passed through a little town called Sandy Run. It is thought that the rebs will make a stand at Columbia; others think we will pass around the place & tear up the R.R. It is thought that there is about 20,000 rebs in our front.

The rebels undertook to make a stand [along?] a deep, narrow creek that empties in [the] Congaree River, but 2 divisions of our Corps drove them out of our [their] works, capturing several prisoners. We have a very muddy camp tonight. The rains have caused the creek to overflow, leaving a deposit of mud, which makes a poor camping ground. Day's march 10 [miles].

Wednesday, February 15.

Camp No. 16. Got up in the rain & soon started forward. There has been heavy skirmishing all day. The rebs had a strong line of works, over 2 miles in length. The 1st Div. charged over a creek, capturing about 100 prisoners.[48] We are encamped in the captured works & there is a continual skirmish going on in front. The 1st & 2nd Divisions are in advance. Day's march 8 miles.

Thursday, February 16.   Near Columbia.

Camp No. 17. We have been in plain view of the city all day. Our line was just on the south side of the Congaree River. We have been supporting the 1st Mo. Battery, which has been shelling the town. At night we crossed the Saluda River. We are now encamped about 4 miles west of the city. I got plenty of Sweet Potatoes.

We move forward in line of battle on the south side of the Congaree, in plain view of the city of Columbia. Our lines gradually drive back the rebels toward the city. They finally retreated across the river into the city. The rebels succeed[ed] in burning the bridge across the river. We made some attempt to lay a pontoon bridge near the burnt one. While this was going on, another part of our Army threw a pontoon bridge across the Saluda River 3 miles above the city. After our batteries had vigorously shelled the city, we suddenly moved up the south side of the Saluda, crossed over and tonight are encamped N.W. of Columbia about 3 miles away.[49]

[This is the final entry in Lewis Roe's second notebook. Entries for February 17 through March 24 are from his original journal.]

Friday, February 17.

Camp No. 18. We started out on a forced march this morning as we thought, but we went through the City of Columbia, which was evacuated last night. Our Division marched through town & are encamped just outside ~~of the city~~. It is now understood that we are to tear up railroads. Half of our boys are up in town, trying to make a raise. The town is on fire & I am afraid it will all burn down. The boys can hardly be controlled. I have heard several wish the "damned town" was burnt up. I hate such Proceedings. I wish the Plunder[er]s were shot. I know it is wrong to burn women & children out of house & home. A great many of the boys are under the influence of liquor, but the 1st Division are doing most of the burning. I had chickens, sweet potatoes, bacon & coffee for supper.

When I hear the screaming & crying of the women & children, I think of home. Are my loved ones safe from harm; I hope so. May God Protect & Shield them from such scenes as I have seen. I hope this war will end soon, so I can return home once more.

Columbia is about as large as Quincy. It is a nice, pretty place. The rebs had placed the bales of cotton in the middle of the street & set it on fire.[50] Most of it was burned. There were several large warehouses filled with provisions burnt up; supplies of all kinds. One large building filled with Sanitary Stores burnt up. We also captured 2 pieces of field artillery.[51] Day's march 4 miles. Distance from Savannah River 139 miles.

Saturday, February 18th.

Camp No. 19. I have been hard at work all day, tearing & burning the railroad running east from Columbia toward Kingsville. The 2nd Div. & ours have burnt 11 miles of R.R. today. It is reported that Charleston is evacuated. I am very anxious to know in what direction we move next. I expect toward Florence.[52] Have plenty of forage such as chickens, meat & meal here on the R.R. Encamped 6 miles east of Columbia. Day's march 16 miles.

Sunday, February 19th.

Camp No. 20. Another day spent in tearing the R.R. It is hard work. The 20th Corps are tearing the road running north from Columbia. We left the railroad about sundown, marched due north about 3 miles & encamped. Columbia has been almost totally destroyed. Every 2 or 3 men in our Regt. has a Darkey to cook for them. Day's march 12 miles.

Monday, February 20.

Camp No. 21. I am very tired tonight. My bones ache & I have a little fever. I think our whole Corps is encamped together. Gen. Howard is with us also. Day's march 22 miles.

Tuesday, February 21st.   [Winnsborough]

Camp No. 22. Started out at 7 o'clock. Encamped tonight between Winnsboro [Winnsborough] & Rocky Mount on the Wateree River. Some think we are going to Charlotte, N.C. The prisoners our Corps have captured passed us today. They are about 200. Day's march 18 miles.

Wednesday, February 22nd.

Camp No. 23. We appear to be getting into a mountainous country. There are high hills on every side. We have turned nearly east. The 1st, 2nd & 3rd Divisions left early; we did not get started until 10 o'clock. Gov. rations has [have] about "Played out;" we live on the country. We have had fine weather for a few days past. Some now think we go to Saulsbury [Salisbury], N.C.; others think we go to Raleigh. I think we will take a direct line to Wilmington. Day's march 8 [miles].

Thursday, February 23.

Camp No. 24. We had to lay over until the other Divisions crossed the Pontoons. It was nearly 2 o'clock before we crossed. Marched southeast through Liberty Hill. We had a hard night's march; did not get into camp until 1/2 past 10 & it commenced raining about 8. Went to bed tired, wet & sleepy. Passed the 1st & 2nd Divisions in camp. Day's march 16 miles.

Friday, February 24th.

Camp No. 25. Got up *all* wet; everything soaked. Hardly had time to boil a little mush for breakfast before we were ordered to fall in. The mud & water knee deep. Tonight I am covered with mud from head to foot. Rained hard all day & still raining. Passed near Camden; the 12th Ills. went into the town & burned several large commissaries. Encamped 4 miles east of Camden. Day's march 18 miles.

Saturday, February 25th.

Camp No. 26. Got up again in a heavy shower. Everything wet. Slept wet & cold; felt miserable & mean. But today we have made a short march; has quit raining. I have time to fix things for the night. Our train is loaded with women & children refugees. Day's march 8 miles.

Sunday, February 26th.

Camp No. 27. This day will ever be remembered by the 4th Division. Last night 1 Regt. from each Brigade started for Lynch's Creek. They got there about 12 at night & succeeded in bagging 110 Johnnies.

This morning our Division came up. The creek was 1/2 mile wide & from 2 to 3 feet deep, but we waded right through. The advance Regt., 2nd Iowa, drove the Rebs from the opposite bank. I am afraid some of the boys will get sick after their cold bath. It will not do me any harm; probably good.

The Johnnies have captured all the foragers belonging to the 2nd Brigade. One man was found with his throat cut & on his breast was pinned a paper with these words "Death to all Foragers." It is reported that they shot 12. If true, we ought to retaliate.[53] It is also reported that Charleston & Wilmington are in our hands. Day's march 7 [miles].

Monday, February 27.

No move today. The train has not yet crossed the creek. We are only 30 miles from Florence. Threw up a line of works in just 20 minutes, the length of the regt. I am anxious to go ahead. I want to get through so that I can hear from home.

Tuesday, February 28.

No move yet. Our train has not yet crossed. Mustered today. Our rations are rather short; nothing but meal & beef. We have a nigger mill for grinding corn, which we keep running night & day.[54]

Wednesday, March 1st.

Camp No. 28. Left camp at 2 P.M., our train having crossed by that time. Marched nearly east. It is said that the Rebs at ~~Cha~~ Florence have been strongly reinforced from Richmond. If so, we may soon expect a fight. Day's march 8 miles.

Thursday, March 2nd.

Camp 29. Only marched about 1 mile when we halted & threw up breastworks. Moved out again in the afternoon. Heard cannon & musketry on our left. It is thought to be the 17th Corps. We hear all sorts of yarns & rumors. One is that the 23rd Corps, [Maj.] Gen. Schofield, is coming up the Great Pee Dee with a provision train. There must be quite a force of Rebs ahead as we move very cautious.

I am in rather a bad fix for marching. My shoes are worn out.[55] I have a large boil on the back of my neck which pains me so I can hardly sleep at night. Day's march 7 miles.

Friday, March 3rd.

Camp 30. Encamped tonight within 5 miles of Cheraw [South Carolina]. The 17 Corps drove the Rebs out about noon today. Passed 2 lines of works the Rebs had thrown up to protect the town. Our whole Corps are together. It has been very rainy & wet for the past week, but now we have a good prospect of fine weather. Day's march 12 miles.

Saturday, March 4.

Camp 31. Marched through Cheraw today.[56] It is about twice as large as Payson [Illinois]. Guards were stationed at every house.

FIGURE 33. Federal troops in Cheraw, S.C.; view along Market Street with the Lyceum, Town Hall, and Moore's Hotel on the left. From *Frank Leslie's Illustrated Newspaper*, April 1865, copy courtesy of Historic Cheraw.

No foraging or straggling allowed. Our forces have captured a large amount of supplies; one large warehouse filled with powder, 25 pieces of field artillery & various other ordnance stores. We have it reported that [Maj.] Gen. Schofield is advancing from Wilmington. I hope it is so. I long for the days of hardtack & coffee again. I am tired of this corn meal & corn meal coffee. Day's march 8 [miles]. Distance from Columbia 160 miles; from Savannah River 299 miles.

Sunday, March 5.

Camp 32. Today our Brigade was taken in town to do provost duty, relieving a brigade of the 17th Corps. 12 of us have 7 houses to guard, to prevent pillaging & burning. Several of the citizens claim to be *Union* but it is hard to tell. All the stores, depots, warehouses &c. are burnt.

Monday, March 6th.

Still on Guard. The house I am at was occupied as the Tory Gen. [Colonel Banastre] Tarleton's Hd. Qrs. during the Revolution. The women living here now are strong Secesh. They are from Charleston. They say the people living here are not as high toned, elegant, & have not the style of the *Charlestonians*.

An awful explosion took place this forenoon. Our forces had been engaged in hauling powder from the rebel magazine & ~~employ~~ emptying it into a small stream, expecting to dam up the stream & thus wet the powder. By some means ~~& the~~ it caught fire & the loudest explosion took place I have ever heard. Every window in town was broke, 3 houses blown down, boards fell in every direction. 9 persons were killed.[57]

Tuesday, March 7.

Camp 33. We remained in town until the last of the Army had crossed the Great Pee Dee. Then pickets were relieved, guards taken off & we crossed. Halted for the pontooniers to take up the bridge, then pushed ahead toward Fayetteville, North Carolina. Encamped tonight near the state line. So, farewell South Carolina. The Northern vandals have eaten & burned you out. They are done with thee for awhile. Day's march 12 miles.

Wednesday, March 8th.

Camp 34. Turned on a cross road leading to the right. 3 miles march brought us to our Div. The day has been very wet & muddy; a poor, wet camp tonight. Encamped near the R.R. leading from Laurel Hill to Wilmington. Day's march 8 miles.

Thursday, March 9th.

Camp 35. Today has been a hard, hard day for us. A constant heavy rain; all the time mud knee deep. After we had our tents stretched for the night, we were ordered 4 miles further. The rain poured. We waded swamps, creeks, but finally got through. I do not think all will get up tonight. We are on the direct road for Fayetteville. Perhaps our campaign will end there for awhile. I will soon be barefooted. Several are without shoes now. Day's march 12 [miles].

Friday, March 10th.

Camp 36. A clear day again. The sun has come out bright & warm. Marched about 3 miles & lay ~~up~~ over for the train to come up. In the afternoon, 1 Regt. was detailed to go ahead to build roads. Ours was taken from the 3rd Brigade; built roads over a swamp 2 miles in length, then went into camp for the night. Day's march 6 miles.

Saturday, March 11th.

Camp 37. We have marched near the whole day over swamp & corduroy roads. Report says that our campaign ends at Fayetteville. I hope so. We are only 13 miles from there tonight. I am very ragged & dirty; have no soap or any way of washing our clothes. Day's march 12 miles.

Sunday, March 12.

Camp 38. Encamped tonight within 2 miles of Fayetteville. Gunboats have come up from Wilmington. Wrote a letter to Louisa. Day's march 10 [miles]. Distance from Cheraw 60 miles. Distance from Savannah River 359 miles.

Monday, March 13.

No move today. I understand we will hold Fayetteville permanently. Rations very short; we keep our nigger mill going day & night. All our refugees & contrabands have been sent down the Cape Fear River. We had nearly a 1,000 with our Division.

Tuesday, March 14th.

Camp 39. Crossed the river this morning about 2 miles below town. Several boats lay at the bridge, loaded with cotton & refugees. Saw a N.Y. Herald of March 6; the first Northern paper I had seen since leaving Savannah. It appears by the paper that the rebs are sure of capturing Sherman's army. Drew 2 days' rations to last 4. We are going ahead & leave our train. Report says we go to Goldsboro. Day's march 5 miles.

Wednesday, March 15th.

Camp 40. Left most of our wagon train under strong guard & started out, our Division in advance. About 4 P.M. we came to a creek, behind which the Johnnies were posted. One Regt. of our brigade skirmished with them & finally succeeded in flanking them out of position.[58] Day's march 12 miles.

Thursday, March 16th.

Camp 41. Came up with the Rebs this afternoon. We went into camp & sent out skirmishers. Rained very hard all day; in fact, has rained every day for a week. Everything wet. I am half sick tonight. Day's march 12 miles.

Friday, March 17th.

Camp 42. Started very early this morning & marched only about 6 miles, halted & threw up works. There must be a heavy force of Rebs near at hand. Our whole Corps is together. Day's march 6 miles.

Saturday, March 18.

Camp 43. Our Division lay into camp until the other Divisions had passed out, when we brought up the rear. Sign boards tonight say only 25 miles to Goldsboro. I suppose we will form a junction with the 23rd Corps in a day or two. I hope we will soon get some rest. I am tired out, ragged & dirty & barefooted. How I would like a good feed of pickles or vinegar; something besides corn meal & grease. Day's march 13 mi.

Sunday, March 19.

Camp 44. Very heavy cannonading & musketry heard on our left. Some think the 14th & 20th Corps have become engaged in a battle, but it does not seem to interfere with us. We marched very slow until 3 in the afternoon. After that time we pushed ahead very fast until 9 at night. About dark, there was a perfect roar of artillery & musketry. We have marched clear around it & are only 10 miles from Goldsboro.[59] They say our Gens. are working strategy. Distance 16 [miles].

Monday, March 20.

Camp 45. Early this morning we turned to our left & marched back southwest. Came up on the rebels & drove them steadily before us until about noon, when we came upon their main ~~line~~ force. We halted & the 1st Division & ours formed the advance line, threw up breastworks & sent out skirmishers.[60] 10 miles.

Tuesday, March 21st.

Another day has past [passed] & another hard fight is over for awhile, or at least the roar of cannon & musketry has almost ceased, although the end is not yet & God only knows what tomorrow may bring forth. Tired, wet, hungry, barefooted, almost without clothes. Covered with swamp mud from head to foot. I am a pretty looking human being tonight. Will this campaign last always? Does Sherman think we are made of iron? Yet, why should I complain? Hundreds of poor fellows are as bad off or worse than I, & I thank God that I still live & have my health. What more does one want? Clothing is only a

FIGURE 34. Battle of Bentonville, N.C., March 20, 1865, 15th Army Corps engaged on the right. W. Waud sketch, from *Harper's Weekly*, April 15, 1865. Collections of the Library of Congress.

luxury & can be done without, especially when one is used to it as we are. I am wet & covered with swamp muck, but when I do get clean & wash up, I suppose I'll feel as well as ever.

"So wait a little longer; there's a good time coming, boys, A good time coming, boys; wait a little longer."[61]

Well, early this morning our company was ordered out to relieve a company of the 57th Ills. then on the skirmish line. We took their places in the rifle pits. Our company skirmish line extended about 20 rods in length & we were about 200 yds. from the rebel pits. Between us & them was a swamp 10 rods wide. Nothing of importance took place until about noon except a few bullets would whistle rather near sometimes.

At noon we were ordered forward to establish a line at the edge of the swamp. Here then was a 100 yds. to cross under a heavy fire & then to hold our line within 100 yds. of their rifle pits. The first thing to do was to pick out a tree to run to. Saw one about 20 yds. in advance. Jumped out of my hole & started. Reached it just in time, for just as I got behind it "*Spat*" came a bullet against the side of it. "You was 1/8 came of a second too late that time, Johnny Reb."

I peered out, saw the smoke of a rebel gun, took as good aim as possible & fired. Loaded & darted ahead again from tree to tree & finally reached the swamp, but right ahead only 100 yds. were the line of rebel pits. Besides, they had a cross fire on us. How I hugged that tree. "Zip," "Zis," "thug," "Spat" came the bullets, striking the tree several times & cutting the bushes on either side. After awhile, I got hold of a spade & in less time than it takes me to write it, I had a hole dug.

Then we felt tolerable safe & commenced yelling at them, "Hello, Rebs, what Regt.?" "47th North Carolina, what yours?" "50 Ills." But they would not talk a great deal. About 3 o'clock in the afternoon, the 66th Ills. came up behind us. We joined them & charged right through the swamp. Took the rebel pits, but only 75 yds. ahead they had their main line of works. The place was too hot. We were ordered back. The 66th went back to their works in [the] rear & we occupied our old holes.

After awhile, we saw that the Rebs did not reoccupy their old works, so we crept forward to them, but again fell back. We were reinforced by several companies of our Regt. & we again went forward to the rebel pits & again fell back. It was impossible to hold them; neither could the Johnnies get to them. Our company having been out, we were relieved & went back to the line. 3 men of our company were wounded. Matthew Leach has his leg off. Frank McCarthy shot through the arm. Iltyd Deer wounded in the head. The 7th Ills. were sent out to occupy our rifle pits. The Rebs made several attempts to charge our works, but were repulsed. Lieut. [James B.] Hawkes, Co. H, was shot through the head & killed behind the works. So was Corpl. [Anderson] Tout, Co. "A." 14 were wounded in the Regt.[62]

Wednesday, March 22.

Tired & wet, I threw myself down amid the roar of battle & slept well, for I was worn out with yesterday's work. I expected a battle today, but this morning tells a different story. The rebs have fled, abandoning their works, which we have occupied. Lots of prisoners have been taken. I have heard no estimate of the number. We have remained on the field all day. Some of the rebel dead lie unburied. Graves are found on every side.

Thursday, March 23.

Camp 45. A congratulatory order from Sherman was read, stating that we should now rest and have all to eat that our own rich & magnificent country can afford.[63] So we started again for Goldsboro. Encamped within 10 miles of the town. Day's march 15 [miles].

Friday, March 24.

Camp 46. Crossed the Neuse River & passed through Goldsboro. Gen. Sherman reviewed the Army as we went through. Encamped 2 miles east of town on the R.R. leading to New Bern [New Berne].

Day's march 10 [miles]. Dist. from Fayetteville 99 [miles]. Dist. from Savannah R. 458 [miles].[64]

Goldsboro, N.C. March 27 1865.   Lewis F. Roe

In spite of the time spent in skirmishing and repairing bad roads, Sherman's Right Wing made amazing progress during the first week of the Carolinas Campaign. From newspaper reports, we learn how a fraction of his army seldom mentioned in official reports kept busy. Soldiers' journals (including Lewis Roe's) and reminiscent accounts confirm the essential accuracy of the following:

> About this time [early February] the foragers began to spread over the country, in irregular and regular parties. These enterprising characters were known by the names of "Bummers," "Smoke-house Rangers," and "Do-Boys." A bummer is an individual who, possessed of a broken-down mule and armed with his musket, makes his way into the enemy's country, . . . not in rear but in front of the army. They went before it like a cloud, being often twenty or thirty miles in advance of the head of the column [and] would fight anything. Three "bummers" together would at any time attack a company of rebel cavalry, and in favorable circumstances would disperse them and capture their booty.
>
> An incident in connection with the capture of the [Charleston & Augusta] railroad is well worth relating. Gen. Howard, in command of the Army of the Tennessee, felt confident that the enemy would make a bold stand in defense of the railroad. Upon our approach the General ordered the columns to deploy so as to be ready for battle. Sitting on his horse, near the head of the column, expecting at any moment to hear a loud crash of musketry, his quick eye caught sight of one of our foragers mounted on a mule and riding at breakneck speed down the road from the front. The forager rode up to the General and at the top of his voice delivered his message, as follows: "Hurry up, General! Hurry up! We have got the railroad and can hold it, if you hurry up!"

The General did hurry up, and found the railroad, as the smoke-[house] ranger had said, in possession of about seven bummers, who were busily engaged skirmishing with a detachment of Wheeler's cavalry. . . . Early the following morning we moved along the railroad, thoroughly destroying it as we went forward. . . .

With the exception of Columbia alone, every town in South Carolina through which the army passed was first entered by the bummers. At Chesterfield they were two days and a half ahead of the army, the whole corps [20th] having congregated at this point. They rigged up two logs for cannon, sent a flag ahead to the town, which was occupied by a detachment of Butler's Division of cavalry, demanded its surrender, frightened off the rebel cavalry, and entered the town in grand procession of broken-down mules, ragged "bummers" and the "Quaker guns." The coat-tails of the rebels disappeared at one end of the town as the "Do Boys" entered at the other.

Sources for the above are the *New York Tribune* and *New York Herald*, as reprinted in the *Cincinnati Daily Gazette* for March 21, 1865, page 3. The incident involving General Howard I have quoted from the version given by Pvt. Myron Loop in the *National Tribune*, June 20, 1901, page 7, in preference to the more highly colored account in the *New York Tribune*.

CHAPTER TEN

The End of the War and Home Again, April–July 1865

L
EWIS ROE DISCONTINUED HIS JOURNAL WHEN THE ARMY ARRIVED AT GOLDSBORO, BUT BY REFERENCE TO THE PUB-LISHED REGIMENTAL HISTORY, THE *WAR OF THE REBELLION, A Compilation of the Official Records* series, and other personal and secondary sources, the final events of the war as Roe witnessed it are easily traced.[1] Two of his letters home, written during June 1865 from his final camp near Louisville, Kentucky, are also available.

At Goldsboro, General Sherman made plans to strike northward toward a railroad junction west of Richmond, Virginia, to place his army between the Confederate forces of Gen. Joseph Johnston and those of Robert E. Lee. Two developments changed all of this. General Grant had already ordered Maj. Gen. George Stoneman to lead a cavalry division through far western Virginia and North Carolina, destroying the railroads, munitions, foodstuffs, and vast amounts of supplies found there. Stoneman did this most effectively, ruining the supply routes to both Lee and Johnston and blocking their lines of retreat.[2] Stoneman's raid rendered Sherman's original plan obsolete even as it was being drafted.

Then on April 6, word reached the western army that Lee had abandoned his trenches at Petersburg and retreated beyond Richmond. Grant's troops had entered the Confederate capital early on the 3rd. Sherman quickly reoriented the three wings of his army, now more than 94,000 strong, and began a rapid march toward Smithfield, North Carolina, at daybreak on April 10. Johnston, waiting at Smithfield, had less than half of the 35,000 infantry and artillerymen Sherman credited him with, and he retreated even faster than Sherman advanced.

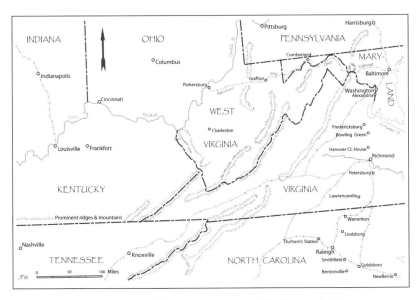

MAP 10. Sherman's Army, Goldsboro, N.C., to Louisville, Ky., April–July 1865.
    Courtesy of author.

On the morning of April 11, the army's Left Wing, the 14th and
20th Army Corps, entered Smithfield. Roe's own 15th corps was in the
Right Wing, and at 9 a.m. the following day, a staff officer came gal-
loping along their lines shouting "Lee has surrendered! Lee has surrendered to General Grant!" For three hours, the men celebrated,
shouting and hugging one another; as one soldier wrote, "the air was
rent with cheers." Finally everyone fell into ranks again, and they
marched steadily until dark, the 50th Illinois bivouacking as the rear
guard of the army.[3] As more than one writer commented, the vision of
every man now turned homeward.

Rains began again, but with this latest news the army set off on a
rapid march toward Raleigh, the capital of North Carolina. April 16
found them camped some twenty miles beyond. Sherman had received
a message from Johnston on the 14th, asking for a cessation of hostilities with a view to negotiating terms of surrender. Sherman responded
at once, and they agreed to meet on the 17th at a point between the
lines. As General Sherman entered a railroad car that morning to
attend the meeting, a telegraph operator handed him a message from
the Secretary of War that announced the assassination of President
Lincoln. Word of the president's death spread rapidly, and as one

Illinois lieutenant put it, "Sherman's great army bow their heads in mournful silence over the startling news of the assassination."[4]

With this cloud of uncertainty hanging over them, Sherman and Johnston worked out the terms of an armistice, a conditional surrender, at Durham's Station, about twenty-five miles beyond Raleigh, North Carolina. They signed it on April 18, and Sherman promptly dispatched his aide, Maj. Henry Hitchcock, to Washington with the text. He reached Washington on the afternoon of April 21, and by midnight Hitchcock was waiting to head back to Raleigh, accompanied by General Grant. The language in the conditional surrender was too lenient, and President Andrew Johnson sent Grant back to show Sherman that only an unconditional surrender, the same terms that Grant and Lee had agreed to, was acceptable. Grant, Hitchcock, and a variety of aides arrived back in Raleigh by April 25, and the next day General Johnston surrendered his army. A controversy over the original terms soon broke out in the newspapers, but eventually this would be laid to rest.[5]

During the ten-day suspension of war, the soldiers kept busy with dress parades and reviews, guard mounts, changing camp locations, and cleaning up new campgrounds. They of course knew what was going on almost as soon as it happened, and groups of paroled soldiers from Lee's army began to pass down the railroad line, heading toward their homes. They found the camp kettles of Lewis Roe's messmates bubbling merrily, full of coffee, with hardtack and sow-belly [bacon] nearby; "'help yourselves,' is the word," and the ragged, hungry Southerners who sat by the fires were heard to say, "this is a rich man's wah and a poor man's fight." Sherman said as much himself in a letter to Gen. O. O. Howard just a few weeks later—"I have realized in our country that one class of men makes war and leaves another to fight it out." For his part, he too was tired of fighting.[6]

Winding down a war with hundreds of thousands of men in the field was almost as complex as running one, but Gen. Ulysses S. Grant had something special in mind before the armies all went home. He voiced this in Raleigh on April 26; the great bulk of Sherman's army would soon start for Washington. Word spread quickly and orders to advance to Richmond were cut the next day. Just four weeks later, Sherman's Army would pass in review down Pennsylvania Avenue before the president and all of official Washington.[7]

Not everyone in this army got to see Richmond and Washington; those who did were in the 15th and 17th Army Corps [the Army of the Tennessee], and the 14th and 20th Corps, the Army of Georgia. Sherman relinquished command of Kilpatrick's cavalry corps and the Army of the Ohio, the 10th and 23rd Army Corps, to Maj. Gen. John Schofield, commanding the Department of North Carolina, who now had more than 52,000 troops under his own orders.

There were some ironies in this, such as the omission of the cavalry corps, including even the hard-riding 1st Alabama Cavalry, former Confederates who served with Lewis Roe's brigade during the Atlanta campaign and afterwards became a part of Kilpatrick's cavalry corps. Also, soldiers typically had little or no money, and when Roe's division was mustered for pay on April 30, this did not mean that a paymaster appeared. Sherman commented weeks later that his men had not been paid for eight or ten months. On the other hand, the disbursing officer with the Confederate Army of Tennessee made token payments of $1.17 45/100 per man, in silver coin, to an estimated 32,174 of Joe Johnston's Confederates the day their surrender was signed. This was probably the only payment in hard money any of them received in the course of the entire war.[8]

Orders for the march to Richmond were drafted even as the negotiators reached agreement on the surrender terms. The Army of the Tennessee started from its camps near Raleigh on April 29, taking roads to the north. All foraging ceased; wagons carried only forage and provisions. Munitions were limited to what soldiers bore in their cartridge boxes. No straggling was permitted, and no rail fences would be converted into campfires. Everyone was on best behavior.

The troops marched rapidly, some as much as thirty miles a day, over good roads. The weather generally remained clear and cool. Confederate soldiers recently paroled from the armies of Joseph Johnston and Robert E. Lee stood quietly by the roads and watched the victors pass. In Virginia, "The people along our line of march had never seen an army, much less a Northern one. In many places they congregated by the roadside and closely observed us as we passed, and I suppose, were surprised to find that Yankees were a little more than half human, barring a want of soap." The march orders directed them toward Louisburg and Warrenton, North Carolina, and on through Lawrenceville, Virginia, until by noon on May 7, the 50th Illinois reached Petersburg, Virginia, after 157 miles on the road in eight days of marching. Twenty-two miles beyond lay Richmond, now a captive city.[9]

At Petersburg the army paused, although not for long, before the lines of earthworks that for nine and a half months had resisted General Grant's siege of Richmond. The boys in the 50th Illinois wandered over the fortifications, now empty of defenders, but were unimpressed by comparison with the defenses at Savannah and those around Atlanta. They passed through Petersburg on the 9th, urged on by the repeated cry "On to Richmond," delayed only by rain and Union officialdom. At Manchester, just across the James River from Richmond, Sherman received orders to continue his march on to Alexandria, Virginia.[10]

Maj. Gen. H. W. Halleck, commanding at Richmond, prompted another delay when he ordered Sherman's Army to halt before the city and parade before him (Halleck). Sherman, still seething from insults offered him at Raleigh, told Halleck that "I will march my army through Richmond quietly, and in good order . . ." and that Halleck had best stay inside and out of the way if he wanted to avoid trouble. After a confrontation with the provost guard, General Halleck gave in. May 13 saw Lewis Roe and the boys cross the James River on pontoons, pass by Castle Thunder and Libby Prison, march into the city and by the capital and Gen. Robert E. Lee's residence, before continuing for twenty miles over very bad roads to a camp on the banks of the Chickahominy.[11] As Roe tells us later, everyone stayed in ranks, and he had no opportunities to look around or collect souvenirs.

It was right at this time, May 12, that Maj. Gen. O. O. Howard, commanding the Army of the Tennessee, was relieved and assigned to duty as head of the newly created Freedmen's Bureau. Another well-liked and familiar officer, Maj. Gen. John A. Logan, then moved up from the 15th Army Corps to command the Army of the Tennessee for the last two and one-half months of its existence.[12] The daily marching orders kept the 15th Corps moving northward to Hanover Court House, Bowling Green, and Fredericksburg, the other corps following or taking parallel roads. On May 16, Sherman asked General Grant if a grand review had been determined on, to which Grant replied not yet, but the commands were to concentrate at Alexandria, Virginia. Then finally on May 18, the headquarters of the army issued a Special Order for a review of the Army of the Potomac and Sherman's Army on May 23 and 24, respectively, passing along Pennsylvania Avenue in front of the president's house. Sherman, while not displeased, was a bit miffed to read about this first in the newspapers.[13]

One week after passing through Richmond and 140 miles beyond that city, the 50th Illinois marched through Alexandria, Virginia, and went into camp. This had been another hard march, the first half of which saw the army once again slogging through rain storms and rising creeks. But then came three days of rest and refurbishment, May 21–23, during which a number of officers from the Army of the Potomac eyed the ragged ranks they called "Sherman's Wolves" and "Sherman's Bummers." Nothing daunted, the western soldiers returned the looks of "the lordly, soft-bread and butter and paper collared 'Potomacers'" with some skepticism that these "splendid looking creatures" were real soldiers.[14]

Modern readers might find it incredible that in five days all orders were issued and arrangements completed for an army of 65,000 to prepare itself to pass in review "in the greatest of all reviews the world has ever seen." Nonetheless it was done and apparently with little or no confusion, in part because Sherman commanded what was by now a very well-honed military machine, the parts of which had long been accustomed to coordinating with one another, and also because most of the men had ample experience with reviewing, up to the corps level. What they would be doing now differed in scale rather than in kind, and the orders made clear how the units would all come together.

General Orders No. 23 for the Fourth Division, 15th Army Corps, specified the order of march for Roe's division and the uniform of the day, so to speak, on the 24th. While these stated that "Every private should have a neat hat, a clean pair of trousers and blouse, and shoes neatly blacked," the operative word was *should*. The quartermaster began issuing new clothing when he had it, after supplies arrived at Goldsboro in late March. Two months later, the regimental history indicated that the process was still far from complete:

> The boys do not feel very well pleased with the prospect of passing
> in review . . . clad in old and worn out uniforms, and having drawn
> only a part of the clothing necessary, it is found that the contrast
> between the poorly and better dressed is still more marked. . . .
> We would present a more uniform appearance in our old, ragged,
> greasy and worn out clothing, than in the half and half style which
> now characterizes our make-up. . . . Here is a fellow with new hat

FIGURE 35. Grand Review of Sherman's veterans at Washington, D.C., May 24, 1865. From an Alexander Gardner photograph as reproduced in *Harper's Weekly*, June 10, 1865. Collections of the Library of Congress.

and new shoes, pants worn off nearly to the knees, with his coat in nearly as bad condition, possibly sleeveless. Here's a "bummer" sporting a new pair of pants, too large, rolled up at the bottom, while his "bunky" has a new coat. . . . This description is of the Fiftieth, and of course represents Sherman's army.[15]

Some of the boys obtained passes on the 23rd and observed the "neatly dressed, fat, well kept soldiers of the Potomac" in the city, returning to camp with the opinion that the Potomac fellows were no great shakes in marching. Sherman had watched this review, too, and saw that the troops did not march well because the music had been provided by two civilian orchestras, more familiar with scores for the latest operas. He would fix that. Among themselves his men apparently decided that if they could not outshine the Easterners, they would out-march them.[16]

The 24th dawned clear and cool. The regiments had bivouacked that night south of the Long Bridge across the Potomac, and at daylight began to cross it into the city of Washington. The 15th Army Corps would lead the parade, behind Sherman and his generals and two engineering regiments. The streets were already lined with spectators, and as the men of the 50th Illinois wended their way to the place of rendezvous, a watcher called out, "What regiment is that?" to which some wag in the ranks responded, "the same old regiment, only we've got new clothes." The crowd cheered.

As the leading corps, the 15th marshaled on Maryland Avenue east of the Capitol, near the northern entrance to the Capitol grounds. At 9 a.m., the signal gun fired and the procession started led by Maj. Gen. John A. Logan, commanding the Army of the Tennessee, with his staff and headquarters guard, then the two engineering regiments. The 15th Army Corps followed next, headed by Maj. Gen. W. B. Hazen, with the 1st, 2nd, and 4th Divisions in order. Each division and brigade had its own brigadier general or colonel in front. Lewis Roe, being in the third brigade of the 4th Division, actually had a place quite near the front of the review. Sherman with his staff and Maj. Gen. O. O. Howard joined General Logan as the column moved around the north side of the Capitol building and continued west down Pennsylvania Avenue. Alongside Sherman and his generals rode Mother Bickerdyke, a widow from Galesburg, Illinois, who had overseen major efforts with organizing hospitals and nursing the wounded during Sherman's campaigns as far as Atlanta. She rode sidesaddle on an army horse, a sunbonnet on her head and wearing a calico dress.[17]

This was part review, part parade. Every regiment unfurled its colors during the entire march. Some of these were entirely new, others torn by bullets and reduced to shreds, but all spearheads had been ornamented by flowers, in bouquets or wreaths. The flags borne by the 50th Illinois on the March to the Sea and in the Grand Review were its third set of colors during the war.

Behind the 15th Corps came the 17th Army Corps, the other half of the Army of the Tennessee, commanded by Maj. Gen. Francis P. Blair. After them followed the Army of Georgia, the 14th and 20th Corps. One reporter estimated that the 15th Corps, some 25,000 strong, required one hour and twenty-five minutes to pass the reviewing stand. The entire review took about six hours, with no more than minor delays, and the entire column stretched out for fifteen miles.[18]

It was the marching that drew the attention of the spectators. People were amazed to see such a dirty, unkempt body of men moving with a solid, uniform tread that resulted from hard drilling, striding along with a rolling, swinging gait, eyes forward beneath the wide-brimmed felt hats favored by the western army. The men were good, very good. Cpl. George Cram wrote two days afterward that his 105th Illinois Infantry regiment made frequent stops, when they came to order arms. "At one of these our regiment . . . brought down their guns with such precision that the audience immediately manifested their delight by cheers and clapping of hands."[19]

One oversight in preparations was the lack of any published roster for the Army of the Tennessee, so that many veteran units passed without recognition by the public. People applauded what they saw, however, and the 50th Illinois heard cries of "What regiment is that?" and "Oh! Oh! See what marching!" Flags and banners fluttered from the buildings en route, while roses and flowers in bunches and wreaths were thrown as the soldiers passed. Many of the men wore roses in their buttonholes while Sherman had been presented with two large wreaths, one around his horse's neck and the other hung upon his shoulder. In front of the reviewing stand, the street was ankle deep in flowers. High on the side of the Treasury building, a sign had been painted—"The only debt the NATION can never pay is that of gratitude to its defenders."[20]

When just short of the Treasury building, Sherman turned in the saddle and looked back over the legions behind him—the flashing bayonets, polished sabers, brass cannons, even the pontoons and heavy freight wagons. Long afterwards he wrote, "the sight was simply magnificent. The column was compact, and the glittering guns looked like a solid wall of steel moving with the order of a pendulum. . . . It was in my judgment the most magnificent army in existence." One of his oldest family friends wrote of the westerners that "They march like the lords of the world."[21]

At the head of each division its black pioneers, still clad in the garments worn on the plantation, marched with the same front and formation as the infantry companies, only bearing their axes and spades at right-shoulder shift. Six ambulances, with stretchers, moved at the rear of each brigade, three abreast. Pack-horses and mules loaded with camp equipage and boxes of hardtack, laden also with chickens, turkeys, pigs, a brace of raccoons, and even a pet goat, led by young contrabands, helped to complete the spectacle. These followed at the ends of the corps. The army's own bands accompanied the marchers and provided the music; one band for each division from the Capitol to the Treasury building, while the brigade bands played as their brigades passed the reviewing stand. Everyone cheered and applauded, and laughed at the occasional comic relief.[22]

Finally it was over, and after the 50th Illinois passed the president's home ("White House" is a later term), it wheeled to the right and marched to a new camp near the Soldiers' Home. Sherman's Army was now bivouacked in the fields and forests east of the capital city and north of the Potomac, while the Army of the Potomac relocated itself south of the river. Here for several days the public visited, observed army life, and enjoyed evening entertainments. The U.S. Christian Commission, a sort of predecessor of the World War II–era USO, provided the soldiers with such amenities as writing paper, combs, potatoes, dried apples, canned fruit, and even a barrel of pickles, so that perhaps Lewis Roe finally realized his wish for a good feed of pickles (see entry for March 18, 1865, in chapter 9).[23]

The troops remained at their assigned locations, doing daily drills and dress parades, but the wagon trains and ambulances had been turned in and another movement was in the works. General Sherman retained overall command of the army and would continue to do so until June 28, when he was formally assigned to command the Military Division of the Mississippi, headquartered at St. Louis. On May 30, however, he penned his farewell to the western army, reviewing their operations and successes in the year just passed, bidding them to be good citizens as they had been good soldiers. Their work was done, and he cautioned against seeking new adventure abroad, a clear reference to the then-current French intervention in Mexico. Three days later, General Grant's own farewell to the soldiers of the armies of the United States was read out.[24]

In the meantime, all regiments and batteries in the Army of the Tennessee and the Army of Georgia, except for eastern troops (regiments from east of Ohio) received orders to proceed without delay to Louisville, Kentucky, and rendezvous there without further orders to be mustered out. Railroads would provide transport in the proportion of 7,000 men daily. Why Louisville was made the destination is unknown, though it was a reasonably central point from which the Middle Western regiments could disperse, by rail, to the communities from whence they came.[25]

On June 2, Roe's regiment received orders to prepare seven days' rations for their knapsacks and be ready to move at 8:30 a.m. the following day. They marched to the Baltimore & Ohio Railroad depot near the Capitol, where they loaded on trains destined for Parkersburg, West Virginia. Not all of the 50th Illinois made the same train, and the regimental history indicates that the rail trip continued for two days and three nights, until the morning of June 6. Although vastly preferable to marching the same distance, the trip had few comforts; Roe tells us that he tied himself to the top of a freight car, while a few days later, Pvt. Myron Loop of the 68th Ohio made the same trip in a cattle car. Rail traffic was very heavy but delays were rare; at one stop to fill the tender with water for the boiler, fifteen trains bound for Washington passed the west-bound cars during their three-hour stop. The efficiency of Sherman's command clearly extended to railroad operations. Private Loop and Corporal Roe both enjoyed the hospitality of the U.S. Christian Commission at Cumberland, Maryland, and Grafton, West Virginia, where they found plenty of bread and meat with barrels of hot coffee.[26]

At Parkersburg on the Ohio River, the boys transferred to steamboats for the two-day, two-night run down to Louisville. This did not go smoothly because the water was low and the boats occasionally grounded on the river bottom. By dint of soldier ingenuity, they shifted the load or even lightened the boat by walking along the river bank until the shoal lay behind. The Ohio at this time must have seen a regular convoy of steamers, with people lining the banks and asking "what regiments?" as the boats passed. Finally the 50th Illinois reached Louisville, and landed at noon on June 8. After unloading, they marched east out of the city (Roe says six miles southeast) and once again pitched their little dog tents.[27]

The regiment stayed near Louisville for a little more than a month, engaged mostly in drilling and policing up its camp. Lewis Roe's undated letter sometime in early June tells us a bit about their 860-mile trip from Washington and the chafing among his comrades to return home. At least two episodes broke the monotony of waiting. Pvt. Myron Loop wrote of visiting a theater in Louisville where Miss Maggie Mitchell played a two-week engagement. Night after night, she sang the verses to "When Sherman Marched Down to the Sea," which so affected the soldiers that the opera house fairly trembled, while she herself "was nearly buried in an avalanche of flowers." This song was personal to the men in the western army and also quite a new one, having been composed by the adjutant of the 5th Iowa Infantry in late 1864 or early 1865.[28]

> Camp near [Louisville, Ky.]
>
> June ——— 1865
>
> My Dear Wife
>
> I have just received a letter from you ~~dated~~ mailed June 5th. We are still nearer home but I am afraid I am as near now as I can get for sometime. "What are they going to do with us" is the question asked by everybody. Some say we are going to Texas. Others say that we will remain in camp until fall, & still others say that we will go home on furlough. A great many of the boys say they will not go to Texas, and after we are paid off (which we expect to be in a few days) nearly half of the boys will take a French furlough; that is, go home anyhow with or without leave. I have a big notion to apply for a furlough myself after payday if there is no prospect of being mustered out. I hardly know what to think about it. I expect it will be very doubtful whether I could get one or not if [I] should apply.
>
> We left Washington June 3rd on the Baltimore & Ohio R.R. for Parkersburg Va. We were 2 days & 3 nights crowded on the cars. We were crowded inside & crowded on top. I took up a position on top & managed to get a little sleep at night by tying myself on. We had these freight cars and I tied myself to the board that runs along on top. We passed through 22 tunnels, some of them a mile long. At Parkersburg we were stowed away on boats above & below last night. Today I expect will be a busy day in cleaning & fixing up camp. We are about 6 miles southeast of Louisville. You must not put off writing letters expecting me home, but write very often. I am more anxious about home than ever before. Our *little* Carrie must be getting to be quite a big girl to run about as you say. "Don't spoil her."
>
> I could not bring home anything from Richmond or Washington for our girl. I did think of getting some relics of Libby Prison or Castle Thunder at Richmond, but had no chance. I might find something here if I come home. Have you heard anything of Charley

or Will? I saw in the papers where all the Prisoners that were in Texas were to be sent home. If so, Will must be on his way now. Don't fail to write often.

Yours &c

L. F. Roe

P.S. By Grapevine Telegraph, I have just heard that Gen. Logan says we will all be on our road home inside of 15 days= *Too good to be true*.

L. F. R.

[Editor's note: Charles and William Smith were Lewis Roe's brothers-in-law; both served in the 77th Illinois Volunteer Infantry.]

The other episode was a drill competition among the regiments of the 4th Division, 15th Army Corps, held on July 3, 1865. The prize was a silk banner, reportedly costing $300, and it was the 50th Illinois, the "Blind Half Hundred," that carried away the honors. In later years, this prize banner would be safeguarded by the regiment's Col. William Hanna, to whom the officers and men had given a presentation sword at the same time.[29]

Just where Lewis Roe spent his final weeks in the army isn't clear. In his June 20 letter, he was optimistic about getting a furlough, the date of their final discharge being uncertain. The regimental historian's entry for the same date indicated a liberal furlough policy in effect. Roe hoped to be paid about June 22. And indeed a paymaster finished paying the regiment on June 25. However, Corporal Roe's company muster for May and June 1865 showed him absent on furlough, as did the company muster-out roll on July 13, so his actual whereabouts is unclear.[30] Since his wife was with his mother and stepfather in Adams County, he probably returned there with his regiment.

The 50th Regiment of Illinois Volunteer Infantry formally mustered out of U.S. service at Springfield, Illinois, on July 13, 1865, although they received their discharges and final pay there one week later. Lewis Roe had his last bounty payments coming to him, $210, plus another $190, against which he had overdrawn his annual clothing allowance ($42) and owed the government $25.39. He had ended the war with his health intact and money in his pocket. The train from Springfield rolled into Quincy at 8 p.m. on July 21, and five companies of the Adams

County regiment were greeted with a sumptuous feast and reception by their friends and neighbors, similar to the homecomings given to many other returning regiments.[31]

Louisville, Ky.
June 20th, 1865
My Dear Wife

I received your letter written June 10th yesterday morning. It does seem that I am a great deal nearer home than I was a few weeks ago, but it is only the more aggravating to be so near you & not be permitted to see you.

How thankful, though, we should be that God has spared your life & mine & our little Carrie through all. There was [were] times when I first enlisted last year when it seemed almost impossible that I would escape all the dangers of war; that I would live to see Peace again established through all our land. What has our family sacrificed in this war? Edward was spared, so was I, & so was Warren & your folks are alive. Charley is still alive & *Will*. Although enduring over a year of hard suffering in Prison, yet he still lives. How much better off are we than those thousands of others. I ~~had not~~ have no right to complain, but it does seem so hard to be so near & not be allowed to see those so dear to me. But I suppose there is nothing to do but to wait Patiently, & by next fall I suppose we will get out.

Perhaps I may get a furlough in the course of a month or so. I do not see the use of keeping so many here doing nothing. Already 2 out of each company are allowed to go & it is reported that a larger number can go in a week or two. We expect to be paid off this week, probably day after tomorrow. If so, I shall express my money home as soon as possible. We will receive pay up to the end of April.

There are plenty of rumors afloat about leaving here. Some say we go to St. Louis; others say we are to go away up to Lake Superior. I see in the Papers that Sherman takes command west of the Mississippi. If any more troops are sent to his command, it will be the old 15th Corps. I do not know what may be thought of Sherman at the north, but no General that ever lived was ever thought more of than Billy Sherman is by this Army. I believe he has only the good of his country at heart; a better patriot never lived. No tricky politician about him, but an *honest man*. His very countenance shows it. I know [I] would like to go up to Knox Co. & see your folks & Will & Charley & I would like so well to go with you, but if you feel like risking the journey alone, perhaps you had not better wait until I get home.

I suppose both the boys will soon be home now. I think I certainly will by the 1st of September anyhow. How does little Carrie get along? I should think she would get sick this hot weather. You must write often. I send an account of the 15th Army Corps as it may interest you.

Ever yours
Lewis Roe

General Sherman had remained with the army at Louisville, and he addressed it again on July 4. However, he watched it slowly melt away as the regiments were mustered out, paid off, and put on trains to their homes—the 105th Illinois during the first week in June; the 103rd Illinois near the end of June; the 7th Illinois on July 9; the 68th Ohio and the 7th Iowa on July 11, and the 50th Illinois on July 12. By August they were all gone and the generals had been ordered elsewhere. The 15th and 17th Army Corps and the Army of the Tennessee were discontinued effective August 1, 1865, and the mighty army that paraded in the Grand Review had marched into history.[32]

Paying the Johnnies

Over four hundred thousand dollars in rebel currency was found in one of the wagons captured by us, which has been extensively circulated among the troops. It was designed for the payment of the rebel soldiers, and has been appropriated to its legitimate use by the officers and men in paying large numbers of the prisoners who have been brought in. Such conversations as the following are by no means unfrequent:

"Hallo! Johnny, when were you paid?"
"About six months ago."
"How much do they owe you?"

"Don't know, 'Tain't much 'count any how."

"Here's a couple of hundred. Will that cover it?"

"Yaa's. Thank yer."

"All right. Give the receipt to Jeff when you see him."

The men offer it with much gravity to citizens along the road in payment for chickens, bacon, flour and other articles which, with prudent forethought, they previously get possession of. It is received with a feeble, helpless smile, highly expressive of their appreciation of its value.

From the *Quincy Daily Whig and Republican*, April 26, 1865, page 3. This item, apparently reprinted from another newspaper, must have been contributed by someone in Sherman's Army about the time Confederate veterans were filtering through Union lines on their way home. Confederate currency, of course, was worth nothing wherever Union occupation had superseded the Southern government.

Notes

Introduction

1. A typical instance would have been a three-month expedition through parts of northern Utah, Nevada, and Idaho in the summer of 1859, led by Maj. Isaac Lynde. Roe's company was not included in the scout; see *Report of the Secretary of War, December 1, 1859*, vol. 2, *Affairs in the Department of Utah*, no. 68, 36th Cong., 1st Sess., S. Exec. Doc. 2, Pt. 2 (serial set no. 1024), pp. 240–55.
2. John P. Wilson, *When the Texans Came* (Albuquerque: University of New Mexico Press, 2004), pp. 242–44.
3. John P. Wilson, "Whiskey at Fort Fillmore: A Story of the Civil War," *New Mexico Historical Review* 68, no. 2 (April 1993): pp. 109–32.
4. *War of the Rebellion, A Compilation of the Official Records of the Union and Confederate Armies*, [hereafter *OR*] Series I, vol. 21, pp. 56, 136, 425–26, 931; vol. 25, pt. 1, pp. 163, 181, 536–37; vol. 27, pt. 1, pp. 161, 179, 644–45; vol. 29, pt. 2, pp. 95, 123, 145, 169–70, 622; vol. 34, pt. 2, p. 209; vol. 34, pt. 3, pp. 371–72; vol. 37, pt. 1, pp. 575, 706; vol. 37, pt. 2, pp. 555–56; vol. 43, pt. 2, pp. 318, 516–17, 581, 858–60; vol. 46, pt. 3, pp. 1050–51.

Chapter One

1. Mark Harmon, Downers Grove Park District Museum, Downers Grove, Ill., to John P. Wilson, June 18, 2002.
2. Kay Vander Meulen, Seymour Library, Knox College, Galesburg, Ill., to John P. Wilson, June 19, 2002; and Christine Parks, Office of the Registrar, Western Illinois University, Macomb, Ill., to John P. Wilson, July 3, 2002.
3. John P. Wilson, *When the Texans Came*, pp. 248–53.
4. Donald P. Verene to John P. Wilson, June 13, 1990; *Galesburg Register-Mail*, June 30, 1990.
5. *Knox County Republican*, February 22, 1893, p. 5; August 16, 1893, p. 1; December 6, 1893, p. 1; January 23, 1895, p. 1.
6. *Western Veteran*, December 19, 1888, p. 1; September 11, 1889, p. 8.
7. *Western Veteran*, September 11, 1889, p. 8.

8. Charles F. Hubert, *History of the Fiftieth Regiment, Illinois Volunteer Infantry in the War of the Union* (Kansas City, Mo.: Western Veteran Publishing Company, 1894).

9. *Western Veteran*, October 9, 1895, p. 3.

10. Charles F. Hubert, *History of the Fiftieth Regiment*, p. 525.

11. Roe Family Records; National Archives [hereafter NA], Microcopy M653, Population Schedules of the Eighth Census of the United States, 1860, Roll 155, Adams County, Ill., Free Inhabitants in Burton Township, p. 570.

12. Kay Vander Meulen, Seymour Library, Knox College, Galesburg, Ill., to John P. Wilson, July 17, 2002; Knox College Catalog, 1857.

13. Chapman Brothers, *Portrait and Biographical Album of Knox County, Illinois* (Chicago: Biographical Publishing Company, 1886), p. 711; Janet Hinck to John P. Wilson, January 24, 2003.

14. NA, Record Group 94, Records of the Adjutant General's Office 1780s–1917, Enlistment Record of Lewis F. Roe.

15. Harold D. Langley, ed., *To Utah with the Dragoons* (Salt Lake City: University of Utah Press, 1974), pp. 6–9, 13–15.

16. Dale F. Giese, ed., *My Life with the Army in the West* (Santa Fe, N.Mex.: Stagecoach Press, 1967), pp. 16–23; see also Harold D. Langley, *To Utah with the Dragoons*, p. 12ff. for letters by an anonymous dragoon recruit assigned to the sixth column.

17. Lewis Roe's First Notebook, in Lewis F. Roe Papers, Knox College Archives and Manuscript Collection, Galesburg, Ill.

18. Fred R. Gowans and Eugene E. Campbell, *Fort Bridger* (Provo, Utah: Brigham Young University Press, 1975), p. 180.

19. Robert M. Utley, *Frontiersmen in Blue* (New York: Macmillan, 1967), p. 171.

20. Charles F. Hubert, *History of the Fiftieth Regiment*, p. 525; Gordon Chappell, National Park Service, Oakland, Calif., to John P. Wilson, August 12, 1996.

21. Marriage license, in Lewis F. Roe Papers.

22. Lewis F. Roe Papers.

23. NA, Record Group 94, Military Service Record of Lewis F. Roe, Company Muster Roll, November–December 1864. The actual appointment is included in the Lewis F. Roe Papers.

24. Roe Family Records.

25. Roe Family Records; Western Historical Manuscript Collection, University of Missouri–Columbia, to John P. Wilson, June 15, 2000.

26. NA, Record Group 94, Pension Record of Lewis F. Roe, declaration of February 13, 1907; NA, Microcopy M593, Population Schedules of the

Ninth Census of the United States, 1870, Roll 789, Livingston County, Mo., Medicine Township, p. 14.

27. Lewis F. Roe Papers.

28. Lewis F. Roe Papers; *7th Annual Report* [1872] *of the Superintendent of Public Schools of the State of Missouri* (Jefferson City, Mo.: Regan and Carter; Columbia, Mo.: State Historical Society of Missouri), pp. 36–42, 267–68, 318.

29. NA, Microcopy T9, Population Schedules of the Tenth Census of the United States, 1880, Roll 174, Burton Township, Adams County, Ill., pp. 1, 2.

30. Lewis F. Roe Papers.

31. Henry N. Stone, comp., *Stone's Adams County Directory*, (Quincy, Ill.: Henry N. Stone, 1886), p. 98; Henry N. Stone, comp., *Stone's Tri-County Directory: 1892, viz.: Adams County, Ill., Marion and Lewis Counties, Mo.* (Quincy, Ill.: Henry N. Stone, 1892), p. 80.

32. NA, Record Group 94, Pension Record of Lewis F. Roe.

33. *Knox County Republican*, February 22, 1893, p. 5.

34. Records of the Knoxville Presbyterian Church, Knoxville, Illinois.

35. Dorothy England to John P. Wilson, November 15, 1993; April 24, 1995.

36. *Western Veteran*, September 11, 1889, p. 8; *Knox County Republican*, December 6, 1893, p. 1; January 23, 1895, p. 1.

37. Lewis F. Roe Papers.

Chapter Two

1. W. H. Emory, *Notes of a Military Reconnoissance, from Fort Leavenworth in Missouri, to San Diego in California*, 30th Cong., 1st Sess., H.R. Exec. Doc. No. 41 (serial set no. 517) (Washington, D.C.: Wendell and Van Benthuysen, Printers, 1848); and "Journal of Captain A. R. Johnston, First Dragoons," in W. H. Emory, *Notes of a Military Reconnaissance*.

2. Raymond W. Settle, ed., *The March of the Mounted Riflemen from Fort Leavenworth to Fort Vancouver, May to October 1849* (Glendale, Calif.: Arthur H. Clark Co., 1940).

3. The latter included http://www.geocities.com/peaker59/history.html; and http://www.over-land.com.

4. Janet Lecompte, *Pueblo, Hardscrabble, Greenhorn* (Norman: University of Oklahoma Press, 1978).

5. Lee Whiteley, *The Cherokee Trail: Bent's Old Fort to Fort Bridger* (Boulder, Colo.: Lee Whiteley, 1999); Jack E. and Patricia K. A. Fletcher, *Cherokee Trail Diaries*, vol. 3, *1851–1900: Emigrants, Gold Seekers, Cattle Drives, and Outlaws* (Sequim, Wash.: Fletcher Family Trust, 2001).

6. W. Turrentine Jackson, *Wagon Roads West* (New Haven: Yale University Press, 1952), pp. 33–34, citing Stansbury's own 1851 report; Lee Whiteley, *The Cherokee Trail*, pp, 16–17, 105–8; and especially Marshall Sprague, *The Great Gates: The Story of the Rocky Mountain Passes* (Boston: Little, Brown and Company, 1964), pp. 144–46.

7. W. Turrentine Jackson, *Wagon Roads West*, pp. 145–46; Lee Whiteley, *The Cherokee Trail*, pp. 105–9; Jack E. Fletcher and Patricia K. A. Fletcher, *Cherokee Trail Diaries*, vol. 3, pp. 196–206, 221–25.

8. http://rutnut.com/cherokeetrail/; http://www.over-land.com/otrail.html; Randolph B. Marcy, *The Prairie Traveler* (1859; repr. Williamstown, Mass.: Corner House, 1968), pp. 320–23.

9. See Lee Whiteley, *The Cherokee Trail*, p. 30; also *Report of the Secretary of War, December 6, 1858*, vol. 2, *Affairs in the Department of Utah*, nos. 87, 88, 35th Cong., 2nd Sess., S. Exec. Doc. 1, Pt. 2 (serial set no. 975) (Washington, D.C.), p. 198.

10. Bob Cunningham, "The Mystery of the Missing Army Train," *Password* 38, no. 1 (Spring 1993): p. 29.

11. NA, Microcopy M1120, Registers of Letters Received and Letters Received by Headquarters, Department of New Mexico, 1854–1865, Roll 11, file no. M41, Morrison to A. A. G., October 18, 1860.

12. NA, Microcopy M1120, Roll 11, file no. M19, Morrison to A. A. G., July 28, 1860; NA, Microcopy M1120, Roll 11, file no. L27, Lynde to A. A. G., October 9, 1860; NA, Microcopy M1120, Roll 11, file no. L31, Lynde to A. A. G., October 23, 1860.

13. David H. Wallace, National Archives and Records Administration, Washington, D.C., to John P. Wilson, August 18, 2000.

14. See http://www.over-land.com/otrail.html; http://wyoshpo.state.wy.us/dugspr.htm; and http://wyoshpo.state.wy.us/laclede.htm; also http://www.over-land.com/ctrail.html; and http://rutnut.com/cherokeetrail/. The route from Fort Bridger to Cheyenne Pass is shown on "[Map of the] Territory and Military Department of Utah . . . 1860," in *Atlas to Accompany the Official Records of the Union and Confederate Armies* [hereafter *Atlas*], plate 120.

15. Marshall Sprague, *The Great Gates*, pp. 145–46, 443–44.

16. See http://www.geocities.com/peaker59/history.html; Horace Greeley, *An Overland Journey from New York to San Francisco in the Summer of 1859* (1860; repr. Lincoln: University of Nebraska Press, 1999), pp. 166–78; *Report of the Secretary of War, December 6, 1858*, pp. 182–87, 193–201.

17. See http://www.overland.com/otllpte.html; http://www.overland.com/laporte.html; Alonzo H. Allen, "Early Days in Longmont," *Colorado*

Magazine 14, no. 5 (September 1937): pp. 191–92; David J. Weber, *The Taos Trappers* (Norman: University of Oklahoma Press, 1971), pp. 210–12.

18. Janet Lecompte, *Pueblo, Hardscrabble, Greenhorn*, pp. 222–25.

19. Janet Lecompte, *Pueblo, Hardscrabble, Greenhorn*, pp. 256–58.

20. Janet Lecompte, *Pueblo, Hardscrabble, Greenhorn*, pp. 81, 88, 124–25, 139, 298; Lee Whiteley, *The Cherokee Trail*, pp. 35, 48; http://www.geocities.com/peaker59/history/html.

21. Chauncey Thomas, "The Spanish Fort in Colorado, 1819," *Colorado Magazine* 14, no. 3 (May 1937): pp. 81–85; Janet Lecompte, *Pueblo, Hardscrabble, Greenhorn*, pp. 32, 280.

22. [Map of the] *Territory and Military Department of New Mexico*, compiled in the Bureau of Topogl. Engrs. of the War Dept. . . . 1859, NA, Record Group 77, Sheet W55(1), Records of the Office of the Chief of Engineers. Reproduction available from Tucson Blueprint Co., Tucson, Arizona. [Map of the] *Arkansas River Basin in Colorado . . . surveyed in November 1890*; copy at Bureau of Reclamation, Denver, Colo. Copy courtesy of Brit Storey, BR Senior Historian. See also Marshall Sprague, *The Great Gates*, pp. 22–23, 411.

23. Helen G. Blumenschein, "Historic Roads & Trails to Taos," *El Palacio* 75, no. 1 (Spring 1968): pp. 16–18.

24. Fort Craig, about 28 miles south of Socorro, New Mexico, on the west side of the Rio Grande, is presently maintained as a historic site by the U.S. Bureau of Land Management.

25. Keith Newhouse, ed., "The Diary of Philander Powell," *Flashback* (Washington County Historical Society) 37, no. 3 (August 1987): p. 10.

26. *Rocky Mountain News*, July 18, 1860, p. 1.

27. *Santa Fe Gazette*, August 22, 1860, p. 2.

Chapter Three

1. Probably Eagle Rock or Castle Rock, which overlook Green River, Wyoming.

2. Lewis Roe's Camp No. 7 lay at modern Rock Springs, Wyoming.

3. A march of 22 miles on June 14 would place Camp No. 8 in the area of Thayer Junction. Ten miles the following day to Sulphur Spring led the troops to a point about 1.2 miles by road southeast of Point of Rocks, Wyoming. The spring and the bluff there are well concealed from the rough track along the east side of Bitter Creek and they remain as Roe described them—east and a little south from where the stream turns and bends to the west, in the NW quarter of Section 35, T20N R102W, Sweetwater County, Wyoming.

4. The site of Fort Laclede?

5. Probably the springs in Middle Barrel Springs Draw, where a stone ruin marks the remains of the Dug Springs Stage Station.

6. The stream was Muddy Creek, where the Overland Trail diverges at a point about 2.5 miles southwest from the Washakie Stage Station and continues west. Small units from Kansas and Ohio volunteer cavalry companies reportedly stationed at Washakie Station also garrisoned the stations at Dug Springs, Fort Laclede, and west to Rock Springs in the 1860s, to offer travelers some protection.

7. The Overland Trail crossed the North Platte River in Section 33, T14N R85W, Carbon County, Wyoming.

8. Pass Creek, Medicine Bow River, and Cooper Creek all retain the same names today.

9. The columns had begun marching toward the southeast, rather than due south, on June 30 and continued along the Overland Trail until they crossed the Little Laramie River ("West Fork") on July 2. At that point, they diverged and headed eastward again.

10. Camp Walbach was established in September 1858 by Companies L and M of the 4th U.S. Artillery, commanded by Bvt. Maj. Thomas Williams. The one hundred officers and men endured the winter there sheltered mostly in canvas tents inside low sandstone walls, with a few buildings of pine logs. The winter was rugged but largely uneventful, and on April 19, 1859, the garrison packed up and marched away. See Horace Greeley, *An Overland Journey*, pp. 178–79; Jack E. and Patricia K. A. Fletcher, *Cherokee Trail Diaries*, vol. 3, pp. 225–26; and especially Garry David Ryan, "Camp Walbach, Nebraska Territory, 1858–1859, The Military Post at Cheyenne Pass," *Annals of Wyoming* (April 1963): pp. 4–20.

11. The Eighth U.S. Census (1860) gave Denver a population of 4,726.

12. Jimmy Camp, named for a trader (Jimmy Daugherty) killed here in the late 1830s, was one of the most heavily used campgrounds along the Front Range. It is now a part of Colorado Springs, Colorado. The troops had rejoined the Cherokee Trail at Denver. See http://www.geocities.com/peaker59/JimmyCamp.html.

13. They were now at the site of Pueblo, Colorado, which appears to have been unoccupied at the time.

14. McDowell Park on the crest of the mountains is indeed a beautiful setting. The next day, the subcolumn had an easy march downstream along Sangre de Cristo Creek to the San Luis Valley and Fort Garland.

15. Fort Massachusetts, founded in June 1852, was a two-company post at the base of Blanca Peak, six miles north of the present town of Fort Garland, Colorado. It proved to be poorly sited and difficult to supply. After six years, the garrison moved to establish a new post at Fort Garland,

namesake of the modern town. Although abandoned by the army in 1883, many buildings at Fort Garland have been maintained and restored. The site is now administered as a museum by the Colorado Historical Society. See Herbert M. Hart, *Old Forts of the Southwest* (Seattle, Wash.: Superior Publishing Co., 1964), pp. 103–5.

16. Fort Burgwin, usually called Cantonment Burgwin, has been excavated and rebuilt in part and is now owned by the Fort Burgwin Research Center. Built originally as a two-company post in 1852, it was in poor condition when inspected seven years later. The army abandoned the place in May 1860, except for a sergeant and several privates left to watch over government property. See Lawrence R. Murphy, "Cantonment Burgwin, New Mexico, 1852–1860," *Arizona and the West* 15, no. 1 (1973): pp. 5–26; David Colin Crass and Deborah L. Wallsmith, "Where's the Beef? Food Supply at an Antebellum Frontier Post," *Historical Archaeology* 26, no. 2 (1992): pp. 3–23; and Ronald K. Wetherington, "Cantonment Burgwin: The Archaeological and Documentary Record," *New Mexico Historical Review* 81, no. 4 (2006): pp. 391–411.

17. Roe presumably meant Fort Leavenworth Road, but nine miles north of Santa Fe would have placed the column between Tesuque and Pojoaque Pueblos. There are no roads leading to the east in this area. Perhaps, as with the earlier reference to U.S. Hill, he had bad information or made his entry later than the indicated date and confused the location.

18. Fort Craig, some thirty-three miles south of Socorro, New Mexico, was a major military post in New Mexico at the time. Established in the spring of 1854, it continued in service until 1885. Although abandoned then by the army, a former chief of scouts, Captain Jack Crawford, maintained a general store, ranch, and residence for his family there into the 1890s. The site, mostly reduced to a series of ruin mounds, has been excavated in recent years and is currently administered by the U.S. Bureau of Land Management. See Herbert M. Hart, *Old Forts of the Far West* (New York: Bonanza Books, 1965), pp. 38–40; Darlis A. Miller, *Captain Jack Crawford* (Albuquerque: University of New Mexico Press, 1993); and Peggy A. Gerow, *Guardian of the Trail: Archeological and Historical Investigations at Fort Craig*, Cultural Resources Series No. 15 (Santa Fe, N.Mex.: Bureau of Land Management, 2004).

Chapter Four

1. The bibliography is large and still growing. Accounts by "witnesses" are mostly reminiscences or secondhand. A recent study is Douglas C. McChristian and Larry L. Ludwig, "Eyewitness to the Bascom Affair,"

Journal of Arizona History 42, no. 3 (Autumn 2001): pp. 277–300. For other primary sources, see Benjamin H. Sacks, "New Evidence on the Bascom Affair," *Arizona and the West* 4, no. 3 (1962): pp. 261–78; Constance Wynn Altshuler, *Latest from Arizona! The Hesperian Letters, 1859–1861* (Tucson: Arizona Pioneers' Historical Society, 1969), pp. 171–73; *Los Angeles Star*, March 9, 1861; *Daily Alta California*, February 19, 1861; and *Mesilla Times*, February 16 and February 23, 1861.

2. Bob Cunningham, "Mystery of the Missing Army Train," *Password* 38, no. 1 (1993): pp. 29–41. A civilian, William D. Kirk, was the wagon master.

3. Edwin R. Sweeney, *Cochise* (Norman: University of Oklahoma Press, 1991), pp. 171–73.

4. NA, Record Group 94, Pension Record of Lewis F. Roe.

5. *Los Angeles Star*, June 15, 1861, p. 2.

6. Introduction in Lewis Roe's First Notebook, in Lewis F. Roe Papers, Knox College Archives and Manuscript Collections, Galesburg, Ill.

7. The mouth of Nogal Canyon, a western tributary of the Rio Grande in New Mexico.

8. A number of early travelers mentioned this natural feature, which stood about thirty feet high. It lay in Section 17, T10S R3W, NMPM and collapsed some time following Roe's passage, after which no one refers to it. See Charles S. Peterson et al., *Mormon Battalion Trail Guide* (Salt Lake City: Utah State Historical Society, 1972), p. 29.

9. In the spring of 1859, settlers established a community called Alamosa, or more properly San Ygnacio de la Alamosa, on the west side of the Rio Grande just below the mouth of Alamosa Creek. In the 1860 Census, all of the 321 residents were native New Mexicans. Alamosa became the setting for a skirmish between a company of New Mexico mounted volunteers and invading Confederates on September 25, 1861 (*OR*, Series I, vol. 9, pp. 26–29). Union army correspondence usually called the village Cañada Alamosa.

10. Perhaps what is now called Mescal Spring, at the south end of the Whetstone Mountains.

11. Roe's phrasing suggests that part of the train and escort, perhaps the six wagons destined for Fort Breckinridge, had stayed at the recently abandoned but highly defensible rock-walled Overland Mail station at Dragoon Springs, Arizona, during the outbound journey.

12. Fort Breckinridge lay on the east side of the lower San Pedro River at its junction with Aravaipa Creek.

13. Robert Stapleton's ranch lay near the present site of Tiffany siding, but on the eastern side of the Rio Grande.

14. Introduction in Lewis Roe's First Notebook, in Lewis F. Roe Papers, Knox College Archives and Manuscript Collections, Galesburg, Ill..

15. Baylor gave his own strength as 258 men on the night of July 23 and the number in the Union command as nearly 700 men; see *OR*, Series I, vol. 4, pp. 17–19. The *Mesilla Times* for July 27, 1861, also reported the Fort Fillmore garrison as 700 effective men.

16. NA, Microcopy 617, Returns from U.S. Military Posts, 1800–1916, Roll 261, Post Return, Fort Craig, N.Mex., February 1862.

17. John P. Wilson, *When the Texans Came*, p. 149.

18. John Taylor, *Bloody Valverde* (Albuquerque: University of New Mexico Press, 1995).

19. John P. Wilson, *When the Texans Came*, pp. 243–244; *OR*, Series I, vol. 9, pp. 490–91.

20. John P. Wilson, *When the Texas Came*.

21. NA, Record Group 94, Enlistment Record of Lewis F. Roe; Charles F. Hubert, *History of the Fiftieth Regiment*, p. 525.

22. *OR*, Series I, vol. 4, p. 15.

23. John P. Wilson, *When the Texans Came*, p. 248; but see endnote 37, this chapter, about this alleged escape.

24. Ibid.

25. Lewis F. Roe Papers; John P. Wilson, *When the Texans Came*, p. 250; NA, Microcopy M1120, Roll 29, Unregistered Letters Received, 1862–63, "Report of Killed, Wounded and Missing of U.S. Troops under Command of Colonel B. S. Roberts, 5th N.M. Volunteers," February 22, 1862.

26. Introduction in Lewis Roe's First Notebook, in Lewis F. Roe Papers, Knox College Archives and Manuscript Collections, Galesburg, Ill.

27. Don E. Alberts, "The Battle of Peralta," *New Mexico Historical Review* 54, no. 4 (October 1983): pp. 369–79; Charles F. Hubert, *History of the Fiftieth Regiment*, p. 525.

28. S. C. Agnew, *Garrisons of the Regular U.S. Army, New Mexico, 1846–1899* (Santa Fe, N.Mex.: Press of the Territorian, 1971), p. 67. It was there also that Lewis Roe received his discharge from the army.

29. Lewis Roe's memory did not serve him very well here. Company F formed part of the Fort Craig garrison. Companies C and H were at Fort Buchanan, Arizona, through July 1861, when the army ordered their withdrawal and new posting at Albuquerque, New Mexico. No companies of this regiment served at Fort Breckinridge. Beginning in April 1861, the other seven companies of the 7th Infantry joined the garrison of Fort Fillmore, New Mexico. Together with three companies of the Regiment of Mounted Riflemen, these were the troops that surrendered

to Lt. Col. John R. Baylor's invading Texans at San Augustin Springs on July 27, 1861, and were released on parole.

30. Lieutenant Colonel Ruggles had been on sick leave prior to his resignation and never commanded the Department of New Mexico.

31. Joseph Wheeler, a brevet second lieutenant in Company A of the Regiment of Mounted Riflemen, submitted his resignation and left Fort Fillmore, not Fort Craig, in March 1861. Captain Garland deserted from Fort Fillmore in July. Lieutenant Marmaduke left for the South from Fort McLane, via a leave of absence.

32. The Post Surgeon at Fort Buchanan, Dr. Bernard J. D. Irwin, was a loyal Union man. This leaves Assistant Surgeon Kirtley Ryland, medical officer at Fort Breckenridge, as the apparent author of this letter. What he might have done will never be known as he died on September 22, 1861, after returning to the Rio Grande when the Arizona posts were abandoned late in July; see Constance Wynn Altshuler, *Cavalry Yellow & Infantry Blue: Army Officers in Arizona Between 1859 and 1886* (Tucson: Arizona Historical Society, 1991), pp. 177, 291.

33. The date here is wrong as Sibley arrived in Knoxville, Tennessee, on this day during his journey to the Confederate capital at Richmond, Virginia (Jerry Thompson, *Henry Hopkins Sibley* [Natchitoches, La.: Northwestern State University Press, 1987], p. 216). The circumstances may well have been what Roe reports, as we saw earlier that he departed Fort Craig the day following his arrival (June 2) to catch up with his Company F en route to Albuquerque. Since Sibley left Fort Union, New Mexico, by stage on May 31 and arrived in El Paso, Texas, on June 12, the coincidental meeting that Roe describes may easily have taken place in early June. Sibley was a major at the time, not a colonel.

34. The ruins of old Fort Fillmore, now a pecan grove, lie about five miles south of Las Cruces, New Mexico, and eighteen miles by road north of the Texas state line.

35. Again, the passage of time had evidently clouded Lewis Roe's recollections. The Texans under Baylor left El Paso the night of July 23, 1861, and occupied Mesilla, New Mexico, about six miles from Fort Fillmore on the opposite side of the Rio Grande, on the morning of July 25. That afternoon, Maj. Isaac Lynde led most of the Fort Fillmore garrison in an attack on Mesilla, which was repulsed. See Martin H. Hall, "The Skirmish at Mesilla," *Arizona and the West* 1, no. 4 (Winter 1959): pp. 343–51.

36. The retreat and subsequent surrender of the ten companies of Union troops at Fort Fillmore on July 27 is another highly controversial incident that only recently has been sorted out; see John P. Wilson, "Whiskey at Fort Fillmore," *New Mexico Historical Review* 68, no. 2 (April 1993): pp. 109–32.

37. Actually, twenty-six enlisted men from the 7th U.S. Infantry deserted to the Rebels after the surrender; see *OR*, Series I, vol. 4, p. 15. The intriguing claim that eighteen 7th Infantry privates and noncommissioned officers refused parole at the San Augustin Springs surrender and subsequently escaped is not supported by any documentation that I have been able to find.

38. *National Tribune*, November 3, 1910, p. 7.

Chapter Five

1. Charles F. Hubert, *History of the Fiftieth Regiment*, pp. 21, 50, 56.

2. Ibid., pp. 27–158; *OR*, Series I, vol. 17, pt. 1, pp. 294–95.

3. Charles F. Hubert, *History of the Fiftieth Regiment*, pp. 131, 186, 208, 368–71; Frederick H. Dyer, *A Compendium of the War of the Rebellion*, vol. 1 (New York: Thomas Yoseloff, 1959), pp. 125, 501, 507–8, 520.

4. Charles F. Hubert, *History of the Fiftieth Regiment*, pp. 158–244.

5. Ibid., pp. 213–14, 245–63; *National Tribune*, August 8, 1907, p. 4.

6. Introduction in Lewis Roe's First Notebook, in Lewis F. Roe Papers, Knox College Archives and Manuscript Collections, Galesburg, Ill.

7. This huge brick building, usually called the "Zollicoffer Barracks," occupied a city block in downtown Nashville. Construction began in 1859 and was well along when the war halted the work. It stood five stories tall, not seven. After Union forces occupied Nashville, it served as a prison for captured Confederates and later, as we see, as quarters for federal troops. Finally completed in 1869 and known as the Maxwell House Hotel for almost a century, the building was destroyed by fire on Christmas night in 1961 (from MTAC Go!'s online informational blurb regarding the Millennium Maxwell House Hotel, accessed April 2005; see also Dave Gorski, e-mail correspondence to John P. Wilson, November 17, 1997).

8. Edward was a full brother; the genealogical relationship of cousin Luther Scarborough could not be resolved.

9. At this period the 50th Illinois was part of the third brigade of the 2nd Division, 16th Army Corps, Department and Army of the Tennessee.

10. See *OR*, Series I, vol. 38, pt. 3, pp. 375–79, 397–402, 420–22, 435, 457–58, 461, 615, 714–15, 722–23; pt. 4, pp. 195–97; Eugene W. Jones Jr., *Enlisted for the War: The Struggles of the Gallant 24th Regiment, South Carolina Volunteers, Infantry, 1861–1865* (Hightstown, N.J.: Longstreet House, 1997), pp. 161–63; also *Past Times* (Rome, Ga.: News Publishing Co., 1989), pp. 36–42; Russell K. Brown, *To the Manner Born: The Life of General William H. T. Walker* (Athens: University of Georgia Press, 1994), pp. 227–31; and

websites for battles of Resaca and Lay's Ferry at http://darrellryan.home-stead.com/Resaca.html; http://www.resacabattlefield.org; and http://www.resacabattlefield.org/ForLaysFerry.htm.

11. Charles Wright, *A Corporal's Story: Experiences in the Ranks of Company C, 81st Ohio Volunteer Infantry* (Philadelphia, Pa.: Charles Wright, 1887), p. 102; George Hovey Cadman Papers, Southern Historical Collection, University of North Carolina at Chapel Hill, George Hovey Cadman to My dear Wife, May 19, 1864; H. I. Smith, *History of the Seventh Iowa Veteran Volunteer Infantry During the Civil War* (Mason City, Iowa: E. Hitchcock, Printer, 1903), p. 121; *Cincinnati Daily Gazette*, May 31, 1864, p. 1; *OR*, Series I, vol. 38, pt. 3, p. 401.

12. *Atlas*, plates 48 #1 and 58 #1; *Past Times*, p. 38; William R. Scaife, *The Campaign for Atlanta* (Atlanta, Ga.: William R. Scaife, 1993), opp. p. 48.

13. See Georgia website at http://homepages.rootsweb.com/~ahopkins/nuckolls/georgia.htm; also 1860 Gordon County, Georgia Census, p. 257, at http://www.censusdiggins.com/1860_georgia_census_2.html, and Frix Family Cemetery listing in Papers of Mary Frix Kidd at Rome-Floyd County Library, Rome, Ga., copy courtesy of Mr. Robert Anglea, Rome, Ga.

14. Robert Anglea, personal communication with John P. Wilson, Rome, Ga., June 4, 2009. The property was described as Land Lot #137, 14th Dist. & 3rd Sec., Gordon Co. GA Deed Book "C," pp. 592–93.

15. *Atlas*, plate 61 #12; Glenna R. Schroeder-Lein, *Confederate Hospitals on the Move: Samuel H. Stout and the Army of Tennessee* (Columbia: University of South Carolina Press, 1994); Hugh Greeson, personal communication with John P. Wilson, Chatsworth, Ga., June 15, 2009.

16. See *OR*, Series I, vol. 38, pt. 3, pp. 399–401, 420–22; pt. 4, p. 713; Frix Family Cemetery listing; Eugene W. Jones Jr., *Enlisted for the War*, pp. 158–86, and website for Georgia Civil War Soldier Index at http://files.usgwarchives.net/ga/military/civilwar/gsi/gsi104.txt.

17. *Cincinnati Daily Gazette*, May 31, 1864, p. 1; George Hovey Cadman Papers, George Cadman to My dear Wife, May 19, 1864; *OR*, Series I, vol. 38, pt. 3, pp. 399, 468–69, 471.

18. Charles Wright, *A Corporal's Story*, p. 102; George Hovey Cadman Papers, George Cadman to My dear Wife, May 19, 1864; *Cincinnati Daily Gazette*, May 31, 1864, p. 1; *OR*, Series I, vol. 38, pt. 3, pp. 397, 468–69, 471; H. I. Smith, *History of the Seventh Iowa*, p. 121. Captain Frederick Welker, in nominal command of the artillery batteries, evidently was not on the field. Lieutenant Blodgett died at the Battle of Allatoona in October.

19. H. I. Smith, *History of the Seventh Iowa*, p. 121; Charles Wright, *A Corporal's Story*, p. 102; W. H. Chamberlin, *History of the Eighty-First Regiment Ohio*

Infantry Volunteers (Cincinnati: Gazette Steam Printing House, 1865), p. 94; *OR*, Series I, vol. 38, pt. 3, pp. 377, 401, 423; pt. 4, p. 197.

20. *OR*, Series I, vol. 38, pt. 3, pp. 421–23, 435, 461, 468–69, 471; *Cincinnati Daily Gazette*, May 30, 31, 1864, p. 1; W. H. Chamberlin, *History of the Eighty-First Regiment*, pp. 92–93; H. I. Smith, *History of the Seventh Iowa*, p. 121; Charles Berry Senior to Dear Father, May 17, 1864, in *Civil War Letters and Diary of Charles Berry Senior* [7th Iowa Veteran Volunteer Infantry], Electronic Text Center, University of Virginia at http://etext. virginia.edu/civilwar/senior/; website for 7th Iowa Infantry at http:// civilwar.aea.14.k12.ia.us/Resources/7thinfgue.htm.

21. "War Records, How Old Soldiers Get to Lying About Them," *St. Louis Post-Dispatch*, March 21, 1887, p. 6. Reprinted in John P. Wilson, *When the Texans Came*, pp. 7–8.

22. The 1st Alabama Cavalry, U.S. Volunteers, weave in and out of Roe's narrative. In 1862, Alabama's governor had sent conscription parties into the northern counties, where these Home Guards tried to coerce men into joining the Confederate army while harassing and brutalizing their families. One result was creation of the 1st Alabama Cavalry, mustered into federal service at Corinth, Mississippi, in December 1862. During most of its operational life, the 1st Alabama was part of the 16th Corps, Army of the Tennessee, where it served the traditional cavalry roles of scouting, raiding, flank guard, and screening the army on the march. General Sherman chose this unit as his escort on the March to the Sea. In three years of service, more than 2,000 loyal Southerners served in its ranks, and some 345 had been killed in action. See website for 1st Alabama Cavalry, USV at http://www.1stalabamacavalryusv.com/1stHistory.aspx, and http://1stalabamacavalryusv.com/Roster/Default.aspx; and Glenda McWhirter Todd, *First Alabama Cavalry, U.S.A.* (Bowie, Md.: Heritage Books, 1999); *Past Times*, p. 73.

23. Philip Dale Roddey, a native Alabaman, organized the 4th Alabama Cavalry, Roddey's Regiment (CSA) in 1862 and received increasingly important commands, becoming a brigadier general on August 3, 1863. At the time Roe first referred to Roddey, he commanded a cavalry brigade in the Army of Tennessee. His forces, far less than the 12,000 that Roe mentioned, served mostly in northern Alabama and participated in dozens of skirmishes as well as the larger actions at Chickamauga, Brice's Crossroads, and Athens, Alabama. Roddey's men were a constant thorn in the side of the 50th Illinois. They sought to repel Wilson's raid on Selma, Alabama, in the spring of 1865, with the result that most of the regiment was captured on April 2, 1865. See websites for Philip

Dale Roddey and for the 4th Alabama Cavalry CSA at http://geoci-
ties.com/Athens/Aegean/6349/roddey.htm; http://civilwarhome.com/
roddey4alacav.htm; http://www.geocities.com/Athens/Aegean/6349/
history.htm; and http://geocities.com/Athens/Aegean/6349/actions.
htm; see also Ezra J. Warner, *Generals in Gray* (Baton Rouge: Louisiana
State University Press, 1959), p. 262.

24. The identifications of Roe's messmates, all in Company C, have been
completed by reference to *Report of the Adjutant General of the State of
Illinois*, vol. 3 (Springfield: Phillips Bros., State Printers, 1901), pp. 530–32.
They were Sgt. Jacob Seiter, Sgt. Luther Scarborough, Cpl. Thaddeus W.
Hinckley, Pvt. Illyd Deer, Pvt. Henry C. Cooper, Pvt. Guy W. or Charles
T. Birdsall, Pvt. Francis M. Stewart, Pvt. James Spicer, Pvt. Hiram Cook,
Pvt. David P. Robbins, Pvt. Francis C. or Michael Ward, Pvt. Michael
Sceiter, Pvt. John Jenner, and brother Edward D. Roe. These add up to fif-
teen. Not all were veteran volunteers; Scarborough, Guy Birdsall, Cook,
and Ed Roe mustered out in September 1864 at the end of their original
three-year enlistments, while one recent enlistee, David Robbins, would
die at the Battle of Allatoona in October.

25. This regiment, the 3rd Alabama Colored Infantry [or 3rd Regiment
Infantry (African Descent)] was organized at Pulaski, Tennessee, on
January 3, 1864. It remained attached to the garrison of Pulaski until June
1864, doing duty there and guarding railroads in northern Alabama. Its
designation changed to 111th U.S. Colored Troops as of June 25, 1864
(see websites for the Civil War Archive, Union Regimental Histories,
Alabama at http://civilwararchive.com/Unreghst/unaltr.htm#3rdinf;
and 111th Regiment, United States Colored Infantry at http://rootsweb.
ancestry.com/~alcwroot/infantry_files/111thusctinf.htm).

26. Roe is quoting the title and part of the refrain from the Henry Clay Work
song, "Brave Boys Are They," published in 1861. Work wrote other patri-
otic pieces, including "Marching Through Georgia" and "Grafted into
the Army"; see Richard Crawford, *The Civil War Songbook* (New York:
Dover Publications, 1977).

27. General Sherman's armies began moving south into Georgia from their
winter quarters in and around Chattanooga in early May. He had just
under 100,000 infantry available; Confederate Gen. Joseph E. Johnston
claimed some 44,000 effectives. On May 8, Maj. Gen. James McPherson,
commanding the Army of the Tennessee, passed south through Snake
Creek Gap to Resaca, Georgia. Roe's regiment was in the advance.

Snake Creek Gap was a long north-south defile and Sherman
intended for McPherson to pose a threat to Johnston, who was emerging
from his winter camp near Dalton, Georgia. What followed, beginning

on May 9, was a series of blunders, until by May 13, Johnston had fortified himself north and west of Resaca, Georgia. Roe's brigade took part
in the initial skirmishing on May 9 but not in the Battle of Resaca on
May 13, 14, and 15.

28. The 9th Illinois Mounted Infantry was the lead element in the attack on
May 9.

29. Roe reported secondhand on the Battle of Resaca. On May 14, General
Sherman ordered Brig. Gen. Thomas Sweeny's 2nd Division, 16th Corps,
south (i.e., to the right) to Lay's Ferry on the Oostanaula River to force
a crossing and establish a bridgehead. Roe was mistaken in writing that
they marched initially to Calhoun Ferry.

     Late on the afternoon of May 14, Companies B and C of the 81st
Ohio Infantry and Company I of the 66th Illinois Infantry crossed the
Oostanaula in canvas pontoon boats at Lay's Ferry, opposed by a brigade of Confederate Brig. Gen. William T. Martin's cavalry. Four more
companies from the 81st Ohio soon followed. No sooner was the first
handful of men (from his second brigade) across the river than Sweeny
received two reports that the Confederates were building a bridge near
Calhoun Ferry, some three miles above. He promptly dispatched his
third brigade (including the 50th Illinois) and a battery of artillery to
Calhoun Ferry, while withdrawing his other troops back across the river.
The second brigade indeed suffered severely in this short action, with six
killed and 53 wounded. See Battle of Lay's Ferry website at http://www.
resacabattlefield.org/FoRLlaysFerry.htm; see also William R. Scaife,
Campaign for Atlanta, pp. 33–34; *Cincinnati Daily Gazette*, May 30,
1864, p. 1; and *OR*, Series I, vol. 38, pt. 3, pp. 377, 399–400, 415,
447–48, 460–61. For a Confederate account of the skirmishing on
May 14, see Eugene W. Jones Jr., *Enlisted for the War*, p. 158. The site was
also called Tanner's Ferry.

30. May 15 saw the second crossing or what is usually called the Battle of
Lay's Ferry. By mid-morning, the first two brigades of Sweeny's division
had crossed the river. The South Carolina and Georgia troops opposing them were part of Confederate Maj. Gen. William Walker's division;
they lost forty dead on the field and an unstated number captured. While
Roe gave a very interesting description of this encounter, his third brigade and the battery of 10-pounder Parrott rifles accompanying it only
returned from Calhoun Ferry some time before 5 p.m., after the day's
fighting at Lay's Ferry had ended. See website cited above and William R.
Scaife, *Campaign for Atlanta*, pp. 35–36; *OR*, Series I, vol. 38, pt. 3,
pp. 377–78, 401, 419–22, 714–15; pt. 4, p. 196; *Cincinnati Daily Gazette*,
May 31, 1864, p. 1; and Eugene W. Jones Jr., *Enlisted for the War*, p. 158.

31. This was the Battle of Rome Crossroads, which developed into a more substantial affair than would appear from the principal official reports by Brig. Gen. Elliott Rice and Brig. Gen. John Corse. Corse was present on May 13–15 as an inspector-general and appears to have held overall command on the Union side as General Sherman's personal representative.

    Roe and the third brigade were involved in some heavy skirmishing at one time but mostly found themselves on the perimeter of the fighting. McPherson had already ordered Sweeny to "hold his position strongly," i.e., not provoke a fight. See *OR*, Series I, vol. 38, pt. 3, pp. 396–414, 420–22, 714–15, 722–23; pt. 4, pp. 186–87, 196–99, 212–13, 282; pt. 5, pp. 266, 270.

32. Roe passed through Adairsville without mention of a fierce rear guard action there the day before, at a remarkable two-storied house, octagon in shape, owned by a planter named Saxon or Saxton. See *OR*, Series I, vol. 38, pt. 1, pp. 317–18, 328; Sam Watkins, *"Company Aytch" or, A Side Show of the Big Show* (New York: Plume, 1999), pp. 123–24; William J. K. Beaudot, *The 24th Wisconsin Infantry in the Civil War* (Mechanicsburg, Pa.: Stackpole Books, 2003), pp. 300–303; Lee Kennett, *Marching Through Georgia: The Story of Soldiers and Civilians During Sherman's Campaign* (New York: HarperCollins, 1995), p. 88; *Past Times*, p. 42.

33. Kingston, Georgia, at the time was an important railroad crossroads.

34. On the afternoon of May 17, Maj. Gen. Jefferson C. Davis and his 2nd Division (14th Army Corps, Army of the Cumberland) arrived at Rome, Georgia, to find a division of Confederate Gen. Leonidas Polk's Army of Mississippi entrenched in some existing earthworks there. After heavy fighting, the Confederates withdrew south of the Oostanaula, destroying the main bridges and leaving Davis in control of the town. On May 22, Col. Moses Bane's third brigade (2nd Division, 16th Corps) with about 1,800 men marched into Rome to serve as a garrison; see *OR*, Series I, vol. 38, pt. 1, pp. 505–6, 627–30, 701–2, 709–10, 720–21; pt. 4, p. 236; *Past Times*, pp. 46–49; and William R. Scaife, *Campaign for Atlanta*, pp. 41–42. Lewis Roe's friend Michael Fitzgerald did not survive the war.

Chapter Six

1. *Population of the United States in 1860; Compiled from the Original Returns of the Eighth Census* (Washington, D.C.: Government Printing Office, 1864), pp. 74, 88.

2. *Manufactures of the United States in 1860; Compiled from the Original Returns of the Eighth Census* (Washington, D.C.: Government Printing Office, 1865), p. 68. Wade B. Gassman, "A History of Rome and Floyd County, Georgia in the Civil War" (master's thesis, Emory University,

1966), pp. 5–8; George Magruder Battey Jr., *A History of Rome and Floyd County* (1922; repr. Atlanta, Ga.: Cherokee Publishing Company, 1969), p. 111.

3. Wade B. Gassman, "History of Rome and Floyd County," pp. 23–36.

4. Ibid., pp. 77–79; Larry J. Daniel, "Manufacturing Cannon in the Confederacy," *Civil War Times Illustrated* 12, no. 7 (November 1973): pp. 4–10, 40–46; Larry J. Daniel and Riley W. Gunter, *Confederate Cannon Foundries* (Union City, Tenn.: Pioneer Press, 1977), pp. 40–46, 93.

5. Wade B. Gassman, "History of Rome and Floyd County," pp. 43–54; George Magruder Battey Jr., *History of Rome and Floyd County*, pp. 153–58; Glenna R. Schroeder-Lein, *Confederate Hospitals on the Move*, pp. 62–63, 130–31.

6. *OR*, Series I, vol. 23, pt. 1, pp. 280–95; George Magruder Battey Jr., *History of Rome and Floyd County*, pp. 161–72; Edward G. Longacre, "All Is Fair in Love and War," *Civil War Times Illustrated* 8, no. 3 (June 1969): pp. 32–40; see also http://ngeorgia.com/history/lightingmule.html.

7. Wade B. Gassman, "History of Rome and Floyd County," pp. 55–69, 85–105; George Magruder Battey Jr., *History of Rome and Floyd County*, pp. 158–60, 177, 197.

8. *OR*, Series I, vol. 38, pt. 1, p. 630; George Magruder Battey Jr., *History of Rome and Floyd County*, pp. 175–77, 197; Larry J. Daniel and Riley W. Gunter, *Confederate Cannon Foundries*, pp. 43–45.

9. George Magruder Battey Jr. *History of Rome and Floyd County*, p. 281.

10. Wade B. Gassman, "History of Rome and Floyd County," pp. 95–167; George Magruder Battey Jr., *History of Rome and Floyd County*, pp. 197–99.

11. *Report of the Committee of the Senate upon the Relations Between Labor and Capital, and Testimony Taken by the Committee*, vol. 4, U.S. Congress, Senate Committee on Education and Labor (Washington, D.C.: Government Printing Office, 1885), pp. 311–47.

12. Wilfred W. Black, ed., "Civil War Letters of George M. Wise," *Ohio Historical Quarterly* 65, no. 1: pp. 75–76; Julie A. Drake, *The Mail Goes Through, or, The Civil War Letters of George Drake (1846–1918)* (San Angelo, Tex: Anchor Publishing Co., 1964), pp. 77–79, 120–21.

13. D. Lieb Ambrose, *From Shiloh to Savannah: The Seventh Illinois Infantry in the Civil War* (DeKalb: Northern Illinois University Press, 2003), p. 173.

14. Digital Library of Georgia, Hargrett Rare Book and Manuscript Library, University of Georgia, Cornelius C. Platter Civil War Diary, 1864–1865, pp. 1–5.

15. Letter of September 6, 1864, in Letters of Frederick Sherwood, May 6–October 21, 1864, in Emily D. Sherwood and Family Papers, Special Collections, Hill Memorial Library, Louisiana State University.

16. Julie A. Drake, *The Mail Goes Through*, p. 78. Pvt. Drake meant that their Confederate sentiments were awfully strong as of late May 1864.

17. *OR*, Series I, vol. 39, pt. 3, pp. 729–30; Wade B. Gassman, "History of Rome and Floyd County," pp. 122–24; George Magruder Battey Jr., *History of Rome and Floyd County*, pp. 179–80; Digital Library of Georgia, Hargrett Rare Book and Manuscript Library, University of Georgia, Cornelius Platter Civil War Diary, pp. 2–5.

18. *OR*, Series I, vol. 39, pt. 3, pp. 208, 415; Wade B. Gassman, "History of Rome and Floyd County," pp. 124–25; George Magruder Battey Jr., *History of Rome and Floyd County*, pp. 198–202, 205–9, 277; *Report of the Committee of the Senate Upon the Relations Between Labor and Capital*, p. 339. Among the numerous Confederate reminiscences collected by Mamie Yeary in 1909–1910 is one by former Second Lieutenant S. Rusk Stiles, who served in Company E, 11th Texas Cavalry. Stiles told Yeary that "One of my scouts perhaps did as much execution as any man in the army [the Army of Tennessee], Jack Colquitt, who was killed at the close of the war in 1865." See Mamie Yeary, comp., *Reminiscences of the Boys in Gray, 1861–1865* (Dallas, Tex.: Smith and Lamar, 1912), p. 722. Colquitt was evidently an enlisted man acting as a scout in the same regiment as Lieutenant Stiles, until Confederate authority evaporated in northern Georgia and Sherman's advance to Savannah left the country under no authority at all. Colquitt and others began their plundering, destruction, and murders at that time.

19. Several modern studies confirm this pillaging; see *Past Times*, p. 48; Wade B. Gassman, "History of Rome and Floyd County," p. 115; George Magruder Battey Jr., *History of Rome and Floyd County*, pp. 176, 197. Joseph T. Glatthaar, *The March to the Sea and Beyond: Sherman's Troops in the Savannah and Carolinas Campaigns* (New York: New York University Press, 1985), p. 152, says that some Texans held the town of Rome hostage until they received a ransom.

20. Rome evidently had two hotels at this time: the Buena Vista on Sixth Avenue and the Etowah on Second Avenue. The latter was of frame construction, so the 50th Illinois perhaps occupied the Buena Vista for their first month in Rome; see George Magruder Battey Jr., *History of Rome and Floyd County*, pp. 177–78, 198, 282, 289.

21. Roe's brief descriptions of the three pieces of artillery are intriguing; these may be the "three field pieces" that Bvt. Maj. Gen. Jefferson Davis listed as captured at Rome (*OR*, Series I, vol. 38, pt. 1, p. 630). Any of these *could* have been produced at the Noble Brothers Foundry. The "10 lb. Rifle" technically should have been a 2.9-inch Confederate Parrott rifle, but more probably was one of the twenty-two 3-inch iron

rifles produced at the foundry in 1861–1862 (James C. Hazlett, Edwin Olmstead, and M. Hume Parks, *Field Artillery Weapons of the Civil War* [Cranbury, N.J.: Associated University Presses, 1983], pp. 60–61, 244; Larry J. Daniel and Riley W. Gunter, *Confederate Cannon Foundries*, pp. 41–43). The 12 lb. Brass (smooth) would have been a 12-pdr. field howitzer of cast bronze, of either federal or Confederate manufacture; Noble Brothers cast five of these (James C. Hazlett, Edwin Olmstead, and M. Hume Parks, *Field Artillery Weapons*, pp. 70–87, 286–93; Larry J. Daniel and Riley W. Gunter, *Confederate Cannon Foundries*, pp. 40–43). There is, or was, no such thing as a "steel Parrott piece"; Parrott rifles had a cast iron tube with a wrought iron band around the breech. One Northern manufacturer did make a few three-inch ordnance rifles of "cast steel," an imprecisely defined material (James C. Hazlett, Edwin Olmstead, and M. Hume Parks, *Field Artillery Weapons*, pp. 220, 243). Parrott rifles, 10- and 20-pdr., were manufactured for both Union and Confederate armies, in the conventional iron and wrought iron materials. There appears to be one surviving 2.9 inch Parrott rifle manufactured by Noble Brothers, unrelated to the surviving records of that firm (James C. Hazlett, Edwin Olmstead, and M. Hume Parks, *Field Artillery Weapons*, pp. 109–19, 231–35, 263–64).

22. Brig. Gen. William Vandever arrived at Rome and assumed command of that post on May 27. He also commanded Roe's brigade from June 20 to August 2, 1864, following the resignation of Col. Moses Bane. He held the command at Rome until September 27; see *OR*, Series I, vol. 38, pt. 1, p. 107; vol. 39, pt. 2, p. 500; and Charles F. Hubert, *History of the Fiftieth Regiment*, pp. 275–76, 293. The identification of Rev. John A. Jones is from the testimony of a Mrs. Ward, in *Report of the Committee of the Senate Upon the Relations Between Labor and Capital*, p. 332.

23. Apparently the rumor mill was wrong this time. At the Battle of Dallas on May 28, both divisions of the 16th Corps were involved, the casualties in Brig. Gen. Thomas Sweeny's 2nd Division being very light. See William R. Scaife, *Campaign for Atlanta*, pp. 50–60; also *Past Times*, pp. 55–57; and *OR*, Series I, vol. 38, pt. 3, pp. 403–4, 422–23, 428, 448, 458, 461.

24. Sherman ordered two divisions (10,000+ men) of Maj. Gen. Frank P. Blair, Jr.'s 17th Army Corps east from Huntsville, Alabama, on May 20. They joined the Army of the Tennessee on June 8; see *OR*, Series I, vol. 38, pt. 1, pp. 109–10; pt. 4, p. 269.

25. The published history of the 50th Illinois reports only "a sharp skirmish" on June 8 (Charles F. Hubert, *History of the Fiftieth Regiment*, p. 276). The list of engagements for Roddey's 4th Alabama Cavalry indicates that they were in Mississippi at the time, so Roe is probably correct that

this skirmish, and many of the ones that followed, was with an irregular band of bushwhackers such as Gatewood's Scouts or Colquitte's Scouts. See also 4th Alabama Cavalry Battles and Engagements at http://www.geocities.com/Athens/Aegean/6349/actions.htm.

26. Col. Moses Bane, who commanded the 50th Illinois at the time the regiment was raised in 1861, had been assigned to command the third brigade in December 1862. Earlier that year at the Battle of Shiloh, he was severely wounded, including the loss of his right arm, and he eventually resigned on June 11, 1864, on account of his wounds and impaired health. Roe is mistaken in that Bane never received a brevet of brigadier general; see Charles F. Hubert, *History of the Fiftieth Regiment*, pp. 485–86; Frederick H. Dyer, *A Compendium of the War of the Rebellion*, pp. 507, 508, 520.

27. This skirmish is described in more detail in Charles F. Hubert, *History of the Fiftieth Regiment*, pp. 279–80.

28. See Charles F. Hubert, *History of the Fiftieth Regiment*, p. 280, for names of the captured men. Such raids and skirmishes were almost continual.

29. The regimental history says nothing about this morning raid. Roe evidently took part in the nighttime excursion to trap some of the "johnnies," but it had no results; see Charles F. Hubert, *History of the Fiftieth Regiment*, pp. 280–81.

30. Roe's terminology is very archaic here but is the same as used in the regimental history; Charles F. Hubert, *History of the Fiftieth Regiment*, p. 318. These would have been 8-inch siege howitzers; see endnote 51, this chapter.

31. By modern roads, the distance is closer to sixteen miles.

32. This two-day foraging expedition involved some 300 men and did meet resistance by guerrillas, but was successful; see Charles F. Hubert, *History of the Fiftieth Regiment*, pp. 284–86.

33. Maj. Gen. McPherson was killed on the afternoon of July 22 during the Battle of Atlanta. Maj. Gen. John A. Logan then took command of the Army of the Tennessee; see William R. Scaife, *Campaign for Atlanta*, pp. 99–103. He was shortly succeeded by Maj. Gen. Oliver O. Howard. On the Confederate side, President Jefferson Davis removed Gen. Joseph Johnston from command of the Army of Tennessee as of July 18 and replaced him with Gen. John Bell Hood. Hood had been one of Johnston's four corps commanders.

34. Roe is talking about the Battle of Atlanta on July 22. The Battle of Ezra Church on July 28 involved only the 15th and 17th Corps of the Army of the Tennessee; see William R. Scaife, *Campaign for Atlanta*, pp. 93–110. With reference to his Sunday dinner three days earlier, some of the Illinois soldiers in other regiments ate equally well; see Victor Hicken, *Illinois in the Civil War* (Urbana: University of Illinois Press, 1966), p. 262.

35. The regimental history is silent about this incident.

36. The 44th U.S. Colored Infantry was organized at Chattanooga, Tennessee, and Rome, Georgia, between April and September 1864. Col. Lewis Johnson commanded the regiment, which by late summer contained some 800 black enlisted men. All but a few hundred of them surrendered to Confederate Gen. John B. Hood at Dalton, Georgia, on October 13, during Hood's invasion of Tennessee. See websites for New Georgia Encyclopedia: "Black Troops in Civil War Georgia" at http://www.georgiaencyclopedia.org/nge/Article.jsp?id=h-783; and Tennesseans in the Civil War: "44th U.S. Colored Infantry Regiment" at http://www.tngennet.org/civilwar/usainf/usa44c.html.

37. Luther Roe, twelve years old at the time of the 1860 Census, was a younger cousin of Lewis Roe. Luther Roe enlisted on Feb. 2, 1864, and was probably discharged for being underage or because of family hardship (see Lewis Roe's letter of June 27). See *Report of the Adjutant General of the State of Illinois*, p. 532; NA, Microcopy M653, Population Schedules of the Eighth Census of the United States, 1860, Roll 155, Adams County, Ill., Free Inhabitants in Burton Township, p. 570.

38. This was Sgt. Thomas W. Billington, a veteran volunteer in Company C, 7th Illinois Infantry. Two privates of Company D were wounded as well. Although the records of the Illinois Adjutant General's Office list Billington as a sergeant, the 7th Illinois regimental history says that he was an acting lieutenant at the time he was killed. The soldier "shot while on picket" two days later was from the same company; see Charles F. Hubert, *History of the Fiftieth Regiment*, pp. 287, 288, and D. Lieb Ambrose, *From Shiloh to Savannah*, pp. 173–74, 239–40. The 7th Illinois Volunteer Infantry had joined the rest of Roe's brigade at Rome on July 9.

39. Brother Warren would have been Warren Read, Lewis's half-brother, born in 1845. He had enlisted in one of the hundred-day regiments raised in the summer of 1864, which formed part of the garrison at Memphis. In a daring raid early in the morning of August 21, 1864, Maj. Gen. Nathan Bedford Forrest took 500 prisoners and large amounts of supplies in the "Second Battle of Memphis." The Confederates withdrew after two hours. Brother Warren was unscathed. See website for 137th Illinois Volunteer Infantry at http://uk.ask.com/wiki/137th; see also Jack D. L. Holmes, "The Day That Forrest Visited Memphis," *Civil War Times* 2, no. 9 (January 1961): pp. 16–18.

40. The regimental history mentions this skirmish briefly and also the interest in ordering 360 Henry rifles. A little less than a month later, the strength of the regiment was put at only 264 men in eight companies; see Charles F. Hubert, *History of the Fiftieth Regiment*, pp. 290, 295.

41. The official history gives about the same version of this incident, but omits the casualty figures; see Charles F. Hubert, *History of the Fiftieth Regiment*, pp. 290–91.

42. As of September 23, 1864, the 50th Illinois and the other regiments in the same brigade were reorganized as the third brigade, 4th Division, 15th Army Corps, Department and Army of the Tennessee, commanded by Maj. Gen. Oliver Otis Howard. Brig. Gen. John M. Corse commanded the 4th Division continuing from his previous position as commander of the 2nd Division, 16th Army Corps, from July 26 to Sept. 23, 1864. See Frederick H. Dyer, *A Compendium of the War of the Rebellion*, pp. 486, 497, 501, 507.

43. Roe's comments here are confusing. Brigadier General Vandever commanded the third brigade of the 2nd Division, 16th Army Corps, from June 20 to August 2, 1864, but he never commanded the 2nd Division. He held command of the post at Rome, Georgia, beginning May 27, 1864, and curiously enough was remembered as "a splendid gentleman." As of September 27, he was ordered to turn over the command at Rome to his next in rank and assume command of the District of Marietta, Georgia; see *OR*, Series I, vol. 38, pt. 1, p. 107; vol. 39, pt. 2, p. 500; Frederick H. Dyer, *A Compendium of the War of the Rebellion*, pp. 501, 507–8; George Magruder Battey Jr., *History of Rome and Floyd County*, pp. 177, 277. General Corse established his headquarters at Rome on September 29, 1864 (*OR*, Series I, vol. 39, pt. 1, p. 761; Charles F. Hubert, *History of the Fiftieth Regiment*, pp. 275–76).

44. Lewis Roe's journal account of the Battle of Allatoona Pass on October 5, 1864, was very accurate, though the fighting ended about 4 p.m. rather than 9 o'clock. Roe's brigade, from General Corse's division, arrived just in time to reinforce the garrison at Allatoona, totaling almost 2,000 men, to oppose Confederate Maj. Gen. Samuel French's three brigades of about 3,200 troops. French's immediate objectives were to capture the supplies warehoused there and cut the railroad that supplied Sherman at Atlanta. His attack failed after a full day of heavy fighting. Roe's letter to his wife gave a much more complete description of this action. Lt. Col. William Hanna put the losses of the 50th Illinois at 86 killed and wounded, a 32 percent casualty rate. See *OR*, Series I, vol. 39, pt. 1, pp. 738–39, 748–49, 760–66, 777–86, 813–25; Charles F. Hubert, *History of the Fiftieth Regiment*, pp. 294–315; also Victor Hicken, "Hold the Fort," *Civil War Times Illustrated* 7, no. 3 (June 1968): pp. 18–27.

45. Beginning with the entry for October 9, 1864, we have the original installments of Lewis Roe's journal to draw upon. Installment 30 ran through October 15 and is cited here although the lower left corner of the page is torn away.

46. Roe saw only a tiny part of the overall view. At this point in time, General Hood and the 34,000 or so infantrymen in his Army of Tennessee had already bypassed Rome, crossing the Coosa River about ten miles to the west at Coosaville (now Coosa, Georgia) on their way north in what would become his invasion of Tennessee. On October 12–13, Sherman himself came to Rome with most of his own army, but Hood had already marched beyond via Summerville, and he appeared at Dalton, Georgia, on October 13. The Confederates moved very rapidly and Sherman never caught up with them. By October 28, Sherman had returned to Rome and left the pursuit of Hood to Maj. Gen. George Thomas, whom he placed in command of all federal forces in Tennessee. See *OR*, Series I, vol. 39, pt. 1, pp. 768–70; Charles F. Hubert, *History of the Fiftieth Regiment*, pp. 316–18; Bruce Catton, *Never Call Retreat* (New York: Pocket Books, 1967), pp. 380–90.

47. Evidently the 57th Illinois and another regiment, perhaps the 50th Illinois, carried out this action; see Charles F. Hubert, *History of the Fiftieth Regiment*, p. 317. Roe and the regimental history are wrong about the identity of the captured Confederate officer; he was the inspector-general of Brig. Gen. William W. Allen's division of Maj. Gen. Joseph Wheeler's Cavalry Corps (*OR*, Series I, vol. 39, pt. 1, p. 727; vol. 39, pt. 3, p. 292).

48. Original installment 31 commences October 16, 1864. The lower right corner is torn away.

49. Original installment 32 commences October 28, 1864. In his journal, Roe wrote that Thomas was at Chattanooga "with 30,000 men."

50. Roe had been promoted to corporal on October 1, 1864.

51. These two "8-inch siege howitzers" were almost certainly the same two 8-inch howitzers that Maj. Gen. Jefferson Davis found abandoned at Rome on May 18, 1864. In April 1862, the Noble Brothers Foundry cast and shipped to Savannah six 8-inch siege howitzers. A few weeks later, the State of Georgia rejected five similar pieces due to faulty casting, and these weapons were subsequently buried on the foundry grounds. The two pieces blown up on November 1 would have been from this second lot (see *OR*, Series I, vol. 38, pt. 1, p. 630; Larry J. Daniel and Riley W. Gunter, *Confederate Cannon Foundries*, p. 43; also Charles F. Hubert, *History of the Fiftieth Regiment*, p. 318, who referred to them as 64-pounders). No surviving examples are known (Edwin Olmstead, Wayne E. Stark, and Spencer C. Tucker, *The Big Guns* [Bloomfield, Ont.: Museum Restoration Service, 1997], pp. 56–58, 175, 235; James C. Hazlett, Edwin Olmstead, and M. Hume Parks, *Field Artillery Weapons*, pp. 80–81, 261).

52. Original installment 33 begins with the entry for November 4, 1864.

53. By Copperhead Party, Lewis Roe meant the Democratic Party, whose presidential candidate in 1864 was Maj. Gen. George McClellan.

Chapter Seven

1. Joseph T. Glatthaar, *March to the Sea and Beyond*, pp. 4–7, 134–35; Lee Kennett, *Marching Through Georgia*, pp. 225–27.

2. Joseph T. Glatthaar, *March to the Sea and Beyond*, p. 7; Lee Kennett, *Marching Through Georgia*, pp. 63, 239; *OR*, Series I, vol. 39, pt. 3, pp. 555–57, 570–71; vol. 44, pp. 19–25, 562. The name Army of Georgia apparently came into use about November 27, 1864, although Left Wing continued to be used.

3. *OR*, Series I, vol. 39, pt. 3, pp. 423, 498; Bruce Catton, *Never Call Retreat*, pp. 388–94; David Smith, *Sherman's March to the Sea 1864: Atlanta to Savannah* (New York: Osprey Publishing, 2007), pp. 23–24, 44–48, 89.

4. *OR*, Series I, vol. 39, pt. 3, pp. 496, 627, 701; vol. 44, p. 79; Henry Hitchcock, *Marching with Sherman* (Lincoln: University of Nebraska Press, 1995), pp. 49–50; Charles F. Hubert, *History of the Fiftieth Regiment*, pp. 319–30; Joseph T. Glatthaar, *March to the Sea and Beyond*, p. 101; Lee Kennett, *Marching Through Georgia*, pp. 227, 232–33.

5. *OR*, Series I, vol. 39, pt. 3, pp. 743–62.

6. Charles F. Hubert, *History of the Fiftieth Regiment*, p. 322; Lee Kennett, *Marching Through Georgia*, pp. 246–47; Victor Hicken, *Illinois in the Civil War*, pp. 278–80; *Atlas*, plates 69 #5, 70 #1, 101 #21.

7. Henry Hitchcock, *Marching with Sherman*, pp. 100–101, 149.

8. *Atlas*, plates 69 #5, 70 #1, 101 #21; Lee Kennett, *Marching Through Georgia*, pp. 244–45; Henry Hitchcock, *Marching with Sherman*; David Smith, *Sherman's March to the Sea*, pp. 22–23, 26–32, 38, 71.

9. *Atlas*, plates 69 #5, 70 #1, 101 #21; Charles F. Hubert, *History of the Fiftieth Regiment*, pp. 325–28.

10. David Smith, *Sherman's March to the Sea*, pp. 38, 71.

11. Henry Hitchcock, *Marching with Sherman*, pp. 103–6.

12. *OR*, Series I, vol. 44, pp. 362, 367; David Smith, *Sherman's March to the Sea*, p. 32.

13. *OR*, Series I, vol. 44, pp. 363, 390; David Smith, *Sherman's March to the Sea*, p. 41; see also http://www.usgennet.org/usa/ga/county/taylor/jones/military/griswoldville.htm.

14. *OR*, Series I, vol. 44, pp. 81–90, 369, 390; Lee Kennett, *Marching Through Georgia*, pp. 254–55; Charles W. Wills, *Army Life of an Illinois Soldier: Including a Day-by-Day Record of Sherman's March to the Sea* (Carbondale: Southern Illinois University Press, 1996), pp. 322–24; David Smith, *Sherman's March to the Sea*, pp. 40–42; William M. Anderson, *We Are Sherman's Men: The Civil War Letters of Henry Orendorff*, Western Illinois Monograph Series Number 6 (Macomb: Western Illinois University, 1986), pp. 117–18.

15. *Atlas*, plates 69 #4, 70 #2; *OR*, Series I, vol. 44, pp. 1–2, 7–10, 30, 54–55, 65–71, 94, 125–28, 144–45, 659; David Smith, *Sherman's March to the Sea*, pp. 70–74.

16. William Duncan, "The Army of the Tennessee Under Major General O. O. Howard," in *Glimpses of the Nation's Struggle*, vol. 4, Minnesota Commandry of MOLLUS (St. Paul: St. Paul Book and Stationery Co., 1898), pp. 170–75; Oliver O. Howard, "Sherman's Advance From Atlanta," in *The Way to Appomattox: Battles and Leaders of the Civil War*, vol. 4 (New York: Thomas Yoseloff, 1956), p. 666; *OR*, Series I, vol. 44, pp. 72, 676. In the Carolinas campaign, Captain Duncan, by then captain of Company K, 15th Illinois Cavalry, was part of General Howard's escort and sometimes acted as a scout and led special missions (*OR*, Series I, vol. 47 pt. 1, pp. 46, 200–208).

17. *OR*, Series I, vol. 44, pp. 71, 109–12, 127, 692–93, 703–4; Richard M. McMurry, "On the Road to the Sea: Sherman's Savannah Campaign," *Civil War Times Illustrated* 21, no. 9 (January 1983): pp. 16–21; David Smith, *Sherman's March to the Sea*, pp. 76–82.

18. *OR*, Series I, vol. 44, pp. 713–14.

19. M. B. Loop, "Rounding-up the Confederacy; Veteran Campaigns of the 68th Ohio," *National Tribune*, June 6, 1901, p. 7. Pvt. Myron B. Loop served almost four years in Company I of the 68th Ohio Volunteer Infantry. His experiences, serialized in the *National Tribune*, have recently been edited by Richard A. Baumgartner and published as a book, *The Long Road Home: Ten Thousand Miles Through the Confederacy with the 68th Ohio* (Huntington, W.Va.: Blue Acorn Press, 2006).

20. *OR*, Series I, vol. 44, pp. 128, 146–47, 360–61, 389; Henry Hitchcock, *Marching with Sherman*, p. 167; Charles W. Wills, *Army Life of an Illinois Soldier*, p. 332; Lee Kennett, *Marching Through Georgia*, pp. 269–70, 309; Joseph T. Glatthaar, *March to the Sea and Beyond*, pp. 120, 130; William M. Anderson, *We Are Sherman's Men*, p. 119.

21. *OR*, Series I, vol. 44, pp. 367–68; Lee Kennett, *Marching Through Georgia*, pp. 228–34, 264–65, 273–79; Joseph T. Glatthaar, *March to the Sea and Beyond*, pp. 136–40.

22. *OR*, Series I, vol. 44, pp. 79–80, 146; David Smith, *Sherman's March to the Sea*, p. 85; Victor Hicken, *Illinois in the Civil War*, p. 288.

23. Entries through November 20 are from original installment #33.

24. Roe's estimates were slightly off. More accurate figures are 55,000 infantrymen, 5,000 cavalry in Kilpatrick's division, and about 2,000 artillerymen; see Victor Hicken, *Illinois in the Civil War*, p. 276.

25. Probably the prisoners taken in the skirmishes with Kilpatrick's brigades at Lovejoy's and Bear Creek Stations on November 16.

26. There is no entry for a Camp No. 12 but the dated entries continue without a break. Original installment #34 commences with November 21.

27. By "junction of the Milledgeville Road," Roe meant the junction at Gordon, Georgia, of the Georgia Central Railroad with a branch railroad that ran east to Milledgeville, the state capital.

28. Units of the 1st Alabama Cavalry and the 17th Corps indeed had some lively skirmishing at Ball's Ferry and the Georgia Central Railroad Bridge on the Oconee River; see OR, Series I, vol. 44, pp. 1, 68, 147; and David Smith, *Sherman's March to the Sea*, p. 43. The Confederates withdrew on the morning of November 26.

29. This small community now bears the name Summertown. Maj. Gen. John G. Foster commanded the Department of the South, headquartered at Hilton Head. His troops had wilted earlier in a conflict with the Georgia militia, but he did have supplies ready for Sherman when he reached the coast; see Richard M. McMurry, "On the Road to the Sea," pp. 13–17; David Smith, *Sherman's March to the Sea*, p. 83. Roe's rumor was vastly premature.

30. Original installment #35 begins Sunday, December 4.

31. Major General Howard was driving off the rebels who tried to prevent his crossing of the Ogeechee; see OR, Series I, vol. 44, pp. 2, 70; Henry Hitchcock, *Marching with Sherman*, p. 158.

32. In his diary entry for December 8, Maj. Henry Hitchcock noted that Brigadier General Corse had seized, bridged, and crossed the Savannah canal, an important strategic position, and now had his whole division poised about twelve miles west of the city. See Henry Hitchcock, *Marching with Sherman*, p. 159. *Atlas*, plate 70 #2 labels this the Ogeechee Canal.

33. This was the initial assault on the western end of the Confederate outer defense line around Savannah. See *Atlas*, plate 69 #4 for positions of the 4th Division, 15th Army Corps on December 9, 10, and 11, 1864. The regimental history cited many more instances of skirmishing; see Charles F. Hubert, *History of the Fiftieth Regiment*, pp. 328–30.

34. Roe tells it pretty much as it happened although lacking much of the drama; see OR, Series I, vol. 44, pp. 87–88, 109–12, 114–15, 121–22; Richard M. McMurry, "On the Road to the Sea," pp. 20–21; Joseph T. Glathaar, *March to the Sea and Beyond*, pp. 166–67, 254–55; David Smith, *Sherman's March to the Sea*, pp. 76–82.

   The poem at the end of this chapter is quoted from *The Western Veteran* 9, no. 5 (February 1, 1893): p. 1. These verses were originally song lyrics, composed by Samuel H. M. Byers, Adjutant of the 5th Iowa Infantry, who had been taken prisoner at the Battle of Chattanooga in 1863. He escaped from a rebel prison camp in Columbia, South Carolina, when Sherman captured the city in February 1865. The melody was borrowed from "Old Rosin the Beau" (or Bow), which served also as the melody for the 1860 campaign song "Lincoln and Liberty." See *Cincinnati Daily Gazette*, March 21, 1865, p. 3; Paul Glass and Louis C. Singer, *Singing Soldiers* (New York: Da Capo Press, 1975), pp. 216–18; Olin Downes and Elie Siegmeister, *A Treasury of American Song* (New York: Alfred A. Knopf, 1943), pp. 176–77; http://www.scriptoriumnovum.com/i/p/byers.html.

Chapter Eight

1. *Population of the United States in 1860*, p. 74; *Manufactures of the United States in 1860*, pp. 63–64; *Agriculture of the United States in 1860; Compiled from the Original Returns of the Eighth Census* (Washington, D.C.: Government Printing Office, 1864–65), pp. 22–23; Walter J. Fraser Jr., *Savannah in the Old South* (Athens: University of Georgia Press, 2003), pp. 244–49; http://en.wikipedia.org/wiki/Savannah_georgia.

2. *OR*, Series I vol. 44, pp. 9–13, 719–21; Walter J. Fraser Jr., *Savannah in the Old South*, pp. 332–33.

3. *OR*, Series I, vol. 44, pp. 637–38, 727–29, 740–41.

4. *OR*, Series I, vol. 44, pp. 701, 727–28, 737–38, 959–60, 974; Henry Hitchcock, *Marching with Sherman*, p. 195.

5. *OR*, Series I, vol. 44, pp. 967–70; Alexander Robert Chisolm, "The Failure to Capture Hardee," in *The Way to Appomattox: Battles and Leaders of the Civil War*, vol. 4, pp. 679–80.

6. *OR*, Series I, vol. 44, pp. 718–21, 768; Alexander Robert Chisolm, "Failure to Capture Hardee," pp. 679–80; David Smith, *Sherman's March to the Sea*, p. 84; M. B. Loop, "Rounding-up the Confederacy," *National Tribune*, June 13, 1901, p. 7.

7. Alexander Robert Chisolm, "Failure to Capture Hardee," p. 680.

8. *OR*, Series I, vol. 44, pp. 7–12; Henry Hitchcock, *Marching with Sherman*, p. 198; Alexander Robert Chisolm, "Failure to Capture Hardee," p. 680; Walter J. Fraser Jr., *Savannah in the Old South*, p. 339; Henry W. Slocum, "Sherman's March From Savannah to Bentonville," in *The Way to Appomattox: Battles and Leaders of the Civil War*, vol. 4, pp. 681–83; Richard M. McMurry, "On the Road to the Sea," pp. 22–23.

9. M. B. Loop, "Rounding-up the Confederacy," p. 7.

10. *OR*, Series I, vol. 44, pp. 13, 843; vol. 47, pt. 2, pp. 52–53.

11. M. B. Loop, "Rounding-up the Confederacy," *National Tribune*, June 13, 1901, p. 7.

12. D. Leib Ambrose, *From Shiloh to Savannah*, pp. 203–4; Charles F. Hubert, *History of the Fiftieth Regiment*, p. 338.

13. Perhaps they bivouacked at the same place as the three dismounted companies of the 7th Illinois Infantry, who went into camp at Fort Brown (D. Leib Ambrose, *From Shiloh to Savannah*, pp. 335–36).

14. See website for New Georgia Encyclopedia: Wormsloe Plantation at http://www.georgiaencyclopedia.org/nge/Article.jsp?id=h-2870; also E. Merton Coulter, *Wormsloe: Two Centuries of a Georgia Family* (Athens: University of Georgia Press, 1955), pp. 207–15, 229–34.

15. *OR*, Series, I vol. 44, pp. 701, 726; *Quincy Daily Whig and Republican*, December 30, 1864, p. 3; January 7, 1865, p. 2; Charles F. Hubert, *History of the Fiftieth Regiment*, pp. 331–38; D. Leib Ambrose, *From Shiloh to Savannah*, p. 204. See also Joseph T. Glatthaar, *March to the Sea and Beyond*, p. 92.

16. M. B. Loop, "Rounding-up the Confederacy," *National Tribune*, June 13, 1901, p. 7.

17. William M. Anderson, *We Are Sherman's Men*, p. 120.

18. In a letter dated December 18 from Savannah, Capt. Timothy D. McGillicuddy of Company K wrote that the army was receiving supplies from the fleet and was in fine spirits. The 50th Illinois was "in as good a condition, if not better, than when it left Rome. They are drawing supplies on the oyster beds of the coast." *Quincy Daily Whig and Republican*, January 7, 1865, p. 2.

19. Original installment #36 begins Monday, December 19, 1864.

20. The pastor was Dr. Samuel Edward Axson, commented on favorably by Henry Hitchcock, *Marching with Sherman*, pp. 199–200. Reverend Axson accepted the pastorate of the First Presbyterian Church at Rome, Georgia, in 1866 and evidently remained there until his death; see George Magruder Battey Jr., *History of Rome and Floyd County*, pp. 290–94, 489.

21. Lewis Roe knew precisely what the successions in command of the 50th Illinois Volunteer Infantry had been, but he didn't explain these very well. Lt. Col. William Hanna, commanding the regiment until sometime after the Battle of Allatoona on October 5, 1864, had been seriously wounded at that battle and sent back to Illinois to recover. By October 26, Capt. Henry E. Horn, Company B, had succeeded him and commanded the 50th Illinois until he was mustered out of service on December 18, whereupon Capt. J. W. Rickart of Company D assumed command. Captain McGillicuddy (Company K) actually returned from detached service and assumed command of the regiment on December 23. He in turn mustered out on January 1, 1865, to be succeeded by Capt. Horace L. Burnham of Company C. Burnham then served until January 14, when Lieutenant Colonel Hanna returned from his convalescent leave and resumed command of the regiment. *OR*, Series I, vol. 39, pt. 1, p. 781; pt. 3, p. 565;

vol. 44, p. 850; Charles F. Hubert, *History of the Fiftieth Regiment*, pp. 318, 333, 337, 340, 494, 538–39.

22. Dr. Jones's plantation, Wormsloe, served principally as a country home for its owner.

23. Original installment #37 begins Friday, January 6, 1865.

24. There were even more reviews than the ones Roe mentions. On December 29, 1864, Sherman reviewed the 17th Corps (Maj. Gen. Francis Blair) and on December 30, the 20th Corps (Brig. Gen. Alpheus Williams); see Philip J. Reyburn and Terry L. Wilson, eds., *Jottings from Dixie* (Baton Rouge: Louisiana State University Press, 1999), p. 21, and Henry Hitchcock, *Marching with Sherman*, p. 203.

25. Perhaps these were Florida manatees, once called "sea cows." Adults might weigh as much as 1,000 pounds and measure about ten feet in length. These gentle creatures once ranged northward to the Carolinas; see Craig Pittman, "Fury over a Gentle Giant," *Smithsonian* 34, no. 11 (February 2004): pp. 54–59. Lewis Roe had obviously never seen anything like these before.

26. First Lieutenant Samuel Starrett had also been seriously wounded at the Battle of Allatoona and sent home to recuperate. Doesticks, P. B. was the nom de plume of a Civil War–era satirist and social critic whose real name was Mortimer Thompson (*Quincy Herald*, May 27, 1861, p. 3; April 24, 1865, p. 4). Bill Arp, the pseudonym for Charles H. Smith of Rome, Georgia, was a contemporary Southern counterpart of Doesticks (George Magruder Battey Jr., *History of Rome and Floyd County*, pp. 225–39, 262–66, 282, 545).

27. Bvt. Maj. Gen. Cuvier Grover with his 2nd Division, 19th Army Corps arrived by ship on January 18 from Maryland. On January 21, he was assigned command of the District of Savannah; see *OR*, Series I, vol. 47, pt. 2, pp. 20, 82, 87, 90, 108, 193. Unlike at Atlanta, Savannah remained firmly in federal control, with a garrison of some 4,800 men, when Sherman departed on his campaign through the Carolinas. A number of such districts had been created in the coastal areas of Florida, Georgia, and the Carolinas, all administered by Maj. Gen. J. G. Foster, commanding the Department of the South.

Chapter Nine

1. *OR*, Series I, vol. 47, pt. 2, pp. 3–4; see also Bruce Catton, *Never Call Retreat*, p. 411. Stanton repeated his argument "most forcibly" about the need to bring the war to a close as soon as possible for financial reasons

when he saw Sherman in Savannah on January 12, 1865; *OR*, Series I, vol. 47, pt. 1, pp. 33–34. The government was running out of money.

2. *OR*, Series I, vol. 44, pp. 797–800, 820–21; vol. 47, pt. 2, pp. 3–4, 6–7, 101–2, 154–56.

3. *OR*, Series I, vol. 47, pt. 1, pp. 42, 46–55, 857–58; pt. 2, pp. 27, 114, 156, 622. Although the aggregate number present on January 31 was almost 72,000, the number present for duty totaled 63,678 (see *OR*, Series I, vol. 47, pt. 2, p. 192). The effective strength of the army in the field on January 31 was reported as even less: 60,079. The number present for duty may be the most meaningful figure.

4. *OR*, Series I, vol. 47, pt. 1, pp. 240, 681; pt. 2, pp. 12, 139, 147.

5. *OR*, Series I, vol. 47, pt. 2, numerous letters and orders from pp. 7–193 passim. For details of their route see *Atlas*, plates 79 #3, #80, and #86.

6. *OR*, Series I, vol. 47, pt. 1, pp. 18, 193; pt. 2, pp. 144–49, 154–56; Henry Hitchcock, *Marching with Sherman*, pp. 214, 231, 236–38.

7. *OR*, Series I, vol. 47, pt. 1, pp. 221, 224–25, 336–37; pt. 2, pp. 102–3, 115, 118–19, 133, 137, 144, 149.

8. *OR*, Series I, vol. 47, pt. 1, pp. 19–20, 146, 195–96; pt. 2, pp. 1028, 1079, 1084–85, 1180; *Atlas*, plates 79 #3, 86 #3, 117, 143; Joseph T. Glatthaar, *March to the Sea and Beyond*, pp. 12, 142–43; Wade Hampton, "The Battle of Bentonville," in *The Way to Appomattox: Battles and Leaders of the Civil War*, vol. 4, p. 701.

9. *OR*, Series I, vol. 47, pt. 1, pp. 221, 223–25, 337–38; *Atlas*, plate 79 #3A; *Cincinnati Daily Gazette*, March 22, 1865, p. 1.

10. *OR*, Series I, vol. 47, pt. 1, pp. 20, 196, 225, 378–79. The *Cincinnati Daily Gazette* for March 22, 1865, p. 1, included a graphic description of the destruction at Orangeburg.

11. *Cincinnati Daily Gazette*, March 22, 1865, p. 1.

12. *OR*, Series I, vol. 44, pp. 1012; vol. 47, pt. 1, p. 1058; pt. 2, pp. 1069, 1071, 1084, 1207; Mark L. Bradley, *Last Stand in the Carolinas: The Battle of Bentonville* (Campbell, Calif.: Savas Publishing Company, 1996), pp. 28–30, 82–83; David Smith, *Sherman's March to the Sea*, pp. 64–65, 90.

13. *OR*, Series I, vol. 44, pp. 874–75, 969–76, 979, 984–85, 1008–10; vol. 47, pt. 1, p. 1053; pt. 2, pp. 1032, 1069, 1084–85, 1104–5, 1180–81, 1201–5, 1247; *Cincinnati Daily Gazette*, March 22, 1865, p. 1; David Oakley, "Marching Through Georgia and the Carolinas," in *The Way to Appomattox: Battles and Leaders of the Civil War*, vol. 4, p. 675; Wade Hampton, "The Battle of Bentonville," pp. 700–701; Henry W. Slocum, "Sherman's March from Savannah to Bentonville," pp. 683–85; Mark L. Bradley, *Last Stand in the Carolinas*, pp. 21–24; and Henry Hitchcock, *Marching with Sherman*, pp. 260–66.

14. *OR*, Series I, vol. 47, pt. 1, pp. 20–22, 197–98, 227–28, 243, 1039; pt. 2, pp. 1202–4; *Cincinnati Daily Gazette*, March 21, 1865, p. 3; March 22, 1865, p. 1.

15. *OR*, Series I, vol. 47, pt. 1, pp. 21–22, 198–99, 227–28, 243, 247; pt. 2, pp. 1105, 1201. Some newspaper accounts were even more lurid; see *Cincinnati Daily Gazette*, March 21, 1865, p. 3, also Joseph T. Glatthaar, *March to the Sea and Beyond*, pp. 143–46. In spite of the massive fire, Maj. Gen. Charles Woods, 1st Division, 15th Corps, managed to find and destroy some 1370 bales of cotton stored or piled in the streets of Columbia.

16. *OR*, Series I, vol. 46, pt. 2, p. 1205; vol. 47, pt. 2, p. 1104.

17. *OR*, Series I, vol. 47, pt. 2, pp. 1078–79, 1247–48; also Mark L. Bradley, *Last Stand in the Carolinas*, pp. 44–46.

18. *OR*, Series I, vol. 47, pt. 2, pp., 1223, 1229, 1247; *Cincinnati Daily Gazette*, March 21, 1865, p. 3; March 22, 1865, p. 1; Wade Hampton, "Battle of Bentonville," p. 701; Joseph T. Glatthaar, *March to the Sea and Beyond*, pp. 143–46.

19. *OR*, Series I, vol. 47, pt. 1, pp. 22, 121–22, 133, 135–36, 228–29, 338–39, 859; pt. 2, p. 1222; *Atlas*, plates 80 and 117.

20. *OR*, Series I, vol. 47, pt. 1, pp. 22, 200–201, 229–30, 246, 319, 339, 343, 380–81, 421, 427, 431, 480, 483, 583–84.

21. *OR*, Series I, vol. 47, pt. 1, p. 23.

22. *OR*, Series I, vol. 47, pt. 1, pp. 22–23, 201–2, 381, 663; Mark L. Bradley, *Last Stand in the Carolinas*, pp. 58–65.

23. *OR*, Series I, vol. 47, pt. 1, pp. 182–83, 381; *Cincinnati Daily Gazette*, March 21, 1865, p. 3; March 22, 1865, p. 4; Henry W. Slocum, "Sherman's March from Savannah to Bentonville," p. 687; Mark L. Bradley, *Last Stand in the Carolinas*, pp. 65–66; John D. Martin, "Campaigning with the Western Army," *National Tribune*, February 1, 1900, p. 3.

24. Charles F. Hubert, *History of the Fiftieth Regiment*, pp. 364–66.

25. *OR*, Series I, vol. 47, pt. 1, pp. 23, 137, 202–4, 231–33, 321, 340, 691–93, 861–62; *Atlas*, plate 80 #6–8; Mark L. Bradley, *Last Stand in the Carolinas*, pp. 70–76, 88–102; Wilber S. Nye, "Kilpatrick Caught in His Underwear at Battle of Monroe's Crossroads," *Civil War Times* 3, no. 1 (April 1961): pp. 17–18.

26. *OR*, Series I, vol. 47 pt. 1, pp. 23–24, 137, 203–4; pt. 2, pp. 735, 821–22; Henry Hitchcock, *Marching with Sherman*, p. 264; Mark L. Bradley, *Last Stand in the Carolinas*, p. 78; M. B. Loop, "Rounding Up the Confederacy," *National Tribune*, June 27, 1901, p. 7; Charles W. Wills, *Army Life of an Illinois Soldier*, p. 362.

27. *OR*, Series I, vol. 47, pt. 1, pp. 23, 183–84, 204, 340, 422, 428, 432–33, 585; Mark L. Bradley, *Last Stand in the Carolinas*, pp. 111–13.

28. *OR*, Series I, vol. 47, pt. 2, p. 980; pt. 3, pp. 706–7; Mark L. Bradley, *Last Stand in the Carolinas*, pp. 75–78.

29. *OR*, Series I, vol. 47, pt. 1, pp. 23–24, 204–5, 233–34, 340–41, 343, 365, 422, 1056–57; pt. 2, pp. 822–23, 846–47, 863–64; *Cincinnati Daily Gazette*, April 1, 1865, p. 2; Charles F. Hubert, *History of the Fiftieth Regiment*, pp. 368–69; Mark L. Bradley, *Last Stand in the Carolinas*, pp. 112, 119; D. Leib Ambrose, *From Shiloh to Savannah*, pp. 208–9.

30. *OR*, Series I, vol. 47, pt. 1, pp. 24–25, 43, 422–23, 433, 484, 585–86, 1130; pt. 3, p. 706; *Cincinnati Daily Gazette*, April 1, 1865, p. 2; Mark L. Bradley, *Last Stand in the Carolinas*, pp. 120–32.

31. *OR*, Series I, vol. 47, pt. 1, pp. 25, 205–6, 383; pt. 2, p. 904; *Atlas*, plate 79 #3; Mark L. Bradley, *Last Stand in the Carolinas*, pp. 154, 316–18.

32. *OR*, Series I, vol. 47, pt. 1, pp. 26, 423–24, 485–86, 586–88, 1057–58; *Cincinnati Daily Gazette*, April 1, 1865, p. 2; Henry W. Slocum, "Sherman's March from Savannah to Bentonville," pp. 692–95; Mark L. Bradley, *Last Stand in the Carolinas*, pp. 140–310.

33. *OR*, Series I, vol. 47, pt. 1, pp. 25–26, 206, 234–35, 365–66; pt. 2, pp. 905–6, 916–19; Charles F. Hubert, *History of the Fiftieth Regiment*, pp. 370–71; Charles W. Wills, *Army Life of an Illinois Soldier*, pp. 364–65; D. Leib Ambrose, *From Shiloh to Savannah*, p. 209; Mark L. Bradley, *Last Stand in the Carolinas*, pp. 321–29, 334.

34. *OR*, Series I, vol. 47, pt. 1, pp. 26–27, 206, 235, 341; pt. 2, pp. 916–18; Charles F. Hubert, *History of the Fiftieth Regiment*, pp. 370–71; Mark L. Bradley, *Last Stand in the Carolinas*, pp. 338–40.

35. *OR*, Series I, vol. 47, pt. 1, p. 370; Charles F. Hubert, *History of the Fiftieth Regiment*, pp. 371–74.

36. *OR*, Series I, vol. 47, pt. 1, pp. 235–36, 341, 366, 368–70; Charles W. Wills, *Army Life of an Illinois Soldier*, pp. 365–66; Mark L. Bradley, *Last Stand in the Carolinas*, pp. 358–65.

37. *OR*, Series I, vol. 47, pt. 1, pp. 201, 229, 240, 273, 315, 319, 338, 426–29, 588, 680–99.

38. *OR*, Series I, vol. 47, pt. 1, pp.132, 189–90, 209, 404, 425, 863.

39. *OR*, Series I, vol. 47, pt. 1, pp. 28–30; Charles F. Hubert, *History of the Fiftieth Regiment*, p. 375.

40. Lewis Roe wrote the following introduction to the portion of his journals that covered the Carolinas campaign: "The March of Sherman's Army through the Carolinas. Left Wing consists of 14th and 20th Corps, Commanded by Gen. H. W. Slocum. Right Wing consists of 15th and 17th Corps Commanded by Gen. O. O. Howard. I belong to Co. 'C' 50th Ills. Infty. 3d Brigade 4th Division 15th Corps." Entries to February 4, 1865, Camp No. 5, are drawn from Roe's second notebook.

41. Roe was still in Georgia and west of Savannah. The Georgia Central R.R. ran from Savannah northward through Millen and on to Augusta.

42. From February 4 through 15 (Camp No. 16), entries are available from Lewis Roe's original journal and his second notebook. For some days, as on February 4, 5, 6, 9, 14, and 16, the notebook entries are a substantial addition and are generally included as a second paragraph. The original journal is headed "Journal, Goldsboro N.C. March 27, 1865" at the top of page 1.

   The entries for February 4 in Roe's original journal and in the second notebook (where they are misdated February 3) show a rare conflict or confusion, and I have edited these by reference to the reports of generals John Corse and John Geary (*OR*, Series I, vol. 47, pt. 1, pp. 337, 682–83), who were also present, to make sense of what I believe were Roe's movements that day. The original journal, which was probably not written down until a later time anyway, appears to contain the most conflicts.

43. Joseph T. Glatthaar, *March to the Sea and Beyond*, pp. 112–15, describes at some length the army's problems in crossing the South Carolina swamps.

44. Roe probably meant Robertsville, as Hardeeville lay at least twenty-five miles to the south.

45. On February 3, Maj. Gen. Joseph A. Mower's 1st Division of the 17th Army Corps, joined by Bvt. Maj. Gen. Giles Smith's 4th Division, had a sharp skirmish with the Confederate defenders at River's Bridge across the Big Salkehatchie River, after first wading through three miles of swamp. Federal losses totaled 18 killed and 70 wounded, while the Confederates reported 8 killed, 44 wounded, 45 missing (*OR*, Series I, vol. 47, pt. 1, pp. 19, 194, 376–77, 1076; *Atlas*, plate 76 #3; Charles W. Wills, *Army Life of an Illinois Soldier*, p. 341; Henry Hitchcock, *Marching with Sherman*, pp. 252–53, 267).

46. The battle Roe refers to was the one at River's Bridge six days earlier; see endnote 31. Their Camp No. 10 at the old rebel earthworks was indeed about twenty-five miles southwest of Branchville, but the Combahee River was far downstream, below the junction of the Big and Little Salkehatchie rivers after the two joined before the river flowed into the Atlantic at St. Helena Sound. It did lie west of Charleston, however.

47. The firing of resin pits and barrels of turpentine in South Carolina's turpentine country made a spectacular addition to the ongoing destruction of railroads, plantations, and other property; see Charles F. Hubert, *History of the Fiftieth Regiment*, pp. 350, 358; Charles W. Wills, *Army Life of an Illinois Soldier*, p. 345; David Oakey, "Marching Through Georgia and the Carolinas," pp. 677–78; Victor Hicken, *Illinois in the Civil War*, p. 292; Joseph T. Glatthaar, *March to the Sea and Beyond*, p. 107. The

regimental history went so far as to label the explosion of one turpentine still "a beautiful sight." In his notebook, Roe wrote that one wagon-load of ammunition (in their train) blew up on February 12.

48. This was the battle at Little Congaree bridge across Congaree Creek. Bvt. Maj. Gen. Charles Woods's 1st Division, 15th Corps, flanked the enemy (reportedly some of Maj. Gen. Wade Hampton's cavalry) out of a strong defensive position overlooking the creek, whereupon they retreated about two miles to a second line of works opposite Columbia. Woods lost six men killed and eighteen wounded. Oddly, only Lewis Roe mentioned prisoners. The 2nd Division did find the enemy in considerable strength along the north bank of the North Edisto River, where one regiment flanked and routed him, taking some 80 prisoners. This was on February 12 (*OR*, Series I, vol. 47, pt. 1, pp. 20, 197, 226–27, 273).

49. Lewis Roe's account of their advance is a good one. The correspondent of the *Cincinnati Daily Gazette* who signed himself "Quill" penned a detailed account of the entire campaign through the Carolinas as far as Fayetteville, including the approach by the 15th Corps into Columbia on February 16, in the *Cincinnati Daily Gazette* for March 22, 1865, p. 1. "Quill" almost certainly was Milton P. McQuillian, one of the journalists employed by that paper.

50. Roe's estimate of Columbia's population may have been accurate; the 1860 Census reported 18,307 whites, free coloreds, and slaves for the Richland District (County), which included Columbia, South Carolina, and a population of 13,718 for Quincy, Illinois; see *Population of the United States in 1860*, pp. 88, 452.

51. The Acting Ordnance Officer for the 1st Division, 15th Army Corps listed forty pieces of artillery, which included several siege or garrison guns, captured in Columbia (*OR*, Series I, vol. 47, pt. 1, p. 244).

52. Florence, South Carolina, was a railroad junction about seventy miles east of Columbia.

53. Foraging had become an exceedingly dangerous occupation, and such incidents were not uncommon. The regimental history included this episode in its entry for February 28 but for the 1st Division. Twenty-seven men had been killed in this manner (Joseph T. Glatthaar, *March to the Sea and Beyond*, pp. 127–28; Charles F. Hubert, *History of the Fiftieth Regiment*, pp. 362–63).

54. Charles F. Hubert, *History of the Fiftieth Regiment*, pp. 362, 364, recorded that on February 28, Colonel Hanna discovered a small stone mill, "a regular old fashioned mill run by hand." Mounted on a cart, it became a part of the regimental train and was kept busy day and night, grinding cornmeal.

55. Shoes, or the lack of them, became a problem in the Savannah campaign and a much more serious one during the march through the Carolinas; Joseph T. Glatthaar, *March to the Sea and Beyond*, pp. 115–17.

56. Cheraw, on the west side of the Great Pee Dee River, lay at the terminus of a spur line that led north about fifty miles from the rail junction at Florence. Roe gave a good account of what happened there; his regiment was on provost duty March 5 and 6, but by then the town had largely been plundered and pillaged; see *OR*, Series I, vol. 47, pt. 1, p. 369; pt. 2, pp. 666, 689.

57. The account of this explosion in the *Cincinnati Daily Gazette* (March 22, 1865, p. 4) and other contemporary sources confirms Roe's description.

58. Bvt. Maj. Gen. John Corse led one of the four "light" divisions organized in the Right Wing at Fayetteville, and his 4th Division had the lead when the 15th Corps moved out on the 15th to the South River. Corse met the rebel cavalry there and dislodged them, rebuilt the bridge, moved on the next day, and skirmished again; see *OR*, Series I, vol. 47, pt. 1, pp. 204–5, 233–34, 340–41.

59. The roar of artillery and musketry marked the first day of the Battle of Bentonville, which involved four divisions from the federal 14th and 20th Corps contending with Confederate Lieutenant General Hardee's Corps, in the swamps and woods south of the tiny community of Bentonville, North Carolina. Lewis Roe's own 15th Corps had no part in this.

60. March 20 was something of an intermission between the first day of fighting on March 19 and the full day of battle on the 21st. Still, quite a bit happened, and the 15th Army Corps skirmished its way to the battlefield by noon.

61. Roe is quoting part of the refrain from the Stephen C. Foster melody, "There's a Good Time Coming," composed in 1846, with lines/lyrics from the *London Daily News*.

62. Lewis Roe's excellent account of the events of March 21, the second full day of the Battle of Bentonville, has only one small error. There was no 47th North Carolina regiment in the Confederate order of battle for Bentonville. Depending on the time of day, Roe's regiment would have been opposed by Clingman's Brigade, which consisted of four North Carolina regiments (8th, 31st, 51st, 61st) or Hagood's Brigade, which included both North and South Carolina units. See Mark L. Bradley, *Last Stand in the Carolinas*, pp. 358–65, 377, 442–43.

63. See *OR*, Series I, vol. 47, pt. 1, p. 44. Their campsite on the 23rd was at Cox's Crossroads, where early in the morning of March 20 they bore left toward the battlefield; see *Atlas*, plate 79 #3.

64. And so the Carolinas Campaign and Lewis Roe's Civil War journal came to an end. Sherman's Army arrived at Goldsboro (also spelled Goldsborough) on March 24 in rags and almost shoeless, where they joined Maj. Gen. John Schofield's 23rd Army Corps, 12,000 strong, and Maj. Gen. Alfred Terry's Provisional Army Corps with an additional 10,000 men (*OR*, Series I, vol. 47, pt. 1, pp. 43, 207).

The march through the Carolinas was by far the longest of Sherman's three campaigns in 1864–1865. Sherman himself estimated that the army marched "near 500 miles" while other commanders used that figure or slightly lower ones (*OR*, Series I, vol. 47, pt. 1, pp. 44, 189, 274, 322, 342, 343, 367, 425, 588, 668, 698).

Chapter Ten

1. See especially Charles F. Hubert, *History of the Fiftieth Regiment*, and *OR*, Series I, vol. 47, pts. 1 and 3.

2. *OR*, Series I, vol. 47, pt. 1, pp. 29–30; vol. 49, pt. 1, pp. 25–26, 323–39, 344–45; Edward O. Guerrant, "Operations in East Tennessee and South-West Virginia," in *The Way to Appomattox: Battles and Leaders of the Civil War*, vol. 4, p. 479.

3. *OR*, Series I, vol. 47, pt. 1, p. 30; pt. 2, p. 707; pt. 3, p. 872; Charles F. Hubert, *History of the Fiftieth Regiment*, pp. 382–83; Horace Porter, "Five Forks and the Pursuit of Lee," in *The Way to Appomattox: Battles and Leaders of the Civil War*, vol. 4, pp. 718–19; Jennifer Cain Bohrnstedt, *Soldiering with Sherman: Civil War Letters of George F. Cram* (DeKalb: Northern Illinois University Press, 2000), p. 162.

4. *OR*, Series I, vol. 47, pt. 1, pp. 31–33; Charles F. Hubert, *History of the Fiftieth Regiment*, pp. 384–85; Henry W. Slocum, "Final Operations of Sherman's Army," in *The Way to Appomattox: Battles and Leaders of the Civil War*, vol. 4, pp. 755–56; D. Leib Ambrose, *From Shiloh to Savannah*, p. 213.

5. *OR*, Series I, vol. 47, pt. 1, pp. 31–35; Henry W. Slocum, "Final Operations," pp. 755–57; Henry Hitchcock, *Marching with Sherman*, pp. 301–17.

6. *OR*, Series I, vol. 47, pt. 3, p. 516; Charles F. Hubert, *History of the Fiftieth Regiment*, pp. 384–86.

7. *OR*, Series I, vol. 47, pt. 3, pp. 311, 324–27; Charles F. Hubert, *History of the Fiftieth Regiment*, pp. 386, 393–95.

8. *OR*, Series I, vol. 47, pt. 3, pp. 323–25, 361, 364, 397, 531, 850; Charles F. Hubert, *History of the Fiftieth Regiment*, p. 387. The Confederate soldiers were probably paid with Mexican silver; a silver dollar (eight *reales*), one "bit" (one *real*), and a U.S. nickel would add up to one payment.

9. *OR*, Series I, vol. 47, pt. 3, pp. 323–39, 347–53, 364, 372–73, 381, 389–90, 402, 413–15, 422; Charles W. Wills, *Army Life of an Illinois Soldier*, pp. 372–80; M. B. Loop, "Rounding-up the Confederacy," *National Tribune*, July 4, 1901, p. 7.

10. *OR*, Series I, vol. 47, pt. 3, pp. 448, 453–57; Charles F. Hubert, *History of the Fiftieth Regiment*, pp. 389–90.

11. *OR*, Series I, vol. 47, pt. 3, pp. 446–47, 454–56, 478–79; Charles F. Hubert, *History of the Fiftieth Regiment*, pp. 389–91; Lloyd Lewis, *Sherman: Fighting Prophet* (New York: Harcourt, Brace and Co., 1932), pp. 564–66.

12. *OR*, Series I, vol. 47, pt. 3, pp. 476–77, 517, 532, 679–81.

13. *OR*, Series I, vol. 47, pt. 3, pp. 495–526.

14. Charles F. Hubert, *History of the Fiftieth Regiment*, pp. 392–93.

15. *OR*, Series I, vol. 47, pt. 3, pp. 555–57; M. B. Loop, "Rounding-up the Confederacy," *National Tribune*, July 11, 1901, p. 7; Charles F. Hubert, *History of the Fiftieth Regiment*, pp. 392–94.

16. Charles F. Hubert, *History of the Fiftieth Regiment*, pp. 392–94; Lloyd Lewis, *Sherman: Fighting Prophet*, pp. 572–73.

17. Charles F. Hubert, *History of the Fiftieth Regiment*, pp. 393–94; Lloyd Lewis, *Sherman: Fighting Prophet*, pp. 572–75; "Review of the Armies," *New York Times* [hereafter "Review"], May 25, 1865, p. 1. Mother Bickerdyke had professional training as a nurse, exceptional organizational abilities, and the support of both Grant and Sherman during the war. In later years, she became something of a legend in west-central Illinois, although she lived in Kansas by then. She died November 8, 1901; the *Western Veteran* for November 1901, pp. 5–6, carried a lengthy memorial to her.

18. *OR*, Series I, vol. 47, pt. 3, pp. 526, 540–41, 554–55; Charles F. Hubert, *History of the Fiftieth Regiment*, p. 438; "Review," May 25, 1865, pp. 1–8. A second article in the same newspaper claimed 80,000 marchers.

19. Jennifer Cain Bohrnstedt, *Soldiering with Sherman*, p. 168.

20. Charles F. Hubert, *History of the Fiftieth Regiment*, pp. 394–95; "Review," pp. 1–8; M. B. Loop, "Rounding-up the Confederacy," *National Tribune*, July 11, 1901, p. 7.

21. Lloyd Lewis, *Sherman: Fighting Prophet*, pp. 574–76; "Review," May 25, 1865, pp. 1–8; M. B. Loop, "Rounding-up the Confederacy," *National Tribune*, July 11, 1901, p. 7.

22. *OR*, Series I, vol. 47, pt. 3, pp. 555–57; Lloyd Lewis, *Sherman: Fighting Prophet*, p. 574; "Review," May 25, 1865, pp. 1–8.

23. Charles F. Hubert, *History of the Fiftieth Regiment*, pp. 395–96; "Review," May 25, 1865, pp. 1–8.

24. *OR*, Series I, vol. 47, pt. 1, pp. 44–46; pt. 3, pp. 670–71; Charles F. Hubert, *History of the Fiftieth Regiment*, pp. 396–400; Lloyd Lewis, *Sherman: Fighting Prophet*, pp. 578–80.

25. *OR*, Series I, vol. 47, pt. 1, pp. 1, 78, 80, 83, 89, 94, 102, 107, 108–18; pt. 3, pp. 588–91, 598–600.

26. *OR*, Series I, vol. 47, pt. 3, pp. 601, 606, 614; Charles F. Hubert, *History of the Fiftieth Regiment*, pp. 399–400; M. B. Loop, "Rounding-up the Confederacy," *National Tribune*, July 11, 1901, p. 7; D. Leib Ambrose, *From Shiloh to Savannah*, pp. 217–18.

27. Charles F. Hubert, *History of the Fiftieth Regiment*, pp. 401–2; M. B. Loop, "Rounding-up the Confederacy," *National Tribune*, July 11, 1901, p. 7; William M. Anderson, *We Are Sherman's Men*, pp. 131–32.

28. For "When Sherman Marched Down to the Sea," see chapter 7. The *Western Veteran* newspaper later reprinted the lyrics from time to time. Charles F. Hubert, *History of the Fiftieth Regiment*, p. 402–6; M. B. Loop, "Rounding-up the Confederacy," *National Tribune*, July 11, 1901, p. 7.

29. Charles F. Hubert, *History of the Fiftieth Regiment*, pp. 406–9, 414, 488; *Quincy Daily Whig and Republican*, July 11, 1865, p. 4; July 17, 1865, p. 4; July 22, 1865, p. 4.

30. Charles F. Hubert, *History of the Fiftieth Regiment*, p. 405; NA, Record Group 94, Military Service Record of Lewis F. Roe, Muster Roll, May–June 1865, and Muster-out Roll, July 13, 1865.

31. Charles F. Hubert, *History of the Fiftieth Regiment*, pp. 412–14; *Quincy Daily Whig and Republican*, July 22, 1865, p. 4; NA, Record Group 94, Military Service Record of Lewis F. Roe, Muster-out Roll, July 13, 1865.

32. D. Leib Ambrose, *From Shiloh to Savannah*, p. 219; Jennifer Cain Bohrnstedt, *Soldiering with Sherman*, p. 171; William M. Anderson, *We Are Sherman's Men*, p. 134; Charles F. Hubert, *History of the Fiftieth Regiment*, p. 412; M. B. Loop, "Rounding-up the Confederacy," *National Tribune*, July 11, 1901, p. 7; *OR*, Series I, vol. 47, pt. 3, pp. 679–81.

References

Publications

Agnew, S. C.

   1971   *Garrisons of the Regular U.S. Army, New Mexico, 1846–1899.* Santa
           Fe: Press of the Territorian.

Alberts, Don E.

   1983   "The Battle of Peralta." *New Mexico Historical Review* 54, no. 4
           (October): 369–79.

Allen, Alonzo H.

   1937   "Early Days in Longmont." *Colorado Magazine* 14, no. 5
           (September): 191–98.

Altshuler, Constance Wynn

   1969   *Latest from Arizona! The Hesperian Letters, 1859–1861.* Tucson:
           Arizona Pioneers' Historical Society.

   1991   *Cavalry Yellow & Infantry Blue: Army Officers in Arizona Between
           1859 and 1886.* Tucson: Arizona Historical Society.

Ambrose, D. Lieb

   2003   *From Shiloh to Savannah: The Seventh Illinois Infantry in the Civil
           War.* DeKalb: Northern Illinois University Press.

Anderson, William M.

   1986   *We Are Sherman's Men: The Civil War Letters of Henry Orendorff.*
           Western Illinois Monograph Series Number 6. Macomb: Western
           Illinois University.

Battey, George Magruder, Jr.

   1969   *A History of Rome and Floyd County.* 1922. Reprint, Atlanta:
           Cherokee Publishing Company.

Baumgartner, Richard A., ed.

   2006   *The Long Road Home: Ten Thousand Miles Through the
           Confederacy with the 68th Ohio.* Huntington, W.Va: Blue
           Acorn Press.

Beaudot, William J. K.

   2003   *The 24th Wisconsin Infantry in the Civil War.* Mechanicsburg, Pa.:
           Stackpole Books.

Black, Wilfred W., ed.
    1956   "Civil War Letters of George M. Wise." *Ohio Historical Quarterly*
            65, no. 1 (January): 53–81.
Blumenschein, Helen G.
    1968   "Historic Roads & Trails to Taos." *El Palacio* 75, no. 1 (Spring): 9–19.
Bohrnstedt, Jennifer Cain
    2000   *Soldiering with Sherman: Civil War Letters of George F. Cram.*
            DeKalb: Northern Illinois University Press.
Bradley, Mark L.
    1996   *Last Stand in the Carolinas: The Battle of Bentonville.* Campbell,
            Calif.: Savas Publishing Company.
Brown, Russell K.
    1994   *To the Manner Born: The Life of General William H. T. Walker.*
            Athens: University of Georgia Press.
Bureau of Land Management, Wyoming State Office
    2010?   *Wyoming Historic Trails* (map). Cheyenne, Wyoming.
Catton, Bruce
    1967   *Never Call Retreat.* New York: Pocket Books.
Chamberlin, W. H.
    1865   *History of the Eighty-First Regiment Ohio Infantry Volunteers.*
            Cincinnati: Gazette Steam Printing House.
Chapman Brothers
    1886   *Portrait and Biographical Album of Knox County, Illinois.* Chicago:
            Biographical Publishing Company.
Chisolm, Alexander Robert
    1956   "The Failure to Capture Hardee." In *The Way to Appomattox:*
            Battles and Leaders of the Civil War, 4:679–80. New York:
            Thomas Yoseloff.
Coulter, E. Merton
    1955   *Wormsloe: Two Centuries of a Georgia Family.* Athens: University
            of Georgia Press.
Crass, David Colin, and Deborah L. Wallsmith
    1992   "Where's the Beef? Food Supply at an Antebellum Frontier Post."
            Historical Archaeology 26, no. 2: 3–23.
Crawford, Richard
    1977   *The Civil War Songbook.* New York: Dover Publications.
Cunningham, Bob
    1993   "The Mystery of the Missing Army Train." *Password* 38, no. 1
            (Spring): 29–41.

Daniel, Larry J.
1973 "Manufacturing Cannon in the Confederacy." *Civil War Times Illustrated* 12, no. 7 (November): 4–10, 40–46.

Daniel, Larry J., and Riley W. Gunter
1977 *Confederate Cannon Foundries*. Union City, Tenn.: Pioneer Press.

Downes, Olin, and Elie Siegmeister
1943 *A Treasury of American Song*. New York: Alfred A. Knopf.

Drake, Julie A.
1964 *The Mail Goes Through, or, The Civil War Letters of George Drake (1846–1918)*. San Angelo, Tex.: Anchor Publishing Co.

Duncan, William
1898 "The Army of the Tennessee Under Major General O. O. Howard." In *Glimpses of the Nation's Struggle*, 4:164–75. Minnesota Commandry of MOLLUS. St. Paul: Book and Stationery Co.

Dyer, Frederick H.
1959 *A Compendium of the War of the Rebellion*. Vol. 1. New York: Thomas Yoseloff.

Emory, W. H.
1848 *Notes of a Military Reconnoissance from Fort Leavenworth in Missouri, to San Diego in California*. 30th Cong. 1st Sess. H.R. Exec. Doc. No. 41 [Serial Set No. 517]. Washington, D.C.: Wendell and Van Benthuysen, Printers.

Fletcher, Jack E., and Patricia K. A. Fletcher
2001 *Cherokee Trail Diaries*, Vol. 3, *1851–1900: Emigrants, Gold Seekers, Cattle Drives, and Outlaws*. Sequim, Wash.: Fletcher Family Trust.

Fraser, Walter J., Jr.
2003 *Savannah in the Old South*. Athens: University of Georgia Press.

Gassman, Wade B.
1966 "A History of Rome and Floyd County, Georgia in the Civil War." M.A. thesis, Emory University.

Gerow, Peggy A.
2004 *Guardian of the Trail: Archeological and Historical Investigations at Fort Craig*. Cultural Resources Series No. 15. Santa Fe: New Mexico Bureau of Land Management.

Giese, Dale F., ed.
1967 *My Life with the Army in the West*. Santa Fe, N.Mex.: Stagecoach Press.

Glass, Paul, and Louis C. Singer
1975 *Singing Soldiers*. New York: Da Capo Press.

Glatthaar, Joseph T.

1985   *The March to the Sea and Beyond: Sherman's Troops in the Savannah and Carolinas Campaigns.* New York: New York University Press.

Gowans, Fred R., and Eugene E. Campbell

1975   *Fort Bridger.* Provo, Utah: Brigham Young University Press.

Greeley, Horace

1999   *An Overland Journey from New York to San Francisco in the Summer of 1859.* 1860. Reprint, Lincoln: University of Nebraska Press.

Guerrant, Edward O.

1956   "Operations in East Tennessee and South-West Virginia." In *The Way to Appomattox: Battles and Leaders of the Civil War,* 4:475–79. New York: Thomas Yoseloff.

Hall, Martin H.

1959   "The Skirmish at Mesilla." *Arizona and the West* 1, no. 4 (Winter): 343–51.

Hampton, Wade

1956   "The Battle of Bentonville." In *The Way to Appomattox: Battles and Leaders of the Civil War,* 4:700–705. New York: Thomas Yoseloff.

Hart, Herbert M.

1964   *Old Forts of the Southwest.* Seattle: Superior Publishing Co.

1965   *Old Forts of the Far West.* New York: Bonanza Books.

Hazlett, James C., Edwin Olmstead, and M. Hume Parks

1983   *Field Artillery Weapons of the Civil War.* Cranbury, N.J.: Associated University Presses.

Hicken, Victor

1966   *Illinois in the Civil War.* Urbana: University of Illinois Press.

1968   "Hold the Fort." *Civil War Times Illustrated* 7, no. 3 (June): 18–27.

Hitchcock, Henry

1995   *Marching with Sherman.* Lincoln: University of Nebraska Press.

Holmes, Jack D. L.

1961   "The Day That Forrest Visited Memphis." *Civil War Times* 2, no. 9 (January): 16–18.

Howard, Frances Thomas

1997   *In and Out of the Lines.* 1905. Reprint, Cartersville, Ga.: Etowah Valley Historical Society.

Howard, Oliver O.

1956   "Sherman's Advance from Atlanta." In *The Way to Appomattox, Battles and Leaders of the Civil War,* 4:663–66. New York: Thomas Yoseloff.

Hubert, Charles F.

    1894   *History of the Fiftieth Regiment, Illinois Volunteer Infantry in the War of the Union*. Kansas City, Mo.: Western Veteran Publishing Co.

Jackson, W. Turrentine

    1952   *Wagon Roads West*. New Haven: Yale University Press.

Jones, Eugene W.

    1997   *Enlisted for the War: The Struggles of the Gallant 24th Regiment, South Carolina Volunteers, Infantry, 1861–1865*. Hightstown, N.J.: Longstreet House.

Kennett, Lee

    1995   *Marching Through Georgia: The Story of Soldiers and Civilians During Sherman's Campaign*. New York: HarperCollins.

Kerr, Charles D.

    1887   "From Atlanta to Raleigh." In *Glimpses of the Nation's Struggle*, 4:202–23. Minnesota Commandry of MOLLUS. St. Paul: Book and Stationery Co.

Lane, Lydia Spencer

    1964   *I Married a Soldier*. Albuquerque, N.Mex.: Horn and Wallace.

Langley, Howard D., ed.

    1974   *To Utah with the Dragoons*. Salt Lake City: University of Utah Press.

Lecompte, Janet

    1978   *Pueblo, Hardscrabble, Greenhorn*. Norman: University of Oklahoma Press.

Lewis, Lloyd

    1932   *Sherman: Fighting Prophet*. New York: Harcourt, Brace and Co.

Longacre, Edward G.

    1969   "All Is Fair in Love and War." *Civil War Times Illustrated* 8, no. 3 (June): 32–40.

Loop, M. B.

    1901   "Rounding-up the Confederacy; Veteran Campaigns of the 68th Ohio." *National Tribune*, June 6, June 13, June 20, June 27, July 4, July 11, 1901. Washington, D.C.

Marcy, Randolph B.

    1968   *The Prairie Traveler*. 1859. Reprint, Williamstown, Mass.: Corner House.

Martin, John D.

    1900   "Campaigning with the Western Army." *National Tribune*, February 1, 1900. Washington, D.C.

McChristian, Douglas C., and Larry L. Ludwig

    2001   "Eyewitness to the Bascom Affair." *Journal of Arizona History* 42, no. 3 (Autumn): 277–300.

McMurry, Richard M.

1983   "On the Road to the Sea: Sherman's Savannah Campaign." *Civil War Times Illustrated* 21, no. 9 (January): 8–25.

Miller, Darlis A.

1993   *Captain Jack Crawford.* Albuquerque: University of New Mexico Press.

[Missouri] Superintendent of Public Schools

1873   *7th Annual Report* [1872] *of the Superintendent of Public Schools of the State of Missouri.* Jefferson City, Mo.: Regan and Carter. State Historical Society of Missouri, Columbia, Mo.

Murphy, Lawrence R.

1973   "Cantonment Burgwin, New Mexico, 1852–1860." *Arizona and the West* 15, no. 1 (Spring): 5–26.

Newhouse, Keith, ed.

1987   "The Diary of Philander Powell." *Flashback* (Washington County Historical Society) 37, no. 3 (August): 1–15.

News Publishing Co.

Past Times. Rome, Ga.: News Publishing Co. (1989).

Nye, Wilber S.

1961   "Kilpatrick Caught in His Underwear at Battle of Monroe's Crossroads." *Civil War Times* 3, no. 1 (April): 17–18.

Oakley, Daniel

1956   "Marching Through Georgia and the Carolinas." In *The Way to Appomattox: Battles and Leaders of the Civil War,* 4:671–79. New York: Thomas Yoseloff.

Olmstead, Edwin, Wayne E. Stark, and Spencer C. Tucker

1997   *The Big Guns.* Bloomfield, Ont.: Museum Restoration Service.

Peterson, Charles S., et al.

1972   *Mormon Battalion Trail Guide.* Salt Lake City: Utah State Historical Society.

Peterson, Harold L.

1969   *Round Shot and Rammers.* Harrisburg, Pa.: Stackpole Books.

Pittman, Craig

2004   "Fury over a Gentle Giant." *Smithsonian* 34, no. 11 (February): 54–59.

Porter, Horace

1956   "Five Forks and the Pursuit of Lee." In *The Way to Appomattox: Battles and Leaders of the Civil War,* 4:708–22. New York: Thomas Yoseloff.

Reyburn, Philip J., and Terry L. Wilson, eds.

1999   *Jottings from Dixie.* Baton Rouge: Louisiana State University Press.

Ryan, Garry David

    1963   "Camp Walbach, Nebraska Territory, 1858–1859, the Military Post at Cheyenne Pass." *Annals of Wyoming* (April): 4–20.

Sacks, Benjamin H.

    1962   "New Evidence on the Bascom Affair." *Arizona and the West* 4, no. 3 (Autumn): 261–78.

Scaife, William R.

    1993   *The Campaign for Atlanta.* Atlanta, Ga.: William R. Scaife.

Schroeder-Lein, Glenna R.

    1994   *Confederate Hospitals on the Move: Samuel H. Stout and the Army of Tennessee.* Columbia: University of South Carolina Press.

Settle, Raymond W., ed.

    1940   *The March of the Mounted Riflemen from Fort Leavenworth to Fort Vancouver, May to October 1849.* Glendale, Calif.: Arthur H. Clark Co.

Slocum, Henry W.

    1956   "Sherman's March from Savannah to Bentonville." In *The Way to Appomattox: Battles and Leaders of the Civil War,* 4:681–95. New York: Thomas Yoseloff.

    1956   "Final Operations of Sherman's Army." In *The Way to Appomattox: Battles and Leaders of the Civil War,* 4:754–58. New York: Thomas Yoseloff.

Smith, David

    2007   *Sherman's March to the Sea 1864: Atlanta to Savannah.* New York: Osprey.

Smith, H. I.

    1903   *History of the Seventh Iowa Veteran Volunteer Infantry During the Civil War.* Mason City, Iowa: E. Hitchcock, Printer.

Sprague, Marshall

    1964   *The Great Gates: The Story of the Rocky Mountain Passes.* Boston: Little, Brown and Company.

Stone, Henry N., comp.

    1886   *Stone's Adams County Directory.* Quincy, Ill.: Henry N. Stone.

    1892   *Stone's Tri-County Directory: 1892, viz.: Adams County, Ill., Marion and Lewis Counties, Mo.* Quincy, Ill.: Henry N. Stone.

Strayer, Larry R., and Richard A. Baumgartner, eds.

    2004   *Echoes of Battle: The Atlanta Campaign.* Huntington, W.Va.: Blue Acorn Press.

Sweeney, Edwin R.

    1991   *Cochise.* Norman: University of Oklahoma Press.

Taylor, John
  1995   *Bloody Valverde*. Albuquerque: University of New Mexico Press.
Thomas, Chauncey
  1937   "The Spanish Fort in Colorado, 1819." *Colorado Magazine* 14, no. 3
          (May): 81–85.
Thompson, Jerry
  1987   *Henry Hopkins Sibley*. Natchitoches, La.: Northwestern State
          University Press.
Todd, Glenda McWhirter
  1999   *First Alabama Cavalry, U.S.A.* Bowie, Md.: Heritage Books.
Utley, Robert M.
  1967   *Frontiersmen in Blue*. New York: Macmillan.
Warner, Ezra J.
  1959   *Generals in Gray*. Baton Rouge: Louisiana State University Press.
Watkins, Sam
  1999   *"Company Aytch" or, A Side Show of the Big Show*. New York: Plume.
Weber, David J.
  1971   *The Taos Trappers*. Norman: University of Oklahoma Press.
Wetherington, Ronald K.
  2006   "Cantonment Burgwin: The Archaeological and Documentary
          Record." *New Mexico Historical Review* 81, no. 4 (October): 391–411.
Whiteley, Lee
  1999   *The Cherokee Trail: Bent's Old Fort to Fort Bridger*. Boulder, Colo.:
          Lee Whiteley.
Wills, Charles W.
  1996   *Army Life of an Illinois Soldier: Including a Day-by-Day Record
          of Sherman's March to the Sea*. Carbondale: Southern Illinois
          University Press.
Wilson, John P.
  1988   "How the Settlers Farmed." *New Mexico Historical Review* 63, no. 4
          (October): 333–56.
  1993   "Whiskey at Fort Fillmore: A Story of the Civil War." *New Mexico
          Historical Review* 68, no. 2 (April): 109–32.
  2001   *When the Texans Came*. Albuquerque: University of New
          Mexico Press.
Wright, Charles
  1887   *A Corporal's Story: Experiences in the Ranks of Company C, 81st
          Ohio Volunteer Infantry*. Philadelphia: Charles Wright.
Yeary, Mamie, comp.
  1912   *Reminiscences of the Boys in Gray, 1861–1865*. Dallas, Tex.: Smith
          and Lamar.

Government Documents

Report of the Secretary of War, Dec. 6, 1858. Vol. 2, *Affairs in the Department of Utah*, nos. 87, 88. 35th Cong. 2nd Sess. S. Exec. Doc. 1, Pt. 2 [Serial Set No. 975] (1859). Washington, D.C.

Report of the Secretary of War, December 1, 1859. Vol. 2, *Affairs in the Department of Utah*, no. 68. 36th Cong. 1st Sess. S. Exec. Doc. 2, Pt. 2 [Serial Set No. 1024] (1859). Washington, D.C.

Agriculture of the United States in 1860; Compiled from the Original Returns of the Eighth Census (1864–1865). Washington, D.C.: Government Printing Office.

Manufactures of the United States in 1860; Compiled from the Original Returns of the Eighth Census (1865). Washington, D.C.: Government Printing Office.

Population of the United States in 1860; Compiled from the Original Returns of the Eighth Census (1864). Washington, D.C.: Government Printing Office.

[Map of the] *Territory and Military Department of New Mexico*, compiled in the Bureau of Topogl. Engrs. of the War Dept. . . . 1859. National Archives, RG77, Sheet W55(1), Records of the Office of the Chief of Engineers.

[Map of the] *Arkansas River Basin in Colorado . . . surveyed in November 1890.* Located at Bureau of Reclamation, Denver, Colo.; copy courtesy of Dr. Brit Storey.

War of the Rebellion, A Compilation of the Official Records of the Union and Confederate Armies, Series I, vols. 4; 9; 17, pt. 1; 21; 23, pt. 1; 25, pt. 1; 27, pts. 1, 2; 34, pts. 2, 3; 37, pts. 1, 2; 38, pts.1, 3, 4, 5; 39, pts.1, 2, 3; 43, pt. 2; 44; 46, pts. 2, 3; 47, pts.1, 2, 3; 49, pts. 1, 2 (1882–1897). Washington, D.C.: Government Printing Office.

Atlas to Accompany the Official Records of the Union and Confederate Armies, compiled under direction of the Secretaries of War, 1891–1895. Washington, D.C.: Government Printing Office. Reprinted as *The Official Military Atlas of the Civil War* by Barnes and Noble Books, New York, 2003.

Report of the Committee of the Senate upon the Relations Between Labor and Capital, and Testimony Taken by the Committee. Vol. 4, *Testimony* (1885). U.S. Congress, Senate Committee on Education and Labor. Washington, D.C.: Government Printing Office.

Report of the Adjutant General of the State of Illinois. Vol. 3 (1901). Springfield, Ill.: Phillips Bros., State Printers.

National Archives and Records Service

Record Group 94, Records of the Adjutant General's Office 1780s–1917; Enlistment Record, Military Service Record, and Pension Record of Lewis F. Roe.

Record Group 249, Records of the Commissary General of Prisoners, Misc. List No. 436.

Microcopy 617, Returns from U.S. Military Posts 1800–1916; Roll 261, Fort Craig, N.Mex., March 1854–December 1870.

Microcopy M653, Population Schedules of the Eighth Census of the United States, 1860, Roll 155.

Microcopy M593, Population Schedules of the Ninth Census of the United States, 1870, Roll 789.

Microcopy T9, Population Schedules of the Tenth Census of the United States, 1880, Roll 174.

Microcopy M1120, Registers of Letters Received and Letters Received by Headquarters, Department of New Mexico 1854–1865, Rolls 11, 29.

Manuscript Collections

Roe Family Records. In possession of Mrs. Eleanor Verene, Galesburg, Illinois.

Knox College Catalog, 1857. Seymour Library, Knox College, Galesburg, Illinois.

Lewis F. Roe Papers. Knox College Archives and Manuscripts Collection. Seymour Library, Knox College, Galesburg, Illinois.

Records of the Knoxville Presbyterian Church, Knoxville, Illinois.

George Hovey Cadman Papers. Southern Historical Collection, University of North Carolina at Chapel Hill.

Cornelius C. Platter Civil War Diary 1864–1865. Digital Library of Georgia, Hargrett Rare Book and Manuscript Library, University of Georgia Libraries, Athens, Georgia.

Letters of Frederick Sherwood, May 6–October 21, 1864, in Emily D. Sherwood and Family Papers. Special Collections, Hill Memorial Library, Louisiana State University, Baton Rouge.

Papers of Mary Frix Kidd. Rome-Floyd County Library, Rome, Georgia.

Deedbook "C." Gordon County Courthouse, Calhoun, Georgia.

Newspapers

Cincinnati Daily Gazette, May 30, 31, 1864; March 21, 22, 1865; April 1, 1865.

Daily Alta California, San Francisco, Calif., February 18, 19, 1861; September 8, 1861.

Daily Constitutionalist, Augusta, Ga., May 22, 1864; June 19, 1864; June 26, 1864.

Galesburg Register-Mail, Galesburg, Ill., June 30, 1990.

Knox County Republican, Knoxville, Ill., February 22, 1893; August 16, 1893; December 6, 1893; January 23, 1895.

Los Angeles Star, February 16, 1861; March 9, 1861; June 15, 1861.

Mesilla Times, Mesilla, N.Mex., February 16, 1861; February 23, 1861; July 27, 1861.

National Tribune, Washington, D.C., June 20, 1901; August 8, 1907; November 3, 1910.

New York Times, May 25, 1865.

Quincy Daily Whig and Republican, Quincy, Ill., May 8, 1861; July 12, 1864; December 30, 1864; January 7, 1865; March 22, 1865; April 26, 1865; July 11, 1865; July 17, 1865; July 22, 1865.

Quincy Herald, Quincy, Ill., May 27, 1861; April 24, 1865.

Rocky Mountain News, Denver, Colo., June 6, 1860; June 20, 1860; July 18, 1860.

St. Louis Post-Dispatch, March 21, 1887.

Santa Fe Gazette, Santa Fe, N.Mex., August 22, 1860; April 26, 1862.

Western Veteran, Topeka, Kansas (1884–May 1893) and Kansas City, Mo. (May 1893–September 1904), December 19, 1888; September 11, 1889; February 1, 1893; October 9, 1895; November 1901.

Personal Communications

Robert Anglea, Rome, Ga., June–September 2009.

Gordon Chappell, National Park Service, Oakland, Calif., August 12, 1996.

Dorothy England, Knoxville, Ill., September 1984–February 1999.

Dave Gorski, e-mail correspondence about Zollicoffer House, November 17, 1997.

Hugh Greeson, Chatsworth, Ga., June 15, 2009.

Mark Harmon, Downers Grove Park District Museum, Downers Grove, Ill., June 18, 2002.

Janet Hinck, Downers Grove, Ill., January 24, 2003; October 12, 2003.

Christine Parks, Western Illinois University, Macomb, Ill., July 3, 2002.

Michael F. Knight, National Archives and Records Administration, Washington, D.C., October 28, 2003.

Kay Vander Meulen, Seymour Library, Knox College, Galesburg, Ill., June 19, 2002; July 17, 2002.

Donald P. Verene, Atlanta, Ga., June 13, 1990.

Eleanor Verene, Galesburg, Ill., September 1984–October 2003.

David H. Wallace, National Archives and Records Administration, Washington, D.C., August 18, 2000.

Western Historical Manuscript Collection, University of Missouri–Columbia, June 15, 2000.

Websites

Website about the Cherokee Trail. Accessed July 3, 2002. http://www.geocities.com/peakers59/history.htm.

The Overland Trail. Accessed July 5, 2002. http://over-land.com.

Overland Stage Line and Cherokee Trail information. Accessed July 5, 2002. http://rutnut.com/cherokeetrail/.

The Overland Trail. Accessed July 5, 2002. http://over-land.com/otrail.html.

Jimmy Camp. Accessed July 5, 2002. http://geocities.com/peaker59/JimmyCamp.html.

Battle of Resaca. Accessed March 4, 2007. http://darrellryan.homestead.com/Resaca.html.

Friends of Resaca Battlefield. Accessed July 17, 2004. http://www.resacabattlefield.org.

"The Battle of Lay's Ferry." Friends of Resaca Battlefield. Accessed July 16, 2004. http://resacabattlefield.org/FoRLaysFerry.htm.

Georgia. Accessed May 30, 2009. http://homepages.rootsweb.com/~ahopkins/nuckolls/georgia.htm.

1860 Gordon County Census. Accessed July 17, 2004. http://www.censusdiggins.com/1860_georgia_census_2.html.

Georgia Civil War Solider Index. Accessed June 19, 2007. http://files.usgwarchives.net/ga/military/civilwar/gsi/gsi104.txt.

Civil War Letters and Diary of Charles Berry Senior [7th Iowa Veteran Volunteer Infantry]. Electronic Text Center, University of Virginia. Accessed July 16, 2004. http://etext.virginia.edu/civilwar/senior/.

7th Iowa Infantry. Accessed June 26, 2007. http://civilwar.aea.14.k12.ia.us/Resources/7thinfgue.htm.

1st Alabama Cavalry, USV, History. Accessed June 6, 2007. http://www.1stalabamacavalryusv.com/1stHistory.aspx.

1st Alabama Cavalry, USV, Searchable Roster. Accessed June 6, 2007. http://www.1stalabamacavalryusv.com/Roster/Default.aspx.

Philip Dale Roddey. 4th Alabama Cavalry, CSA. Accessed February 6, 2004. http://www.geocities.com/Athens/Aegean/6349/roddey.htm.

"Roddey's Fourth Alabama Cavalry." Shotgun's Home of the American Civil War. Accessed February 6, 2004. http://www.civilwarhome.com/roddey4alacav.htm.

4th Alabama Cavalry, CSA, History. Accessed February 6, 2004. http://www.geocities.com/Athens/Aegean/6349/history.htm.

4th Alabama Cavalry, CSA, Actions. Accessed February 6, 2004. http://www.geocities.com/Athens/Aegean/6349/actions.htm.

"3rd Regiment Infantry (African Descent)." Union Regimental Histories. The Civil War Archive. Accessed June 2007. http://www.civilwararchive. com/Unreghst/unaltr.htm#3rdinf.

"111th Regiment, United States Colored Infantry." Alabama Civil War Roots. Accessed June 2007. http://rootsweb.ancestry.com/~alcwroot/infantry_ files/111thusctinf.htm.

"The Lightning Mule Brigade: Abel Streight's 1863 Raid into Alabama." About North Georgia. Accessed July 2007. http://ngeorgia.com/history/ lightningmule.html.

"Black Troops in Civil War Georgia." New Georgia Encyclopedia. Accessed July 2007. http://www.georgiaencyclopedia.org/nge/Article. jsp?id=h-783.

"44th U.S. Colored Infantry Regiment." Tennesseans in the Civil War. Accessed July 2007. http://www.tngennet.org/civilwar/usainf/usa44c.html.

"137th Illinois Volunteer Infantry Regiment." eNotes. com. Accessed July 2007. http://enotes.com/ topic/137th_Illinois_Volunteer_Infantry_Regiment.

Griswoldville Georgia. Accessed August 1, 2007. http://usgennet.org/usa/ga/ county/taylor/jones/military/griswoldville.htm.

"Wormsloe Plantation." New Georgia Encyclopedia. Accessed August 20, 2007. http://www.georgiaencyclopedia.org/nge/Article.jsp?id=h-2870.

Sherman Strikes Again

4 large peaches, peeled and sliced
1/2 cup white wine
2 ounces peach or apricot brandy
1 quart peach ice cream

Put the peaches in a pan, add the wine; heat just before serving. Add the brandy and heat. Ignite and serve flaming over ice cream.

Serves 4

Puttin' on the Peachtree
Junior League of DeKalb County,
Georgia

Index